International Studies in Educational Achievement

VOLUME 6

The IEA Study of Written Composition II: Education and Performance in Fourteen Countries

International Studies in Educational Achievement

Other titles in the Series include

TRAVERS & WESTBURY
The IEA Study of Mathematics I: Analysis of Mathematics Curricula

ROBITAILLE & GARDEN
The IEA Study of Mathematics II: Contexts and Outcomes of School Mathematics

BURSTEIN
The IEA Study of Mathematics III: Student Growth and Classroom Processes

GORMAN, PURVES & DEGENHART
The IEA Study of Written Composition I: The International Writing Tasks and Scoring Scales

ANDERSON, RYAN & SHAPIRO
The IEA Classroom Environment Study

ROSIER & KEEVES
The IEA Study of Science I: Science Education and Curricula in Twenty-Three Countries

POSTLETHWAITE & WILEY
The IEA Study of Science II: Science Achievement in Twenty-Three Countries

KEEVES
The IEA Study of Science III: Changes in Science Education and Achievement: 1970 to 1984

The IEA Study of Written Composition II:

Education and Performance in Fourteen Countries

Edited by

A. C. PURVES
State University of New York at Albany, USA

Published for the International Association
for the Evaluation of Educational Achievement by

PERGAMON PRESS

OXFORD • NEW YORK • SEOUL • TOKYO

U.K.   Pergamon Press Ltd, Headington Hill Hall, Oxford
            OX3 0BW, England

U.S.A.   Pergamon Press, Inc., 660 White Plains Road,
            Tarrytown, New York 10591-5153, U.S.A.

KOREA   Pergamon Press Korea, KPO Box 315, Seoul 110-603,
            Korea

JAPAN   Pergamon Press Japan, Tsunashima Building Annex,
            3-20-12 Yushima, Bunkyo-ku, Tokyo 113, Japan

Copyright © 1992 I.E.A.

First edition 1992

Library of Congress Cataloging-in-Publication Data

(Revised for volume 2)
The IEA study of written composition.
(International studies in educational achievement ; v.6)
Vol. 2 edited by A.C. Purves.
Includes bibliographies and index.
Contents: 1. The international writing tasks and scoring scales -- 2. Education and performance in fourteen countries.
1. Composition (Language arts). 2. Comparative education. I. Gorman, T. P. II. Purves, Alan C., 1931-   . III. Degenhart, R. E. IV. International Association for the Evaluation of Educational Achievement.
LB1575.8.I38 1988   808'.007   87-35980

ISBN 0-08-041397-8 (v. 2)

British Library Cataloguing in Publication Data

A catalogue record for this book is available from the British Library

Printed in Great Britain by BPCC Wheatons Ltd, Exeter

Contents

vi   *Contents*

Foreword

Tjeerd Plomp
Chairman, IEA

This volume on written composition edited by Professor Alan Purves is the second of two books reporting on the results of IEA's Study of Written Composition. IEA, the International Association for the Evaluation of Educational Achievement, was founded in 1959 for the purpose of conducting comparative studies focusing on educational policies and practices in various countries and educational systems around the world. IEA has grown over the years from a small number of countries until today it includes a group of nearly fifty and has a Secretariat located in The Hague, The Netherlands. IEA studies have reported on a wide range of topics, each contributing to a deeper understanding of educational processes and especially the nature of teaching and learning subject-matter. The Written Composition Study is one such project shedding light on the way children view writing and the way they perform various writing tasks.

With the publication of this volume, The Written Composition Study, begun in 1980, is now completed. The database derived from this study will soon be available via the IEA Secretariat to qualified researchers around the world. Unlike other school subjects, written composition is a domain that has hitherto been clouded by a lack of understanding about the way children perceive writing skills. Where the first IEA volume on written composition clarified the domain under study, this present volume presents the efforts of many international authors to analyze the richest source of international data on composition and its teaching ever collected.

The international costs of the study were primarily supported by two grants from the Spencer Foundation. In addition, grants were received from the Center for Statistics of the Office of Educational Research and improvement of the United States Department of Education. Much support was given to the International Coordinating Center by the University of Illinois Graduate Research Board, the University of Jyväskyäla, Finland, the Academy of Finland, and the Research Foundation of the State University of New York. To each of these organizations as well as to the organizations and individuals that supported the national phases of the study in 14 educational systems (Chile, England and Wales, Finland, Germany, Hungary, Indonesia, Italy, Netherlands, New Zealand, Nigeria, Sweden, Thailand, and the United States), I would like to express IEA's deepest gratitude for making the project a success.

This volume results from many individual efforts. A special thanks must go to Professor Alan Purves who took the challenge of editing this volume which could not be completed without his dedication. The various contributors to the book likewise have made the findings useful to the general public. I would also like to express my gratitude to IEA's Publications and Editorial Committee, chaired by Dr, Richard M. Wolf, and to the external reviewers: Dr. Ina Mullis of the Educational Testing Service, and Dr. Karen Greenberg of the City University of New York for their contributions. Finally I would like to thank Pergamon Press for their support in realizing this important volume. Those readers wishing additional information on this or and other IEA project may direct correspondence to IEA at the following address:

IEA Executive Director
14 Sweelinckplein
2517 GK The Hague
The Netherlands

Editor's Preface

As editor, I should like to add a brief preface extending the thanks that are begun in the Foreword. This volume was delayed for a number of reasons; the primary one was a lack of funding from 1986-1990 for the analyses necessary to write the volume. Nonetheless certain people carried out the analyses on their own and it is their effort for which I am grateful--particularly Kari Törmäkangas, Rainer Lehmann, Michael Green, and Ruth M. Schick. I am also grateful to those authors who are listed in the various chapters for their efforts and drafts. The errors of interpretation are my own.

The final writing and editing of the volume was undertaken from the period April 1991 to January 1992. In addition to the IEA Board and the reviewers, I am grateful to Sauli Takala, Kimmo Leimu, Hannu Saari, and Elaine Degenhart for their comments. I am also grateful to James Bradley for his editing and to Linda Papa for work on the manuscript.

Alan C. Purves

1

Background to the Study

Alan C. Purves

The IEA Study of Written Composition in fourteen countries is based on the premise that "good writing" is a culturally defined phenomenon but that there are cross-cultural aspects that admit of comparison across languages and cultures. Good academic writing in particular is a complex concept in that it partakes both of a particular culture and of a broader academic structure fostered by the "Western" academic tradition which has come to dominate schooling around the world. One implication of this assumption is that when we talk about "growth" or "development" in writing, we are disguising the fact that what we are referring to is acculturation and deliberate instruction.

Theoretical Underpinnings of the Study

The activities of being literate carry with them the burden of acceding to and employing a large body of common knowledge and conventional wisdom. This act of accession and use may be seen as entering into a contract with the world of text, an act not unlike the act which social philosophers have referred to as the social contract. Being literate, in this sense, is a deliberate and social activity, one that takes place in the world and is not to be seen as a mental state or condition.

In her history of writing, Gaur (1985) begins by saying that all writing is information storage. She shows how, from the earliest invention of writing, the main function of the text was to store information, usually commercial but also governmental and later religious information, so that it could be retrieved by the writer or by some other person at a later date. Of necessity, then, written language had to be standardized so as to allow access to the information contained within the graphic code.

In early civilizations, writing was done by scribes who perfected the system and made advances in the technology of writing such as shifting from the stylus to the brush or pen. The scribes also set forth standards for penmanship, conventions of writing such as word boundaries and sentence boundaries, and even text structures and matters of morphology, grammar, and syntax for the written language. Some of the conventions they set were

1

for efficiency, and some were for elegance. From the earliest times, therefore, the various scribal groups established a contractual arrangement for being literate, a contract that was clearly social and that clearly transformed the individual from a state of natural existence to a state of textuality.

As a result of the development of moveable type and the availability of cheap paper, the scribal world opened up to a vast new group of people-- the middle class--during the seventeenth and eighteenth centuries and simultaneously or consequently more and more people became literate. The kinds of information stored increased to include the literary arts and popular literature as well as the news of the day and advertising. Changes in the structures and forms of written language came slower, and in most societies the textual contract of prescribed text structures and standards for words, syntax, and text structures continued in constantly but slowly modified forms as different groups took on scribal responsibilities and different fields of knowledge took on their own scribal functions. In addition, the scribal traditions often prescribed standards as to how texts should be read as well as indited. To some extent these standards arose from religious practices such as a reverence for the exact wording of the text (as opposed to a tolerance for individual interpretation) and the piling of commentary upon commentary, but scribal practices in the reading of lay texts, such as in the reading of law in England or the *explication de texte* in France, also had their influence (Purves and Purves, 1986).

Alphabets and Other Textual Conventions

One of the persistent aspects of text from the days of the clay pouch and cuneiform tablet to those of the electronic message is that all texts have in common certain qualities, to which we may ascribe the term *convention* (Goody, 1977, 1986, 1987). Among these conventions are the use of a visual symbol system comprising marks and spaces. This system became standardized early in the history of any writing system and as various writing systems, means of transcription, and surfaces have been developed or discarded, the conventions have become modified in more or less obvious ways. The reason for the standardization of writing emerges from the very pragmatic fact that written language stores information so that it can be retrieved by the writer or someone else at a later time or in a different place. That being so, it has been necessary for the symbols to have a standardized core of reference. As is the case today, much early writing was commercial and the various bills of lading had to be standard both as to the number of jars and the type of wine or oil in those jars. As time has progressed, the number and types of conventions in writing have increased, since the medium has come to be used for an increasing number of functions beyond the commercial and historical, and as the society using writing has become more and more complex and subdivided.

We may divide the conventions into three broad categories: spatial, linguistic, and structural. The spatial characteristics range from the direction or flow of the visual display. In Western culture it currently runs from upper left to lower right with some minor exceptions such as warnings written on road pavements. The spatial characteristics of text are particularly notable in the relation of text to blank space. These relations act as cues for the reader, often telling the reader what sort of text is presented. The greater the proportion of white space to text, the more likely the text is to be poetry. In a Shakespeare play the more dense the text appears the more likely it is to be comic. Columns of text signal certain kinds of information; newspapers, for example, use column spacing and type size to indicate the distinction between news and advertisement. In some types of text, type size and color can indicate the importance of the message or the loudness of the noise represented by the letters. Other visual devices such as boldface, italics, and the like have particular referents given the place in which they are situated. In a text such as this, boldface indicates a division; in a telephone directory it may indicate a commercial establishment.

In many languages linguistic conventions begin with the alphabet. It is an unknown feature of oral language, but is necessary to written language and is important both for its graphic representation of the phoneme and for its order. In all alphabetic written systems the very order of letters has been standardized, and most have added other standard symbols as well to mark such conventions of written language as sentence and paragraph boundaries, as well as questions, insertions, or quotations. Because of the consistent order of the alphabet, such works as directories and indices can be created, not to mention dictionaries. Other linguistic conventions peculiar to written language include spelling and punctuation as well as certain aspects of syntax and grammar. Uninflected written languages, for example, normally demand the placement of modifiers near what they modify, a demand not made by the oral language with as great a degree of stringency.

Structural conventions of texts include such matters as order and arrangement of segments of the message. Some of these may have counterparts and antecedents in oral language, but in many cases they have evolved into their own format. The recipe form is a good example of such an evolution. Although the sequence of the text resembles that of the narrative in that it is time bound and sequential, the modern recipe begins with a list of ingredients, which is not a necessary part of the sequence, although the information is requisite. Other structural conventions can be seen in the telephone directory with its segregation of alphabetical and occupational listings, the newspaper article with its initial summary followed by elaboration, or the scientific report with its prescribed order of presentation and its demand for an elaborate description of the experimental conditions.

The Relation of Culture to Discourse

Two recent comparative studies of writing, Scribner and Cole's *The Psychology of Literacy* (1981) and Heath's *Ways with Words* (1983), examine the relation of culture to discourse and particularly to written discourse. Scribner and Cole study the Vai of Liberia, among whom there are three types of literates as well as nonliterates (those literate in the indigenous Vai, those literate in Arabic, and those literate in English). Heath examines two groups of poor Appalachians in the United States, one black and one white, and contrasts them with the urbanized middle-class blacks and whites. Both studies point to the fact that written texts, and the ways in which they are used and perceived, vary according to the cultural group to which an individual belongs.

Together, the studies point to two aspects of that variation: the content that is written and the forms or structures used to encode that content constitute the surface manifestations of those cultural differences. In Heath's study the two Appalachian groups differ as to what should be included in a story. For one group the story must contain only "true" events and it should not have direct speech; for the other embellishment and fantasy are permitted and dialogue is a staple. The two groups also differ in the nature of the formulae that are used to open and close a tale. Scribner and Cole show the formulaic nature of Vai letters and how those letters differ from the formulae used by the English writers. The variations in content and form have been studied by many researchers in the areas of comparative literature and contrastive rhetoric.

Behind these surface manifestations of cultural difference lie three other aspects of discourse, and particularly of written language, that Heath and Scribner and Cole also suggest. The first of these aspects is the relative stress given to the functions of discourse. If we adopt Jakobson's listing of functions: expressive, referential, conative, metalingual, poetic, and phatic, we see that in both of Heath's groups writing is seen as primarily referential, as it is among the Vai literates in Liberia. There is also some metalingual and phatic use of written language. These functions and the consequent stylistic characteristics differ from those of speech in the same communities. In the Liberian Qu'ranic writers, the use of literacy is primarily phatic. In the Black Appalachian group of Heath, much oral discourse is poetic, but there is little poetic discourse among the white group. To a certain extent, these functional demands of discourse dictate both the content and the forms it will take. Such seems to be particularly true of written discourse.

Closely connected with function, however, and perhaps influencing it, there exist two other aspects of written discourse that seem to vary according to culture and that seem to affect the content and form. One of these aspects we may think of as the cognitive demand of the discourse (Vähäpassi, 1982; Hairston, 1986), which is to say the degree to which the writer must "invent" either the content of the written text or the form of the text. Much writing is transcription, in which the writer has both the content and the form and has simply to transcribe them. This is done in copying from oral or written discourse or filling in forms, and much of the writing in all of the cultures these authors study is transcription. Another large segment of writing involves the organization or reorganization of material that is known to the writer--shopping lists, brief reports such as directions, and the like. The form into which the material is to be placed may also be well known to the writer but the writer has to select it from among a variety of forms. The demand, then, is to select an appropriate form and put the material into the proper places.

A third kind of writing involves the invention or generation of both the content and, in many cases, the form or structure, although that may be a conventional form such as the story or the rhyme or the proposal. Invention in this sense appears to play little part in the lives of any of the groups of writers studied by Heath or Scribner and Cole, although the Black Americans do engage in invention in their talk and may even be inventive in their lexicon in early writing. It seems clear that Heath's townspeople are encouraged in secondary school to invent in their writing.

The last area in which cultural variation plays a part might be defined as the pragmatics of discourse. Written discourse, like oral discourse, occurs in a social setting, and there exist rules of behavior with respect to writing. In Heath's White Appalachian community, a child should write a thank-you note for a present; in the Black community, such an obligation does not exist. In the Vai community it was hard for the Vai language writers even to conceive of engaging in some of the tasks that Scribner and Cole asked them to do. Because they had difficulty conceiving of it, they did not know what to write or how to write it.

We may represent the interaction of these aspects of cultural variation as in Table 1.1. It is clear that the three cultural variables interact with each other and that the particular situation in which a writer writes may also determine the pragmatics and the function, which may, in turn, affect the text produced. That is to say that writing in a business setting may become a different sort of activity than writing at home or in a community.

Table 1.1

A Generalized Model of Writing in its Cultural Context

Socio-cultural Determinants of Literacy

Functions of Discourse	Cognitive Demand of Discourse	Social Function of Discourse	Textual Consequents
Expressive	Reproduction/Recognition	Person	Type and amount of
Referential	Reorganization/Following	Time	Information
Conative	Organization/Summar- izing	Occasion	Formal Characteristics
Metalingual	Generation/Interpretation Evaluation	When	Constituent
Poetic		Audience	Tools
Phatic		Outcome	

We may extend this position from broad cultural groups such as those studied by Scribner and Cole to the narrower subcultures that constitute academic disciplines. The philosopher of science, H. Tornebohm (1973), has shown that the disciplines are "inquiring systems," or communities that have their own carefully defined ways of reporting to each other. Throughout school, students are taught to be members of rhetorical communities, both the specific disciplinary ones and the broader cultural ones. It is primarily in schools that students learn to write according to certain conventions, many of which have little to do with the structure of the language and more to do with the literary and cultural heritage of the society, or the academic subcommunity. That is to say that many aspects of texts are not bound by the morphology and grammar of a particular language, but by custom and convention.

In many academic disciplines, as well as in certain professions that demand a great deal of writing, individuals learn to write according to certain explicit and implicit conventions that affect patterns of organization, syntax, and phrasing, and even the selection from the lexicon. It is apparent that the scholarly article in a given academic discipline has properties demanded by the history of that discipline. In the humanities, references to previous research on the topic come at the beginning of an article or are sprinkled throughout the text when needed; in psychology they always occupy the second of five sections of the article; and in the biological sciences they occur in separate articles from the report of a particular piece of research. In addition to structural conventions, disciplines differ in the degree to which they allow the writer to use the first person, the degree to which the passive is tolerated, and the degree to which interpretation or inference is permitted, to name but three instances. As we shall see, running across these disciplinary differences, there appear to be certain common strands which form a general type of academic discourse as it is construed by those who judge entrants into tertiary education.

This depiction of cultural variation supports the idea that written language and the activities involved in composing or reading and responding are highly conventional. Convention and need dictate the occasions for writing or reading and the functions of discourse appropriate to those occasions. From these two sources the writer or the reader then applies knowledge of both the content and form appropriate to a function on an occasion, and conducts the appropriate search of the long-term memory. At that point, the writer goes on to certain text-producing as well as discourse-producing activities (Takala, 1983). The text-producing activities include the more mechanical or physical; the discourse-producing activities include those related to the selection and arrangement of content. The reader goes on to certain decoding activities and certain types of response to the text material. Again these activities are bounded by convention (Purves, 1987), not unlike the conventions of response to literature that were set forth in Purves, Hansson, and Foshay (1973).

The reader, however, performs one additional and crucial act, and that act forms the basis for the argument of this study. The reader judges the adequacy of the text to the text model or models that exist in his/her head (Purves & Purves, 1986). Such a judgment may extend from whether the particular text is a good approximation to the model, to whether the text indeed falls within the broad or narrow range of the model. The reader's judgment may range from "this is a good story," to "this isn't even a story." This judgment of value is and has been one of the most powerful forces to shape the nature of writing throughout history. The judgment may be based upon a variety of facets of the perceived text, but particularly the clarity (or type of information) and the effectiveness of the text (or formal characteristics) based on the reader's sense of appropriate function and cognitive demand, and the pragmatics of the context for the writing. Judgments of texts based on mental models have informed rhetoric and poetics and continue to inform writing pedagogy and the various rhetorical communities of the world, be they religious, commercial, social, or academic. The use of these models can have a beneficial or a deleterious effect; they can serve to include or exclude people from rhetorical communities, and they are imperfectly understood. It seems that these models are learned by student writers as they get various forms of feedback from their teachers. The result is that in various examination situations including term papers and theses--when the writing counts--the students will use these models. It is the quasi-automatic use of these models that determines such concepts as "writing skill" or "writing ability."

The Special Nature of School Literacy

Much of the evidence behind what we have so far advanced comes from an examination of the reading and writing of students in primary and secondary schools. There seem to be some differences between what goes on with respect to literacy training within these institutions as opposed to what goes on outside of them (Scribner and Cole, 1981; Heath, 1982). In exploring these differences, which tend to be less great in a society like the United States than one like that of the Vai of Liberia, we shall elaborate upon this first approximation of a definition of what constitutes the twin domains of school reading and school writing as forms of acculturation into the textual contract.

Kadar-Fulop (1988) describes three major functions of the language curriculum in school basing her argument on a survey of writing curricular goals and aims in the countries in the IEA Study of Written Composition (see also Weinreich,1963). The first of these functions is the promotion of *cultural communication* to enable the individual to communicate with a wider circle than the home, the peers, or the village. Such a function clearly calls for the individual to learn the cultural norms of semantics, morphology, syntax, text structures, and pragmatics as well as procedural routines so as to operate within those norms and be understood.

The second function is the promotion of *cultural loyalty* or the acceptance and valuing of those norms and the inculcation of a desire to have them remain. A culturally loyal literate would have certain expectations about how texts are to be written or read as well as what they should look like, and would expect others in the culture to follow those same norms. Because Americans had a loyalty to certain norms in the 1960s, for example, they reacted strongly when a cigarette advertisement substituted "like" for "as," and one suspects the advertiser was fully conscious of this loyalty. Today that particular loyalty has been lost, thanks to some extent to the persistence of the advertisement.

The third function of literacy education is the development of *individuality*. Once one has learned to communicate within the culture and has developed a loyalty to it, then one is able to become independent of it. Before then, deviation from those norms and values is seen as naive, illiterate, or childish (Vygotsky, 1956; Markova, 1979). For example, teachers of English in the United States will accept a sentence fragment in a student's composition only when they know that the student is fully aware of the rules and the effect of breaking them. In some societies, particularly those of emerging nations, individuality in reading and writing does not form any part of the curriculum; in "romantic" postindustrial societies it is given great lip service but not really tolerated except in a select few.

Already in the IEA Study of Literature Education in Ten Countries (Purves, 1973), secondary school students in each of the cultures demonstrated that they were aware of the norms and standards of school reading, such as the importance of history or figurative language, or that school texts necessarily contain hidden meanings. They have acquired norms and cultural values concerning the appropriate response to a text. Whether they could live up to these norms and standards when asked to criticize a text was another matter. Probably many could, some could not, and some chose not to. The important bond they share is a general understanding and acceptance of those norms and standards. Students *know*, by and large, and accept as valued more than they might have the skill to do. They know they should "watch their language," even if they make the most egregious errors. The IEA Study of Written Composition in part seeks to explore this aspect of literacy education with respect to the production of discourse and texts. Some of that exploration will be found in chapter 5 of this volume.

As formal educational institutions, then, schools set out to make literacy learning serve both broad societal purposes and purposes specific to the subculture of schooling and the academy. School writing asks of the individual: (a) articulateness according to certain conventions, (b) fluency, (c) flexibility in moving from genre to genre, and (d) appropriateness, suiting what is done to the norms of the genre and the situation. The competence aspect includes two sorts of competence: one relating to the motor acts in producing text, the other relating to the acts involved in discourse production. Again, schools focus a great deal of attention on writing preferences; not all writing activities are approved in schools (e.g., graffiti, love notes), despite the various sorts of ingenuity with language they might display. Writing in school must follow particular conventions, and the conventions appropriate in one subject are not always those in another. Students must be apprenticed to as many as five or six rhetorical communities seriatim during the day or the week.

In school writing, then, we can see that students are expected to learn not only the practices and preferences of a larger cultural community of writers but also those of several specialized academic communities. As they progress through the academic world to the university, they will learn the even more specialized practices and preferences of various scholarly communities. As they go into various occupations, they will learn the conventions of literate behavior in the various institutions that make up a complex society. A large number of these people accept the conventions of the community and even seem to thrive comfortably within them. For them as consumers of the culture, familiarity and conventionality are comfortable. They can retreat to an orderly and predictable world of text. Many others, however, find such conventions boring.   Some of them are artists; some are teachers and academics; all of them are the ones who test conventional wisdom and common knowledge, and prevent them from becoming totally stagnant and sterile.

General Design of the Present Study

In order to explore these contentions about written composition, the IEA Study of Written Composition sought to obtain extensive data about writing in the countries or systems of education participating in the study. The procedure involved the following steps:

1) securing national case study data in the form of historical sketches, questionnaires on literacy and schools, sample examinations and texts;
2) completing a curriculum questionnaire;
3) testing samples of students including an average of three compositions per student, each composition scored at least twice by national teams of raters trained according to international standards (Gorman, Purves, & Degenhart, 1988);
4) gathering questionnaire data from students teachers and school administrators.

The original intention of the study was to examine students at that point in school just before a large number left formal common schooling. The median age of the students and the number of years of prior schooling varied across systems and it was decided to limit strict cross-system comparisons in favor of studying populations considered significant in each system.   This population is designated as B.

To this plan were added as subsidiary populations:

Population A: students at or near the end of primary education in self-contained classrooms;

Population C: students at or near the end of pre-university schooling.

Because direct measures of writing performance over several tasks were desired, sample sizes could not be large (costs of scoring are high). It was also determined that the samples at all levels should be intact classes (for ease of administration). The proposed minimum sample sizes internationally are Population B, 100 classes; Population A and C, 50 classes each. In general, classroom effects are to be examined only in Population B.

Selection and Rotation of Tasks

The selection of tasks included in the IEA study is based on the analysis of school writing and the developed model of school writing (Gorman, Purves, & Degenhart, 1988). The model was built to take a balanced account of the three major factors that influence writing: (a) aims of writing including purpose and audience, (b) level of cognitive processing involved in writing, and (c) the content (topic) of writing.

The two main dimensions of the model are the purpose of writing and the level of cognitive processing involved in writing. The model has been illustrated and tested by classifying different writing products (text types) according to the cells.

The tasks used in the study have been chosen in order to cover the basic elements of the domain of writing. Another determinant in the selection of tasks has been the curriculum. Inspection of curricula and examinations shows that school-based writing appears to have three major objectives: (a) acquisition, reproduction and restructuring of knowledge through writing; (b) expanding and building up one's view of reality, including the development of logical thinking; and (c) practice in writing that enhances one's ability capacity to function as an effective member of society.

Taking into account the educational objectives and the domain of school-based writing, nine tasks were chosen to form the dependent variable of the study (See Table 1. 2). The formulation of writing assignments was based on the task specification system adopted for the study. The final selection of assignments was based upon pilot studies conducted in the participating countries.

Table 1.2

Summary of Tasks and Task Rotation

Population	Common	Functional	Rotated	Optional
A (Primary) Ages 10-12	Personal Narrative	Note to Parent Description of Article Self-Description Note to School Head	Argument Summary/ Paraphrase	Description
B (Secondary) Ages 15-17	Expository Letter	Description of Article Self-Description Note to School Head Letter of Inquiry	Personal Narrative Argument Reflective Essay	Description Summary Open Task
C (Pre-University) Ages 17-19	Argument	Letter of Advice Letter of Inquiry	Reflective Essay	Description Summary Open Task

In order to identify factors that are related to patterns of writing performance, a large amount of information on schools, teaching, and students was collected through questionnaires administered to students, teachers, and school heads.

Since educational systems offer instruction in several tasks and since students are taught several different kinds of writing, it was decided to sample student writing across tasks in order to cover the domain well. Each student was to write on three assignments representing different cells in the domain. Getting several writing samples from each student was considered necessary also in order to be able to study the structure of the writing ability. Limitations of testing time made some task rotation necessary, however. In spite of task rotation, populations were linked so that in most tasks, the same task was common to two populations (A and B, or B and C), one task was the same for all three populations, and two tasks were meant for Population A only.

Similarly, students were linked so that there was one common (core) task in all three populations, that is, all students within a given population were assigned the same task. This task was a narrative for Population A, an expository letter of advice for Population B, and an argument/persuasion for Population C. Within each population, and partly also across populations, the task order was standardized so as to control the possible task order effect. Within the above-mentioned constraints of being able to link students within populations and across populations, task rotation was based on the following principles: (a) each student should write on as many different types of tasks (different cells of the domain) as possible, and (b) rotated tasks should require approximately the same amount of writing time.

Scoring

One main problem to be solved in the study was the method of scoring. The following steps were undertaken:

1. Development of a scoring scheme. This first involved identification of the universe of dimensions of a composition considered important in each of the systems in the study. Second, the universe was reduced to a set of common dimensions across systems. It was clearly determined that some of these common dimensions were language specific. The international dimensions that emerged were content, organization, style and tone, and personal reaction of the rater. These dimensions are intercorrelated but their order of importance varies by task and by rater. To these dimensions was added one for overall impression. This scheme was piloted and revised in December 1982.

2. Development of scoring scales. These scales were to consist of comparable sets of benchmark composition to illustrate poor, adequate, and good performance on each of four dimensions (Overall Impression, Content, Organization, Style and Tone.). It has been estimated that personal reaction would be rater-dependent and, therefore, not reliable. The reason for developing comparable sets was that large-scale translation was not desirable and the use of bilingual supranational raters was not feasible. The sets were

developed by asking each national center to submit twelve compositions per assignment and translate them into English. These twelve were to be selected to represent poor, average, and excellent compositions in terms of overall impression, content, organization, and style and tone.

An issue arose as to how to treat assignments given to two or three populations in a system. Since those systems were concerned with "growth" or change, and since costs could be reduced, it was decided to conflate populations on some tasks, but not all tasks. It should be noted that creating an internationally common pool from an age range of up to three years potentially restricted the particular score range of any one population in any one national system. By adding additional populations the overall range was expanded and any one population's range on some tasks should not be effected much beyond the effect of an international conflation.

The international scoring sessions were intended to accomplish two purposes. First, to "validate" with an international jury the scales proposed by a particular system and to make adjustments to those scales. The compositions on these scales were to be used nationally as "benchmark" and "reference" sets of compositions to indicate scale points on each dimension. The second goal was to generate a small (12-20) set of compositions that would be scored by raters in all countries. This "calibration set" was intended as a modest check on the comparability of national scores.

The results of these two scoring sessions produced two disquieting observations: (a) The international jury was divided into four subjuries whose leniency or strictness varied to some extent, and (b) the international subjuries reversed the relative scores of national juries in 10% of the cases. Although the overall success was high, these two observations suggest that internationally the scoring metric is too elastic to allow robust cross-national comparisons of scores on any one task or group of tasks. Nonetheless, it was hoped that the study could produce some comparisons and replications across the participating centers. To that end, data of the magnitude as represented in Table 1.3 were analyzed:

Table 1.3

Overall Data Pool IEA Written Composition Study

Population	Students	Teachers	Schools	Scripts
A	9,117	482	407	25,666
B	26,132	1,100	1,079	72,640
C	8,314	412	412	18,291
TOTAL	43,563	1,994	1,898	116,597

Summary

The IEA Study of Written Composition explores many of the aspects of the conventions held by national and regional communities and also explores the community of school writing and teachers as it intersects with the other communities that students inhabit. The other chapters in this volume take up the nature of the beliefs and conventions of the school writing community as they are expressed in general curricular statements (chapter 3), in the beliefs and practices of teachers (chapter 4), in the perceptions of students (chapter 5), in the resultant performance of students (chapters 6, 7, and 8), and in the scoring practices of the raters (Appendix B).

In a sense, this study begins from the premise that the school subject writing is perhaps unique among school subjects in that it represents what we might think of as a cultural-determined inquiring system wherein all members (curriculum planners, teachers, students, and raters) subscribe to a common set of norms and values and participate in a common set of practices. To attempt a cross-cultural study in the IEA tradition, then, means that the standard international measure may not allow for straightforward comparisons because the systemic differences may provide too strong an interference. The original intention of the study was to try to pierce these cultural barriers at the same time to portray the cultural variation. The extent to which this effort was a success is in part the subject of this volume.

2

The Educational Context of Writing Instruction

Wilfried Hartmann and R. Elaine Degenhart

This overview of the fourteen systems included in the IEA study on written composition is based on information received from the national centers, as given in national context questionnaires, additional sets of questions to the research coordinates, and the school questionnaires. At certain points, information from previous IEA studies was used as well. The country and school-system chapters in the various international encyclopedias, as well as a number of monographs, serve as more exhaustive treatments of the educational systems.

Historical Background to Written Composition Instruction

Each of the systems of education involved in the IEA study completed an historical sketch of its literacy and literacy education. A review of these reports indicates that the systems may be divided into the European vernacular group and the Eastern group. In the first would be placed Chile, England, Finland, Hamburg, Hungary, Indonesia, Italy, The Netherlands, New Zealand, Nigeria, Sweden, the United States, and Wales. In the second group would be placed Thailand. One might wonder whether some of the postcolonial systems (Chile, Indonesia, New Zealand, Nigeria, and the United States) belong in the European group, but the reports suggest that, although there may be some attempts to fuse a new-found indigenous literacy with the colonial tradition, or to establish a new and unique rhetoric, the colonial tradition prevails. This is true even in a country like Indonesia, which consciously selected a language of instruction and developed a local literature, but which at the same time kept what might be termed Western rhetoric. Indonesian prose traditions appear to derive more from the Dutch than they do from the Arabic.

Indonesia, however, differs from the other systems in the study in that it has an official dual education system in which the parts differ strongly from each other. There is a secular "public" school system and a religious system based on the Muslim madrasseh, both with ministries. Other countries such as Chile also have dual religious and secular systems but they are generally informed by the same philosophy and the religious schools are not directly run by the government. In Indonesia, the religious system is dominated by study of the Qu'ran, although in other aspects of study there are attempts to make subject matter curricula parallel (Diah, 1982). The effect of Qu'ranic teaching on mother-tongue and views of literacy has been outlined in such works as Scribner and Cole (1981) and in Wagner (1987). In general the effect can be seen in greater emphasis on memorization and recall of text, and on writing to reflect that sort of learning. However, the fact that there are attempts to harmonize the religious and secular curricula mean that students are not rigidly separated from the sorts of instruction in narrative and report writing that would occur in the secular curriculum.

The Thai language curriculum has quite different roots from the other systems in the study. It is derived from the Buddhist temple tradition, in which the making of the temple and the production of sacred texts for the temple library was part of the strong monastic tradition. This education was endorsed and expanded by the monarchs, who remained close to the world of the temple. The temple dominated education for both the monks and the laity, for it was the center of education from the 10th century on. Literacy was a part of the monastic life, and was used for copying texts and for essay and verse composition. Education beyond the most rudimentary was almost exclusively for males, and in some of the major temples, there was a level of education appropriate to an extensive library with medicine, governmental administration, philosophy, astrology, and other subjects. Such education can be seen as literary and religious with an emphasis on writing as an art, particularly the writing of verse. The Buddhist tradition dominated Thai education from 1257 to 1868, which is the time of educational expansion.

At the time of expansion, the King was influenced by Mrs. Leonowens and her importation of English education. Literacy came to be a desirable goal for more of the people, and was expanded throughout the country over the next eighty years. This meant the gradual establishment of a secular school, with European principles of compulsory primary education and voluntary and selective secondary education. The curriculum also became secularized and westernized, although the older poetic traditions did not disappear.

In each of the other systems in the study, a vernacular literacy replaced a latinized one as the subject of study. In the European countries, the change occurred sometime during the eighteenth or nineteenth century. In Chile, New Zealand, and the United States, the vernacular colonizing language became the main language of instruction from the beginning. In some of the systems in the study, this change involved a dual transition with an intervening language (which was that of the ruler of the country, such as German in Hungary or Swedish in Finland) becoming the language of instruction. In colonies, the colonial vernacular became the language of instruction from the beginning of "westernized" schooling, although Latin, Greek, and Hebrew might have been reserved for a smaller group. Recently in several of the systems there has been greater attention to the vernacular languages of either indigenous native groups or recent immigrants, so that questions of bilingual or multilingual and multicultural education are matters of great debate.

The patterns of development of vernacular instruction are outlined by Van de Ven (1987), who suggests a parallel development across systems of education as they move from a literary-religious rationale to a technical rationale in the 19th century, to a social rationale that began in the middle third of the 20th century. The first of these stems from a view that language should be studied from the perspective of the "true" or the "good" or the "beautiful." It is seen as an elitist view of the curriculum that focuses on the classics and an aristocratic or academic approach to style and composition. The technical rationale sees the curriculum in terms of technology and science and aims at producing people who can use the language in "everyday life." It can be seen as a bourgeois or meritocratic view that sees literature and art as clearly secondary. The social view provides an alternative to the technical by examining the relationships among social institutions with a view to changing them. It is a view that assumes the curriculum can"emancipate," or at least help people "understand" the social reality of their language. It aims to help students by making them more reflective, emotional, and expressive, and by enabling them to communicate competently within varied social situations.

In the light of what we have presented so far, the technical approach focuses on cultural communication, the literary-religious on cultural loyalty, and the social on individual expression. Each of these is a matter of emphasis, of course, and most national and actual curricula are hybrids of the three views as we shall see in chapter 3. Historically, most of the systems in the study appear to have adapted the technical approach during the past fifty years and in many systems it dominates, for it is attacked by the literary-religious group on the right and the social group on the left.

School Authority

In all countries three different levels of authority and responsibility are to be distinguished: national/federal, state/regional, and district/local. On the highest level we find a national policy institution, which can be a single ministry or multiple ministries, each responsible for a different segment of the systems (religious and secular or special populations). The policies issued by these ministries might have the status of law or of recommendation.

In general, we find a single ministry with high influence in those countries either with a strong central government (as in Chile, New Zealand at the time of the study, Sweden, or Thailand), or where in the course of history the unity of education was an important tool in gaining and preserving national independence (as in Finland, where the ministry is represented by two ministers in the Government), or where regional autonomy is stressed (as in the Welsh Office of the Department of Education and Science). The influence of the central ministry is weaker in federations like the United States, Nigeria, and Hamburg. More than one ministry is to be found in Indonesia, where the Ministry of Education and Culture is responsible for the secular schools, and the Ministry of Religion for traditional and modern Islamic schools. The latter have their roots in non-fee-levying boarding schools attached to mosques and offer the chance of education to the poorer rural population, but are now distinguishable from the state's schools only by a curriculum offering more than 50% of Islamic instruction.

The second level can be described as an intermediate regional level. The size and the political power of these regions may vary from states (as in the Federal Republic of Germany), through states, counties, and districts (as in the United States) to municipalities (as in England). Wales has a local education authority corresponding to the administrative county. There are educational offices in the 27 provinces of Indonesia, but they have little power because of the strong central authority. In Italy, despite constitutional attempts to overcome the traditional central structure, the influence of the 20 regions and the cities and provinces is poorly developed. A multilayered system exists in Chile, where there are regional secretaries of the Ministry of Education both for provinces and for communities; in Federal Republic of Germany, states, regions, and municipalities; in Finland, provincial departments and municipalities. In Hungary, 19 counties and the capital form one layer, local education authorities, the second. The Netherlands has two intermediate layers, provinces, and municipalities, which play an unimportant role. In New Zealand there are three regional offices and--for the primary school administration--10 district education boards. In Nigeria there exist state ministries of education under a commissioner and local government councils. In Sweden Municipal Education Committees and Local Education Authorities share the intermediate responsibilities with 24 County Education Committees. In Thailand there are twelve educational regions besides Bangkok for which the Ministry takes responsibility; Provincial and District bodies are also to be found.

The lowest administrative level to be taken into account is the actual school or district level. Individual schools or school districts subserve a higher level in Chile, Hamburg, Hungary, Nigeria, and Sweden. They are administered and governed locally in England, Finland, Indonesia, Italy, The

Netherlands, New Zealand, Wales, and the United States. A system of cooperative school groups exists in Thailand, where 8 to 10 schools in the same area may cooperate in educational policy.

School Finances

In most countries each of the three levels of government contributes to the financing of the school system. This fact makes it impossible to give a precise percentage of the public money used for the funding of education, or even a percentage of GNP so as to compare these expenditures.

Since all systems except Indonesia and New Zealand report that schooling is free of charge from primary education onward at "official" schools, and only Thailand charges for secondary schooling, in general a free basic education is guaranteed in all countries in the study. In more than half of the systems learning materials like books and handouts are provided free of charge or for a nominal fee when required as part of a syllabus (free: Hamburg, Finland, Hungary, Sweden, Wales, the United States, and Chile, where even paper, pencils and biros are provided free of charge; nominal fee: England, Wales, and New Zealand). In many systems other costs such as transportation, meals, and uniforms are also provided.

Role of Private Education

In addition to free education at the state-governed schools, all the participating countries except Nigeria allow private schools. For these schools, education is not free of charge, except for The Netherlands. The rights, number, and importance of the private schools vary considerably. The general pattern seems to be that it is at least advisable for these schools to follow the official syllabi or to make use of a core curriculum in order to receive subsidies (as reported from Chile, England, Hamburg, Indonesia, Italy, New Zealand, Sweden, Thailand, and Wales), to meet the standards of supervising state-commissions (Italy, Sweden), or to prepare their students in an adequate way for examinations (Finland, Hungary, Hamburg, England, The Netherlands, United States). The schools are free to add certain subjects, special programs, and extracurricular activities; to follow a specific philosophy; or to experiment with and make use of alternative methods. At times they operate under the restriction that the greater the deviation from the official syllabus, the lower the government subsidies (the extreme example being Indonesia, where schools with no restriction to the autonomy of their curriculum receive no state money at all). In the United States the individual private school is free to decide about its policy, but most belong to voluntary accrediting agencies that monitor their curricula.

The state contributes in some way to the costs of the private schools in six of the thirteen systems:

- grants, loans, or bursaries are obtainable by the students, as reported from Sweden and New Zealand,

- subsidies are given to the schools, as in Chile, Sweden, New Zealand, Hamburg and Indonesia, where private schools receive a certain percentage of their funding from the state.

- all costs are covered, as in The Netherlands.

- part or all of the money is earned from fees, as reported from Chile, England, Hamburg, Finland, Indonesia, New Zealand, Sweden, Thailand, and the United States.

The number of students at private schools varies, as is shown in Table 2.1. No percentage was obtainable for Indonesia, but it was reported that more private institutions exist at the secondary than at the primary level. Much of the data results from the influence of religious schools. New Zealand private schools are run by religious or philosophical organizations or by private individuals. In the United States, two thirds of the private school population comes from Roman Catholic elementary and secondary schools. Most Chilean private schools are religious. The large percentage found in The Netherlands (68%) is explained by the fact that the majority of all schools in the country are considered to be either Roman Catholic, Protestant, or secular private schools; these are considered private, but they too offer free education and are financed by the state. It should be noted that some of the data in Table 2.1 represents attendance at only secondary schools, while other countries' figures encompass both primary and secondary schools.

Though a number of the private schools are religious or denominational, one should be careful not to equate private with religious and mistake the given percentage as indicative of the number of religious schools. Official schools may be religious schools, and private schools may be not religious. Two examples illustrate these facts. In Indonesia, as mentioned above, dual ministries exist: the Ministry of Education and the Ministry of Religion, so that of the number of "official" schools, 25% are Islamic. In Hamburg, the International School, the French school, and the Japanese School, as well as 14 German schools, are private, but not religious.

Table 2.1

The Number of Students in Private Schools

Chile	34.2%
England	5%
Finland	< 1%
Hamburg	5%
Hungary	1.1%
Indonesia	NA
Italy	7%
The Netherlands	68%
New Zealand	3%
Sweden	< 1%
Thailand	12.5%
United States	> 10%
Wales	3.5%

Structure of the Systems

The age at which school life begins ranges from age 3 (The Netherlands, where since 1985 nursery and primary schools are combined; Chile) to 7 (Finland, Sweden, Thailand). Since all countries have a fixed beginning of the school year, the usual arrangement either requires the entrance into Grade 1 at the next official starting date after reaching the prescribed age (as in England or Finland), or allows the beginning of schooling at a certain point for all children who will reach the required age during the next n-months (as in Hamburg). In New Zealand, where by law all must start school at age 6, most children start school on the day after their 5th birthday (see Figure 2.1).

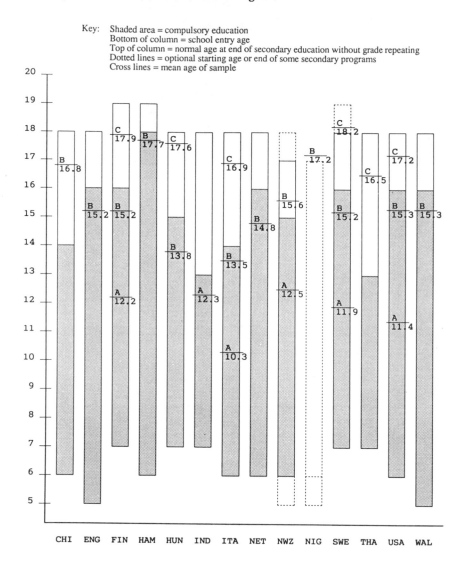

Key: Shaded area = compulsory education
Bottom of column = school entry age
Top of column = normal age at end of secondary education without grade repeating
Dotted lines = optional starting age or end of some secondary programs
Cross lines = mean age of sample

Figure 2.1: **Legal Starting Age, Length of Compulsory Education, End of Secondary Education, and Approximate Age of Tested Populations**

The normal duration of basic education, a span of 6 or 8 years, defines population A in the writing study, students at or near the end of primary education and the self-contained classroom. Secondary education includes all opportunities for schooling during the time from leaving basic schooling to the time when most students who want to continue education leave the secondary school system. On the whole, secondary education stretches over a varying number of years, so that total schooling from the first grade of basic education to the end of secondary education adds up to 12 years (Chile, Finland, Hungary, Indonesia, The Netherlands, Nigeria, Thailand, the United States) or 13 years (England, Hamburg, Italy, New Zealand, Sweden, Wales).

During the last two or three years all countries have allowed students to leave school, depending on a minimum of years spent in the school system, or on age (e.g., in New Zealand students are allowed to leave school on the day they turn 15 years of age; in Hungary, when they are older than 13 and have successfully finished Grade 8, or at the age of 16, no matter what grade they have reached). In such cases a certificate is issued, perhaps with the consequence of restricted access to tertiary education (e.g., in Finland the certificates after 1, 2, or 3 years of upper secondary school entitle the students to different types of further schooling or careers).

In all countries secondary education is not considered to be a monolith, but usually consists of two smaller blocks, the first of which, usually called junior, lower secondary, or middle school, tends to be comprehensive or - if an early differentiation takes place - offers easy opportunities to revise the original choice by changing track or programs. Track in this context is used for a line of study that is separated by a different philosophy or curriculum, has a different final examination, and has a group of students who share all or most of the activities (whether in a separate building, or administrative framework, or not). Program means an alternative for which the separation is less rigid, such as choices offered to replace one subject or a group of subjects by equivalents, normally inside the same school. The upper secondary block usually offers different choices, aiming at the threshold qualification to enter programs in post-secondary education, and the curricula often take into consideration the intended careers and professions of their students.

This structure explains why it is impossible to define a population by a grade number. Instead, a point of time where the students have reached an important transition point in their academic career is used. It is for this reason that we have focused the population in the study as we have.

Selectivity

Given the diversity of the school systems and the variety of choices within each system, the questions arise of how the stream of students is split up or forced into different branches; how it is regulated by locks and dams or connected by canals; and finally how it is brought together again to form the big river of the adult, working society. We find complicated systems of open or hidden examinations or other selection instruments sometimes within a school for tracking or promotion. At other times this occurs in the school system as a whole, to govern the transition from one level to the next, or from one track to the next (such as to the more prestigious or more academically demanding one).

Different attitudes towards automatic or restricted promotion explain the fact that in two countries with the very same school entrance age and a similar system of grade numbering, we might nevertheless find students from considerably differing age cohorts in the respective classes (e.g., Chile reports that in Grades 5 and 6, almost 50% of the students are one or more years older than the modal age for these grades). Therefore, it is necessary to know the patterns of promotion: where it is automatic, where it depends on achievement, and how it is monitored and tested.

In New Zealand, Sweden, Wales, England, and Nigeria, promotion with the year-group to the next grade is automatic and takes place simultaneously for all subjects. In Chile, Finland, Hamburg, Hungary, Indonesia, Italy, The Netherlands, Thailand, and the United States, promotion depends in some way upon achievement. Mixed forms occur, as in New Zealand, where the more able students tend to pass through the junior classes faster than those of average ability. In Finland promotion is automatic for the first ten years and only admission to the last two years of academic schooling is based on achievement.

In daily classroom work the responsibility for the measurement of student achievement lies with the teacher. Teachers normally prepare and administer tests, control the daily classroom work or homework and keep track of the students' success or failure. All countries also use a system of annual, semiannual, or term report cards or certificates, usually formal marks based on a point scale, though this system may be used only for the older students. But the consequences of these grades differ considerably from country to country.

In England and Wales such grades may place students in an appropriate teaching group (set or stream) for each subject, though their promotion with the year-group remains an automatic one. In the United States automatic promotion is widespread; not more than about 4% of 8-year-olds were below modal grade in 1979. In some countries, like The

Netherlands, Chile, Thailand, and Hamburg, the students have to qualify for promotion to the next grade year after year. In Hamburg the minimum marks to be achieved are prescribed, with a complicated system balancing good marks in one subject or subject area against poor marks in others. In Thailand students have to collect points in different subjects once a semester or a quarter that add up to the determination of pass or fail. In The Netherlands students in the bottom quartile of performance are not promoted, and in Chile students have to reach a minimum average of all the subjects they have studied, with a compulsory minimum mark in mother-tongue and mathematics required for promotion.

In other countries decisions about promotions are only made after certain grades, such as Sweden's examinations at the end of Grades 8 and 9, where marks on a five-point scale serve as a basis for the decision about upper secondary school entrance. Annual tests in Thailand are used for promotion from primary to the lower level of secondary after Grade 6 and to upper secondary after Grade 9. In New Zealand movement into the equivalent of Grades 11 or 12 is dependent either on performance in national examinations, or awards or on the discretion of the school principal.

In some cases, the basis for these decisions lies at the school level, as in Italy or Hamburg where the individual teacher's observation or self-designed test is decisive. In Nigeria there is school-based assessment; in The Netherlands, norm-referenced tests are used. In Thailand and Indonesia the tests are external, such as school-leaving examinations at the end of primary school and junior and senior high school.

In spite of the differences mentioned above, the transition from primary to secondary education in most countries (Chile, England, Finland, Hamburg, Hungary, New Zealand, Sweden, United States, and Wales) is done without special examinations, but through student choice (although there may be placement tests). Only a limited number of countries (Indonesia, Nigeria, Italy, and Thailand) rely on special "secondary school entrance" or "primary school leaving" examinations.

Where there is a separate upper secondary, postcompulsory phase, the general pattern is one of separation by ability or interest: Chile (end of Grade 8), England (age of 16), Hamburg (Grade 10), Finland (Grade 9), Hungary (Grade 8), the United States (end of Grade 9), Sweden (end of Grade 9 for admission to upper secondary), Wales (age of 16), New Zealand (Grade 10). Some countries use a more rigid examination at this phase: Indonesia (Grade 9), Italy (Grade 8), Thailand (Grade 9) Nigeria and The Netherlands.

Language Policy

As far as the language situation is concerned, three different groups of countries can be identified in this study:

Group A: the language of instruction is the only official national language (Chile, England, Hamburg, Hungary, Indonesia, Italy, The Netherlands, Sweden, Thailand, the United States).

Group B: the language of instruction is one of the official national languages (Finland, New Zealand, Wales) and can be considered to be the native language of most of the students taught in that language.

Group C: the language of instruction is one of the official national languages (Nigeria) but not the native language of most of the students.

Although the situation seems to be more or less common for most countries except Nigeria, the following complications of the general pattern should be kept in mind:

Group A

Chile. In Mapuche communities (Araucanians) initial primary education is given in their language, besides Spanish.

Hamburg. Though German is the only official language, because of bilateral agreements there are Danish schools for the children of that minority. The children of migrant laborers form a considerable percentage in some parts of the country school population (e.g., the children of more than 1.5 million Turks) and are taught during the first years after they enter the school system in their mother-tongue, as well as in German.

Hungary. Though Hungarian is the native language of 98% of the population, the Hungarian constitution (section 61.3) states: "All minorities living in the country have the right to use their mother tongue, have a right to education in the mother tongue and to the preservation of their ethnic identity." Therefore besides Hungarian, the following languages are used as the medium of instruction at primary level: German (0.5%), Serbo-Croatian (0.3%), Slovenian, Slovak, and Romanian.

Indonesia. In Indonesia 669 living languages are listed, and the national language, Bahasa Indonesia, is not the native language of most students (it is spoken by less than 10% as their first language). But it is used as the language of instruction above the second grade of primary school; some local languages are used for instruction during the first two primary grades.

Italy. Besides Italian, the following regional languages are used in school: Cimbrian, French (0.2%), German (0.4%), Sardinian.

The Netherlands. Although Dutch is the official language, Frisian is used as the language of instruction during primary education (Grade 1 through 6) in Friesland (500,000 million people). Bilingual education for migrant worker minorities, like Moroccans, Turks, and Indonesians, also exists.

Sweden. Swedish is the only official language, but almost all immigrant students as well as the children of the Finnish (3%) and Lapp minorities are also taught their home language.

Thailand. Over 80 languages are reported, but officially only Central or Standard Thai is used in schools.

United States. Besides the official language, English, many other languages are taught in bilingual programs, particularly Spanish, Native American, and Asian languages.

Group B

Finland. In Finland two national languages exist, Swedish and Finnish, but there are two parallel school systems and the general pattern shows students whose mother-tongue is Swedish at schools where Swedish is the language of instruction, and Finnish-speaking students at Finnish schools. At Lapp schools the instruction is given in that language only during the first two years of primary school.

New Zealand. Although English is dominant, Maori is taught in bilingual programs.

Wales. Welsh is the official language in Wales, and its use is being encouraged in schools. In Wales, Welsh was the native language of approximately two thirds of the students in the sample, but this proportion varies from school to school.

Group C

Nigeria. In Nigeria we find 413 living languages; besides English three official languages are used (Hausa, Ibo, and Yoruba). English and one of the non-mother-tongue official languages are compulsory subjects for every student. During the first three grades of primary education a local language serves as language of instruction in schools. In senior classes of primary education and onwards, English is the language of instruction.

In all participating countries instruction in the mother-tongue covers about one forth of the total teaching time, followed by mathematics, with far less time allocated to social sciences and natural sciences. A second modern language besides the first language is taught in the following countries: Chile (from Grade 7 onwards, competent staff provided), Hamburg (Grade 5, English, French, or Latin), Finland (Grade 3, second national language or English), Indonesia (Grade 1, Bahasa Indonesia), Hungary (Grade 4, Russian), Nigeria (English), Sweden (English from Grade 3 onwards).

Teacher Training

The systems can be compared in legal requirements for teacher education, as shown in Table 2.2 on the next page.

Nigeria, Italy, and Indonesia are the only countries in the study where no further training beyond secondary schooling is required to obtain a primary teacher's license. This impression is true as far as the number of years is concerned, but teacher training courses are offered as special tracks during secondary education.

A more reliable view looks at the number of years primary teachers undergo education from grade one to the first teaching certificate, as shown in Table 2.3. The total training for upper secondary school teachers tends to be slightly longer (e.g., one year more in chile, one or two years more in Hungary) than for primary school teachers.

Table 2.2

Years of Required Postsecondary Training
for Teaching at Various Grade Levels

Country	Primary	Lower Secondary	Higher Secondary (if distinct)
Chile	4	5	
England	3-4	5	
Finland	4	4	
Hamburg	3-4	4	
Hungary	3	4	5
Indonesia	-	3	
Italy	-	4-5	
Netherlands	4	4	4.5-5
New Zealand	3	4-5	
Nigeria	-(3)	-4	
Sweden	3.5		4.5
Thailand	3	3	
United States	4	4	5

Table 2.3

Number of Years of Education for Primary School Teachers,
from Grade 1 to First Teaching Certificate

Nigeria	8-12
Italy	11-12
Indonesia	12
Sweden	12.5
Hungary	15-16
New Zealand	15-16
Thailand	15-16
United States	15-16
Chile	17-18
England	17-18
Finland	17-18
Hamburg	17-18
The Netherlands	17-18
Wales	17-18

During the past 15 years in almost all of the participating countries
a change in teacher training can be observed. The general trend is towards
professionalization, university education, and longer times of study for all
teachers. Parallel to this development, the lines of study become more and
more alike, which means the total time of study for primary and higher
secondary school teachers is converging. Primary school teachers get a more
intensive subject training (e.g., the course leading to a bachelor's degree in
education in Colleges of Education has been lengthened in the British systems
from 2 years to 4 years; in Finland from 1979 onwards, all teachers have been
trained at universities) and secondary teachers are offered more courses in
pedagogy.

Selected Characteristics of Schools in the Sample

In addition to the broad contextual features of schooling, we must mention something of the schools in the sample in this study. Some of the aspects of the schools are covered in the sampling discussion (Appendix 1). Other aspects are highlighted in Table 2.4.

Table 2.4

Selected Characteristics of Schools in Sample

	Pupils	%Girls	%Spk Lang.	No.M-T Tch	No. Days	Avg. Per.	%with Lib.
POPA							
FIN	192.2	50	97.2	8.1	190.0	45.0	88
IND	423.1	50	48.6	6.7	251.9	40.1	99
ITA	686.2	49	97.4	NR	214.8	60.0	100
N-Z	443.6	50	95.7	12.1	196.1	43.2	99
SWE	349.1	50	97.1	7.6	178.0	40.0	96
USA	640.2	55	90.1	14.7	179.6	46.7	99
POPB							
CHI	1480.6	59	98.0	8.7	191.3	44.7	97
ENG	933.4	53	96.8	9.1	193.4	41.8	86
FIN	374.1	50	98.0	3.3	190.0	45.0	78
HAM	537.6	55	94.9	14.1	NR	45.0	91
HUN	334.5	86	NR	2.6	180.0	45.0	95
ITA	517.4	47	95.6	16.8	213.9	59.1	99
NET	NR	NR	88.2	NR	NR	NR	87
N-Z	866.9	51	95.7	11.4	189.1	56.8	100
NIG	1056.8	67	32.1	4.9	214.5	39.0	99
SWE	558.6	49	97.3	6.8	178.0	40.0	100
USA	1321.8	51	93.1	21.9	180.3	51.3	99
WAL	722.3	50	51.6	9.8	196.1	37.4	100

	Pupils	%Girls	%Spk Lang.	No.M-T Tch	No. Days	Avg. Per.	%with Lib.
Table 2.4 (Cont'd.)							
POPC							
FIN	283.9	60	98.0	2.2	190.0	45.0	98
HUN	301.8	64	NR	4.3	180.0	45.0	100
ITA	1001.4	48	97.7	18.2	210.8	53.5	
SWE	940.1	46	98.0	1.0	178.0	40.0	
THA	2549.8	53	94.2	14.8	209.2	50.0	
USA	1596.4	51	89.8	25.0	180.7	51.5	

One aspect of this table is clear: the average size of the schools varies considerably from system to system. Finnish schools tend to be much smaller than those in other systems, and the schools in the United States, Chile, and Thailand tend to be larger than average. When one goes from size to the ratio of teachers to students in mother-tongue, one notes that the ratio would seem to favor Hamburg and Italy, which have fewer students per mother-tongue teacher. This topic will be taken up in chapter 4, where teaching load is discussed in detail.

A second feature of note concerns the proportion of girls in school. In Population A the proportion is nearly equal except for the United States. In Population B, the percentage of girls is noticeably high in Chile, Hamburg, Hungary (where the figures may result from the fact of single-sex schools), and Nigeria. In Population C, the proportion of girls rises for Finland and Hungary. It would appear that in these systems, girls tend to stay in school longer and to be more successful. How this finding relates to the achievement results remains an interesting question, which we will explore further in chapters 6-8.

The popular media in many countries have expressed the belief that differences in achievement can be attributed to the amount of instructional time, particularly the length of the school year, and it has become an item of concern to policy makers in many systems of education. Table 2.4 shows the number of school days and the average length of class period per subject. The difference in the length of the school year is greatest for Population A, where Indonesia has nearly two more months of schooling than any other system in the study. Of the industrialized countries in the study, Italy has the longest school year and Sweden the shortest. Within the school day, however, the amount of instructional time per subject is quite uniform, never rising above an hour. As we shall see in chapter 4, though the amount of writing time may extend beyond a class period in some systems of education, so that the bare figures of time mask perhaps deeper differences in the use of that time.

A final note of comparison deals with access to books in the school. Nearly all the schools in the study report having libraries; the sole exception is Finland for Populations A and B, where municipal libraries serve the schools. Unfortunately, however, we did not gather information concerning the size or use of the libraries. We have visited schools in many countries in the study and have noted wide disparity both in size (from ten to several thousand volumes), and in availability of books. It would seem that there are books and other resources available to some degree throughout the systems in the study, but real divergence underlies apparent uniformity.

Conclusion

As is true in so many other aspects, the broad context of schooling in the systems of education in the Written Composition Study contains diversity within apparent uniformity. Schools are generally instruments of the state or the church; they are subject to national control in addition to having varying degrees of autonomy. The schools clearly implement a national language policy, which may or may not reflect the linguistic situation of the country. Teachers normally receive training, but primary teachers usually receive less training than advanced secondary teachers. The length of schooling both annually and over the life of the student shows fluctuation that is only partly explicable by the degree of industrialization.

3

The Curriculum in Mother-Tongue and Written Composition

Hannu Saari and Alan C. Purves

In the initial stage of the Written Composition Study, a questionnaire was devised to elicit information on the intended curriculum in composition (and in mother-tongue in general). The questionnaire was sent to each research coordinator to be filled out either on the basis of published documents or a series of interviews and examinations of textbooks and other documents. The International Coordinating Center collated and transformed the data and the analysis was performed at The University of Jyväskylä.

The questionnaire moved from the general -- dealing with control over the curriculum and overall policy -- to specific questions dealing with goals and specific features of the curriculum. It was based on prior studies of the curriculum, both those performed by IEA and those performed nationally. Much of this background is reported in Kadar-Fulop, Pezeshkpour, and Purves (1982). Centers usually responded for all populations even if only one was tested. In addition, three centers, Australia, Kenya, and Scotland, responded although they later dropped out of the study. Their responses are included so as to broaden the picture of writing curriculum in the 1980s. At a later point in the study a questionnaire was sent to the teachers of the classes participating in the study. Some of the items dealt with the curriculum as well, and their results elaborate on the curriculum questionnaire data.

The analyses examine the language curriculum generally and then the specifics of the composition curriculum as an aspect of language instruction. In general, the analysis will rely on quantitative information in order to make comparisons easier, but narrative background will be used where it is appropriate. One must keep in mind the fact that although questionnaire responses from representatives of different educational systems allow for comparison, such comparisons are extremely rough indices of consensus or lack of it. There are fundamental differences among school systems that work to prevent ready comparison: a system with local autonomy and an examination system for those students who wish to sit for the examinations (as in England and Wales) is quite different from a system with a centrally developed curriculum that includes texts and teaching materials (as in Indonesia). Generalizations are easier to make about the latter than about the former. Again, different systems interpret the same terms differently, so that "student needs" has a psychological meaning in one system and an economic meaning in another. With these caveats, one may make some tentative conclusions about trends across systems and differences between systems based on questionnaire data. When we say "In system X ...," we are saying it is probably more the case in system X.

Curriculum Control

As was discussed in chapter 2, each of the systems except Nigeria has some kind of legal requirement for schooling, touching on matters ranging from the length of the school year or school days, to specific aspects of curriculum and instruction. It is important here to add a note on the nature of the control concerning the curriculum, particularly the composition curriculum (Table 3.1). In the majority of systems, the central government sets these legal requirements, although four systems report a regional establishment, and the USA reports that both regional and local authorities set the requirements. In Australia, England and Wales, and Finland for Population C, the pre-university year schooling is voluntary but the programs are subject to conditions set by universities or their examining board.

One of the major thrusts of the curriculum questionnaire was to determine the broad curriculum goals, particularly in composition, and the extent to which these goals were supported by specific objectives and practices. Based on the theoretical review reported in Kadar-Fulop, Pezeshkpour, and Purves (1982), which examined various depictions of the curriculum in mother-tongue in general and writing in particular, three major thrusts were identified. The first of these was called knowledge-based or heritage curriculum, in which schooling in language was to make the student aware of and knowledgeable about the literary and rhetorical heritage. The emphasis was on learning and using a body of information and/or a set of traditional models of the best way to write. The second was called a competence or skills curriculum, which focused on the acquisition and development of a number of skills in reading and writing. The purpose would be to bring students to a common level of competence deemed useful by society. The third thrust was called the personal growth model, and it takes a generally developmental and individualistic approach to language and writing. The emphasis was on the development of powers of individual expression with a lesser emphasis on common skills or common knowledge. To these three was added a fourth broad goal of education which appears in language curricula as well: that is a goal which explicitly focuses on the inculcation and strengthening of values.

Question or Item

Table 3.1

Population /	AUS	CHI	ENG/WALES	FIN	HAM	HUN	IND	ITA	KEN	NET	N Z	NIG	SCO	SWE	THA	U S
	ABC	ABC	ABC	ABC	ABC	ABC	ABC	ABC	ABC	ABC	ABC	ABC	ABC	ABC	ABC	ABC
Is there a set of legal requirements for schooling in general?	S/X SS/- S/X	NNN	N NNX N	NNN	SSS	NNN	NNN NNN NNN	N NNN N	N--	'YES'	N NNN	XXX	---	N NNN N	NNN	S/LO
Is there a curriculum for the teaching of 'mother tongue' or language instruction?	L/S SL/- L/S	NNN	L LLL L EB	NNN	SSS	NNN	NNN NNN NNN	N NNN N	N--	X XXX X	N NNN	NNN	NNN	NNN	NNN	L SLL L
Does it include a specific section on writing or composition?	L/S SL/S L/S	NNN	L LLL L EB	NNN	SSS	XNX	XNN XNN XNN	N NNN N	N--	X XXX X	N NNX	NNN	NN-	N NNN N	NNN	L SLL L
Is there a curriculum for foreign language teaching that explicitly includes a section on writing?	L/S XL/- L/X	L LLL	XLL L (EB)	NNN	XSS	XXX	XXX XXX XXX	N XNN N	N--	X XXX X	X XXX	XNN (E)	NNN	XXX	N NNN N	- X--
Is there a discussion of writing in the curriculum documents of other subjects?	X/S XX/- X/X	XNN	L LLL L (EB)		XXX	XNX	XXX XXX XXX	N XNN N	X--	X XXX X	X XNX	XXX	XXN	N XXX N	NNN XXX	- X--
Is there a curriculum for writing in special subjects (e.g. business, remedial, education, special education)?	X/X XX/- X/X	NNN	L LLL L (EB)		XS		XXX XXX XXX	N XXX N		X XXX X	X XXX	XXX	XXX	X LLX X	XXX	- LLX X

N = by a National Curriculum Agency
L = by a Local DistrictSchool
- = no information given

S = by a State or Region
X = Does not exist
EB = Examination Board

The procedure adopted in the questionnaire was to ask directly about the emphasis in general educational aims and in the aims of language instruction. These questions were followed by a number of questions to which certain responses or emphases would indicate that the general thrust was supported by such matters as: the assumptions about students' prior knowledge; the emphasis in statements surrounding these goals; the role of texts and other materials; and specific classroom and instructional policies.

The assumption underlying the development of the questionnaire was that if an educational system espoused a particular goal, that system might logically follow that goal through its general policies and practices. On the other hand, it was also postulated that many curricula represented less a set of deductions from an ideological position and more a series of compromises brought about by changing and shifting ideologies over time, and by the recognition that ideology must be tempered by the practical world of the school and society. The purpose of the questionnaire was, then, to determine the consistency of the curriculum in terms of its premise, but not to judge whether or not consistency was superior to inconsistency. As a consequence, three analyses of the responses were performed: (a) an analysis using the logical framework, (b) a cluster analysis of responses, and (c) a factor analysis. The last two allow for an empirical look to compliment the logical one. These analyses were performed for the general aims of the curriculum, for the language arts curriculum as a whole, and for the writing curriculum in particular. We will briefly present the first two, then go into more detail. A detailed report on the analyses is available in Saari (1991).

Logical Analysis of Curricular Goals

In order to perform the logical analysis, each item associated with a curricular thrust was scored and assigned a value on a scale. For the heritage (knowledge) thrust there were 40 items; for skills (competence), 41; for personal growth, 35; and for values, 11. The scores were summed for each curricular thrust, then converted to percentages of the total possible score for the thrust, so that comparable scores for each could be assigned to a system of education for a population. To check the independence of the four thrusts, the items for each thrust were divided into two parts and correlations were obtained between the percentages across systems and populations within systems. The mean correlation between split halves was .89, and only for the values thrust did the correlation fall below .9 (.79). The correlations between thrusts were also high (about .70), which suggests that in very few cases did the curriculum for a population follow one strong thrust. But correlations do not show the absolute weight of the approaches. Some of the items were not found relevant in all countries. Therefore the procedure was not to use percentages but the means of existing observations.

An examination of the results across countries for each population (Figures 3.1-3.3) reveals that, overall, the four approaches are seen as equally important, although the values approach is slightly more heavily emphasized and the knowledge curriculum is the least heavily emphasized. The reason for the latter can be explained by its low weight for Population A. In fact, the results clearly show that for Population A, most systems of education value growth more highly and do not see the transmission of knowledge as important. By Population C, most systems claim to strike a balance among the four approaches.

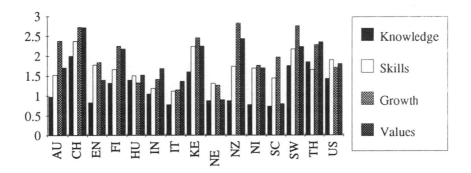

Figure 3.1: Curriculum Goals, Population A

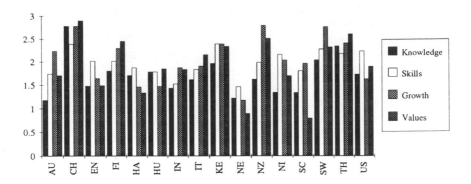

Figure 3.2: Curriculum Goals, Population B

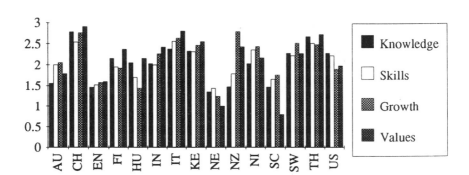

Figure 3.3: Curriculum Goals, Population C

Differences among countries are apparent in the results of this analysis. In part this is an artifact of the ratings within countries. Chile, Thailand, and Kenya especially rate all approaches high and The Netherlands, Scotland, and England rate them low. Whether this results from a response set on the part of the National Study Committee or from the reality of the curricula is unclear. On the other hand, Finland, Italy, Nigeria, Indonesia, and the United States emphasize the shift in the rating of the knowledge approach between populations more than do other countries. Italy, Indonesia, Hungary, and Nigeria report a increasing emphasis on values in the curriculum for the older populations. There are some shifts across populations for skills and growth as well, but they are less clear-cut than the shifts for knowledge and values.

At the most global level, no one thrust appears clearly dominant in any national curriculum. Most countries appear to have a mix of approaches, although most appear to display a shift in emphasis across populations. One suspects that this shift across populations represents the fact that the university system exerts an academic-literary pressure (emphasizing the transmission of knowledge about texts and authors and genres) on the secondary curriculum in mother-tongue teaching, but that such pressure is mitigated. The mitigating forces might be a realization that students will enter a variety of faculties and that therefore schools should emphasize not simply knowledge, but skills, growth, and values as well.

Cluster Analysis of Curricular Goals

In order to probe more deeply into the issues raised by this first analysis, a second set of analyses, using the technique of cluster analysis, looking across populations and centers, was performed. The analysis divided the questionnaire into three parts. The first analysis is based on the set of questions determining the overall educational objectives based on the purposes of instruction and those emphases behind those purposes. The second is based on the objectives of mother-tongue education, and the third on a set of questions measuring students' aesthetic, affective, and moral development.

The results tend to confirm the logical analysis in finding that the logical groupings remain more or less consistent. They also point to the differences between Population A and Populations B and C in the curricula of most countries, as well as the differences in national weightings of the variables. A secondary analysis shows that the age differentiation becomes increasingly clear. Both Populations A and C distinguish themselves for their particular mixture of the four curricular approaches. In the analysis of the aesthetic, moral, and affective goals, Australia, Chile, New Zealand, Thailand, Sweden, The Netherlands, and Scotland appear to make less of a distinction among populations than do the other countries.

The cluster analyses, therefore, tend to advance the picture of the curriculum beyond that set forth in the first analysis. They suggest that there are certain consistent trends in thinking about curriculum and instruction in the mother-tongue that go beyond the traditional curricular ideologies. The next analysis seeks to probe these trends further.

Factor Analysis of Curricular Goals

The third form of analysis of these goals was a factor analysis. The analysis was carried out in two stages, first producing "first order factors" using small collections of variables and then running a second-order factor analysis based on the results. The first-order analysis examined the general objectives of education (15 items), the mother-tongue objectives (15 items), the acquisition of knowledge (14 items), skills and attitudes (30 items), and general ethos (8 items). From these analyses were developed 21 scale scores on the relevant items; included as well were some single variables that were considered worthy of investigation (the social competence objective of education, listening comprehension, speaking, reading and literature, and writing).

From this exercise emerged seven factors that explained 81.7% of the variance. The factors could best be labelled: (a) Personal Growth and Language Development, (b) High-level Mastery of Language and Literature, (c) Student-Centered Language Learning, (d) Teaching Language Knowledge and Use, (e) Training the Basics in Mother Tongue, (f) Competence and Proficiency, and (g) Trust in Children's Abilities and Knowledge. The factor eigenvalues and percentages of variance accounted for appear in Table 3.2. Only the first two factors account for more than 10% of the variance and thus they should be the only ones considered as important internationally.

Table 3.2

Factors: Curriculum Goals

Factor	Eigenvalue	Percent of Variance
Personal Growth	9.82	36.4
High-level Lang/lit	3.76	13.9
Student-centered Lang	2.49	9.2
Teaching Lang Knowledge	2.02	7.5
Training in Basics	1.44	5.3
Competence and Proficiency	1.41	5.2
Trust in Children	1.12	4.2

When one examines the scores on Factors 1 and 2 for the various countries and populations, the results show some differences that had not been found in the earlier analyses (Table 3.3). Factor 1 divides the curricula into high, middle, and low groups. The low and middle groups are made up of the industrialized countries and the high group, the developing countries. On this factor, the countries' population differences are minimal and national factors outweigh age factors. For Factor 2, the differences are not between developing and industrialized countries, but again between Population A and Population C.

Table 3.3

Factor Analysis of Scale Scores

Score	Factor I Personal Growth and Development	Factor II High Level Mastery of Language and Literature	Factor III Student-Centered Language Learning	Factor IV Teaching of Language Knowledge and Use
-3		NIG-A		
-2.9				
-2.8				
-2.7				
-2.6				
-2.5				
-2.4		IND-A	HUN-C	
-2.3				
-2.2				
-2.1			HUN-B	
-2				
-1.9			THA-A	
-1.8		NIG-B		
-1.7				
-1.6			THA-B	
-1.5			HUN-A	
-1.4				N-Z-A AUS-A

	Factor I Personal Growth and Development	Factor II High Level Mastery of Language and Literature	Factor III Student-Centered Language Learning	Factor IV Teaching of Language Knowledge and Use
Score				
-1.3	USA-C			N-Z-C THA-A N-Z-B
-1.2	SCO-C	NET-A IND-B		KEN-AB
-1.1	NET-B	ITA-A NET-B		AUS-C
-1	USA-B FIN-C	SCO-A		AUS-B THA-B SCO-A
-0.9	AUS-B	HUN-A NET-C		
-0.8	HAM-B NET-C SCO-A		NET-C	ITA-A SWE-A
-0.7	AUS-C	AUS-A		SCO-B NET-A
-0.6	NET-A	USA-A	NET-B HAM-B FIN-C IND-A AUS-C	KEN-C SCO-C
-0.5		HAM-B	SCO-C KEN-C	SWE-B

Table 3.3 (Cont'd.)

Score	Factor I Personal Growth and Development	Factor II High Level Mastery of Language and Literature	Factor III Student-Centered Language Learning	Factor IV Teaching of Language Knowledge and Use
-0.4	SCO-B HUN-ABC USA-A	SCO-B ITA-B	IND-B KEN-B	FIN-B FIN-A HAM-B
-0.3		HUN-B	USA-B IND-C ITA-B	
-0.2	FIN-B AUS-A NIG-C	NIG-C FIN-A	USA-C ITA-A	
-0.1	N-Z-C		NET-A	HUN-A
0	N-Z-AB	HUN-C USA-B	USA-A	
0.1	FIN-A	SCO-C THA-A IND-C	AUS-B KEN-A	HUN-B
0.2	ITA-A			ITA-B
0.3	SWE-BC	N-Z-A		IND-A
0.4	SWE-A	KEN-AB AUS-B	SWE-C	USA-A SWE-C
0.5		CHI-A	CHI-BC AUS-A FIN-B	
0.6		AUS-C		NET-B
0.7		THA-B ITA-C	FIN-A SCO-B	IND-B NIG-A

Table caption (top of table): Table 3.3 (Cont'd.)

	Table 3.3 (Cont'd.)			
Score	**Factor I** Personal Growth and Development	**Factor II** High Level Mastery of Language and Literature	**Factor III** Student-Centered Language Learning	**Factor IV** Teaching of Language Knowledge and Use
0.8	CHI-BC IND-C	SWE-A FIN-C KEN-C		
0.9	KEN-C CHI-A		CHI-A SCO-A	USA-B HUN-C
1	IND-AB ITA-B	SWE-BC N-Z-B FIN-B USA-C		NIG-B
1.1	ITA-C NIG-B			
1.2			N-Z-BC NIG-C	CHI-A
1.3	NIG-A THA-B			IND-C
1.4	KEN-AB		N-Z-A NIG-B SWE-AB	FIN-C
1.5				NIG-C
1.6		CHI-C		USA-C
1.7	THA-A	CHI-B	NIG-A	
1.8				ITA-C CHI-C
1.9				CHI-B

The factor scores on the other factors tend to portray individual countries, groups of countries, or populations. Hungary and Thailand score low on factor 3 (Student-centered); factor 4 distinguishes Population C. The other factors show unclear differentiations.

Summary of General Mother-Tongue Curriculum Analysis

The scope of a mother-tongue curriculum can be quite wide. It may contain "the language," "the student," "the teaching," and "the relationship" of these with society. These elements are present in the four approaches used in planning the questionnaire: the knowledge-based (heritage, language), the skills (competence), the personal development (growth), and the values approaches.

All of the four general approaches are well represented in the curricula of the countries taking part in the Study of Written Composition. The approaches receive rather equal weight of importance. The values approach can be said to be most important, and the transmission of knowledge the least important, but the differences between them are not large. All these approaches are important elements in curricula.

Between countries (school systems), there are some systematic differences. One group of countries, Chile, Thailand, Kenya, and Sweden, is a high-scoring group. England, Australia, Scotland, and The Netherlands form a low-scoring group. It is not clear whether this difference is a function of the detail with which the written composition curricula are presented, or of the way the items were rated.

Concerning general aims, the general objectives of mother-tongue teaching, the acquisition of knowledge and skills, and the objectives of aesthetic, moral, and affective development, clustering (using cluster analysis) of curricula tends to show that a school system's (country's) three populations often appear together in the same cluster. The series of cluster analyses also show that clusters are not simply based on the differences of "high and low scoring countries." Depending on the nature of the variable (e.g., general objectives or aesthetic objectives), different systems and populations group together. At the same time, the analyses consistently show that the curricula for different populations do differ from each other.

The description of the mother-tongue curricula based on factor analyses makes an alternative to the description based on "the four approaches." They are necessarily overlapping, because of the common data base, but also informative. As written documents, intended to guide the whole school systems, curricula naturally contain "good and valuable" aspirations. The analyses show that both the students and the subject are given high value, but the balance between these two depends in part on the industrialization of the country or the level of education in focus. The student and the language, the language and literature (on a demanding level), student-centered curricula, teaching the proper use of language, teaching the basics, competence and proficiency--these form some of the competing themes in mother-tongue curricula of the participating countries in this study. There are common elements in these concepts and in the description based on the four approaches, and we may conclude that the participating centers in this study display common tensions concerning these various values in mother-tongue education.

The Analysis of Writing Curricula

The curriculum study and the curriculum questionnaire were based conceptually on three broad curriculum approaches: the Growth model, the Competence model and the Heritage model. These three approaches and the added Value model, were analyzed in the preceding sections of this chapter. Are these approaches also relevant for writing as a distinct part of mother-tongue instruction? Do curricula of school writing differ in respect to these approaches? Do countries differ in their writing curricula with regard to these approaches? Subjecting the writing section to a separate analysis will give a more focused description of the approaches, and possibly describe differences among countries and populations.

The analysis was done using the same classification of questions as in the earlier analysis, but excluding the questions concerning mother-tongue teaching in general. Three variables were created measuring "Knowledge about Writing" (18 items,the Heritage-approach), "Skills in Writing" (28 items, the Competence approach), and "Personal Growth in Writing" (18 items, the Growth approach). A fourth variable, "Values in Writing" was also created, but because it included only two items, it was given less emphasis and is not discussed. For each country and population, the mean of existing observations was calculated for each variable. The results are described in Figure 3.4.

Knowledge about Writing, or the Heritage approach, holds to the concept that writing can be done "correctly" and students are to be presented good and valued models of writing. There are appropriate style(s) of rhetoric; stylistic conventions; various genres of prose; style(s) of classical or contemporary authors; abstracts, summaries, notes, or outlines. Grammatical conventions exist and are important. Skills in Writing, or the Competence model, measures, among other things, the students' capacity to communicate and students' strengths and weaknesses in writing. It teaches students to record, report and narrate, to summarize, argue, convey information, present a point of view, and learn how to write and practice for examinations, how to evaluate their products and to improve them. Personal Growth in Writing, or the Growth model, contains items measuring whether the curriculum allows students to develop their expressive capabilities so that they can present their thoughts and feelings. Other items measure the extent to which students can freely play with ideas; organize and clarify their own experiences, thoughts and feelings; write personal essays; keep a diary, etc. Expressing the writer's personality, originality, and individuality or imagination may be accepted standards for writing in school and are included for this approach.

The results of these analyses are given in Figure 3.4. The scale may vary between about 0.5 and 3.0, with the mean 2.0, meaning approximately "some emphasis or occasionally emphasized." Countries are ranked by the combined population means (stacked means) for each of the three approaches. At the country level, the rank of countries is mainly the same as in the overall description of this "conceptual analysis". This means that writing is seen as a part of mother-tongue teaching and not differentiated in any major way within it. Some changes in the rank between countries do occur, but the differences in means between these countries are not of importance, so it is not necessary to give much attention to these changes. Scotland, New Zealand, and Kenya rank a bit higher for Knowledge about Writing than for the total scale Transmission of Knowledge. For the scale Skills in Writing, Italy and Australia rank a bit lower than in the total scale Skills and Competencies. For the scale Personal Growth (in writing), there are a few minor changes in the rank of countries when compared to the total Growth scale.

Between approaches there are differences so that Knowledge about Writing is the least emphasized (total mean over countries and populations is 1.59) and Skills in Writing and Personal Growth are more emphasized and have equal means (1.89 and 1.94). Knowledge about Writing is not an important approach for Populations A and B. Even for Population C there are several countries not emphasizing this approach. For England, The Netherlands, New Zealand, Scotland, Australia, Indonesia, Hungary, and Nigeria, the Population C mean does not exceed 2.0.

Skills in Writing is less emphasized for Population A than for the other populations, for which Skills and Personal Growth have equal weight. In most cases, the means do not exceed 2.0, giving rise to the interpretation that none of the approaches are predominantly emphasized. Individual countries may differ from each other, but there is the problem of possible response set as mentioned several times earlier. High-scoring countries tend to score high in all respects and vice versa.

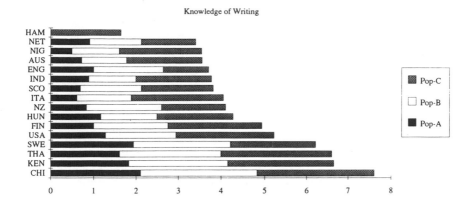

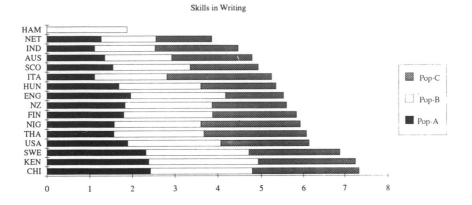

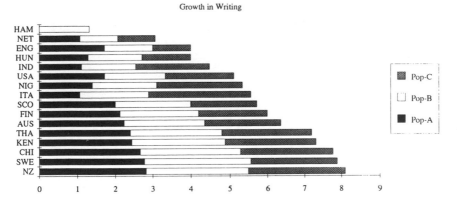

Figure 3.4: Emphases of Writing Curricula

In addition to the questions that could be classified according to the models, there were two separate questions that characterize the general approach towards instruction in composition. One aimed to measure three often cited general objectives: (a) a practical goal emphasizing communicative competence, (b) a cultural goal emphasizing cultural loyalty, and (c) a personal goal emphasizing individuality (see Kadar-Fulop, 1988). The practical, communicative goal is given attention in nearly all of the curricula and is often rated as having "major" emphasis in composition teaching. The personal, individual goal is also highly emphasized and these two goals have almost equal "weight" as seen in Table 3.4. Among populations, there are no clear differences in these two goals; both appear equally often in all different age level populations. So, the capacity to communicate effectively and the development of students' individual capabilities are important goals throughout the school systems. The goal of cultural loyalty is mentioned considerably less than the other two goals. The other question dealt with whether composition is seen as an art, a craft, a skill, or a process. Almost without exception composition is seen as a skill in all systems and at all population levels.

Table 3.4

General Goals in Writing Curricula

	Writing Seen as ...				Emphasized as Goal...			R A N K
	Art	Craft	Pro-cess	Skill	Cult.	Pers.	Prac.	
ITA-C	Yes	Yes	Yes	Yes	some	Yes	Yes	-9
KEN-A	Yes	No	Yes	Yes	some	Yes	Yes	-8
KEN-B	Yes	No	Yes	Yes	some	Yes	Yes	-8
KEN-C	Yes	No	Yes	Yes	some	Yes	Yes	-8
THA-B	Yes	No	Yes	Yes	some	Yes	Yes	-8
THA-C	Yes	No	Yes	Yes	some	Yes	Yes	-8
AUS-C	No	Yes	No	Yes	some	Yes	Yes	-7
CHI-A	No	Yes	No	Yes	some	Yes	Yes	-7
CHI-B	No	Yes	No	Yes	Yes	some	Yes	-7
NIG-B	Yes	No	Yes	Yes	some	some	Yes	-7
NIG-C	Yes	No	Yes	Yes	some	some	Yes	-7
SWE-A	No	Yes	No	Yes	some	Yes	Yes	-7
SWE-B	No	Yes	No	Yes	some	Yes	Yes	-7
THA-A	No	No	Yes	Yes	some	Yes	Yes	-7
USA-C	No	Yes	Yes	Yes	some	some	Yes	-7
FIN-B	No	No	Yes	Yes	some	some	Yes	-6
FIN-C	No	No	Yes	Yes	Yes	some	some	-6
HUN-B	No	Yes	No	Yes	Yes	some	some	-6
N-Z-B			Yes		some	Yes	Yes	-6

	Writing Seen as ...				Emphasized as Goal...			RANK
	Art	Craft	Process	Skill	Cult.	Pers.	Prac.	
NIG-A	No	No	Yes	Yes	some	some	Yes	-6
SCO-A	No	Yes	Yes	Yes	No	Yes	some	-6
SCO-B	No	Yes	Yes	Yes	No	Yes	some	-6
SCO-C	No	Yes	Yes	Yes	No	Yes	some	-6
USA-B	No	Yes	Yes	Yes	No	some	Yes	-6
AUS-A					some	Yes	Yes	-5
AUS-B					some	Yes	Yes	-5
CHI-C	No	Yes	No	Yes	some	some	some	-5
FIN-A	No	No	Yes	Yes	No	Yes	some	-5
HUN-C	No	Yes	No	Yes	Yes	No	some	-5
SWE-C	No	Yes	No	No	some	some	Yes	-5
USA-A	No	No	Yes	Yes	No	some	Yes	-5
HAM-B	No	No	No	Yes	Yes	Yes		-5
HUN-A	No	No	No	Yes	Yes	No	some	-4
IND-B	No	No	Yes	Yes	No	No	Yes	-4
N-Z-A			Yes		No	Yes	some	-4
ENG-A					No	Yes	some	-3
ENG-B					No	Yes	some	-3
IND-A	No	No	Yes	Yes	No	No	some	-3
ITA-A	No	No	No	Yes	No	No	No	-1
NET-A					No	No	some	-1

Table 3.4 (Cont'd.)

Table 3.4 (Cont'd.)							
	Writing Seen as ...				Emphasized as Goal...		R A N K
	Art	Craft	Pro-cess	Skill	Cult.	Pers.	Prac.	
NET-C					No	No	some	-1
ENG-C					No	No	No	0
	-9	-17	-25	-34	-33	-60	-69	

Factor-Analysis of Writing Objectives

In the spirit of the general thinking on the curriculum questionnaire, a series of questions were written to measure objectives of writing instruction. Twenty-nine questions asked "to what extent do the following reflect the objectives of writing instruction in your country?" The items represent roughly the competence, growth, heritage, and value approaches. In order to give a condensed description of the objectives, these variables were subjected to a Principal Component factor analysis. Varimax rotation of seven factors was found best for interpretation, although there are still several variables having moderate loadings on two or more factors. The decision was made to include these kinds of variables in more than one factor, hence they are used more than once in the interpretation of factors.

Table 3.5 shows the results of the factor analysis and lists the items. As a general comment on the results it can be said that items written to measure a given approach do not load on one particular factor only. Most of the factors are interpretable, however, and the four approaches can be partially recognized in the empirical classification of items in the factor analysis results. As the second general comment, it is a common observation that principal components factor analysis often gives one strong or general factor and a series of weaker factors (in terms of percent of explained variance), and this is the case in this analysis too. The first factor explains 46.6% of total variance; the six other factors each explains 7.6% to 4.2%. It is clear that the factors extracted after the first one are specific. Some 81.0% of total variance is explained by all seven factors.

Table 3.5

Writing Objectives Factors.
Rotated Factor Matrix.

	I'	II'	III'	IV'	V'	VI'	VII'		Item
	i								
2006	82	20	18	29	23	-7	-6	expr	play with language (words, syntax, etc.)
2023	74	16	20	35	16	34	3	heri	recognize and write in various poetic and other literary genres.
2029	71	31	14	29	40	11	7	valu	value the scholarly honesty and to avoid plagiarism.
2022	66	21	40	15	-16	43	-24	heri	recognize and write in various genres of prose.
2001	54	45	13	20	55	-6	-6	expr	play freely with ideas that occur to them.
2015	49	44	32	28	44	6	20	cogn	develop reflective thinking through writing and then reading their
	ii								
2004	13	81	10	28	12	22	10	expr	feel a sense of ach. at having produced smth. themselves.
2005	20	72	21	19	28	11	10	expr	become more aware of their ideas and feelings by seeing them on paper.
2002	32	68	35	32	1	6	34	expr	express their feelings and attitudes.
2025	38	67	34	7	-21	3	28	valu	trust and value their own expression.
2008	7	60	20	51	5	-8	-29	cogn	record, report and narrate events and information.
2007	-48	54	20	20	30	38	-11	cogn	diagnose indiv. students' strengths and weaknesses in writing.
2014	31	49	29	-6	36	39	-14	Cogn	write products which they can evaluate and try to improve.
			iii						
2016	-2	31	81	18	17	0	-5	cogn	learn how to write in various functional situations (business, pers.
2020	38	25	76	12	1	18	2	cogn	examine the motives in commercial writing and other propaganda.
2010	15	5	71	21	27	35	11	cogn	present, report, convey information, events etc. with pers. concl.
2011	25	29	63	22	9	-9	46	cogn	present points of view or ideas in order to persuade.
2003	41	35	49	30	11	12	43	expr	org. and clarify.... own exps., thoughts and feelings.
				iv					
2027	7	23	-10	79	-1	16	7	valu	value accuracy and correctness in writing.
2021	33	25	26	71	8	13	-8	heri	learn stylistic conventions.
2028	49	19	31	68	7	9	-8	valu	value the traditions of writing and literary expression.
2009	10	13	33	66	0	34	0	cogn	summarize information, arguments, etc.
2018	42	6	44	60	29	-8	10	cogn	develop lexical variety.
2017	27	14	45	59	50	10	-4	cogn	develop syntactic variety.
					v				
2026	10	10	13	0	82	9	12	valu	value the lang. and style of people who speak oth. dial. or lang.
2024	2	16	5	22	3	77	1	heri	imitate the style of various classical and contemporary authors.
2013	35	19	45	18	24	52	30	cogn	explore and develop varying points of view.
2012	-17	14	5	-13	6	0	85	cogn	learn how to write and practice for examinations.
2019	32	-21	10	10	39	41	45	cogn	learn how to write academic papers
	46.2	7.6	7.2	5.6	5.3	4.5	4.2	per cent of total variance. Cum Percent = 81	

The first factor is one of learning about academic language and writing. Playing with language, recognizing and writing in various poetic and other literary genres as well as in various genres of prose, valuing scholarly honesty, playing freely with ideas and developing reflective thinking, valuing the traditions of writing and literary expression, organizing and clarifying students' own experiences, thoughts, and feelings, and developing lexical variety are all objectives of writing instruction having high loadings (in descending order) on the first factor. "Diagnosing individual students' strengths and weaknesses in writing" has a moderate negative loading on the factor. The factor characterizes language and writing as "a subject to be known and practiced." The factor might be named "Academic Writing as a Humanistic Value." The factor includes important elements of skill and knowledge of writing as a school subject, but can best be interpreted as allied with the Knowledge approach.

The second factor concentrates on the development of the student by his/her writing at school. Among the important objectives of teaching writing are: allowing students to feel a sense of achievement at having produced something themselves, allowing them to develop an awareness of their ideas and feelings by seeing them in written form, providing possibilities to express feelings and attitudes, and trusting and valuing their expression. Different kinds of writing concerning events and information should be offered in school to be evaluated by students themselves in order to improve their texts. At the same time, students' strengths and weaknesses in writing can be diagnosed.

Students should have possibilities to play freely with ideas occurring to them, and to develop their reflective thinking through writing. The factor reflects ideas of personality development and is here understood to represent the Growth approach and is named "Personal Growth Factor."

The third factor stresses the practical understanding of different types of writing, intentions, and motives in functionally different writing. These include how to write for business, personal correspondence, and for other purposes; examining the motives in propaganda (e.g., commercial writing); how to write about information and events with personal conclusions, comments, and evaluation; how to persuade; how to organize and clarify one's own experiences, thoughts and feelings; and others. A competent, skillful, informed writer in practical situations of life tends to be the generalized meaning of these objectives of teaching writing. The factor was named "Writing as a Practical Skill."

The fourth factor is a description of a rather demanding attitude toward the learning of writing. Accuracy and correctness in writing are to be valued and stylistic conventions and traditions of writing and literacy expression are to be learned and valued. Students are allowed to develop lexical and syntactic variety and they are allowed to record, report, narrate, and summarize events, arguments, and information. The factor was named "Disciplined, Advanced Writing."

The third and fourth factors describe the skills and competencies approach, the former more for practical purposes, the latter more for literary purposes.

The fifth and sixth factors are of minor importance and are not interpreted here.

The seventh factor is a specific "writing for academic purposes" factor. Students are expected to learn how to write and practice for examinations, and how to write academic papers. They are allowed to present their points of view in order to persuade and to organize and clarify experiences, thoughts, and feelings. This kind of writing is useful mainly at school.

Factor Scores of Writing Objectives

Factor scores for "Objectives of Composition Writing" are presented in Table 3.6 for each population of the participating school systems. In interpreting the results, the location of a curriculum (country/population) on the factor score scale may be checked, being either "high," "average," or "low." Although the analysis gives exact figures, they are not to be taken so literally. Ranking of the curricula is the main result. Several countries and/or populations have missing values in the measured variables. Therefore, they appear as missing cases in results. It was attempted to overcome this problem by also calculating scale scores. Scale scores were calculated as the mean of existing items for a curriculum in the respective factor. Scale scores are not the same thing as factor scores, but they give the possibility to estimate whether a particular curriculum belongs to the "high," "average," or "low" group of curricula.

Table 3.6

Objectives in Teaching Writing. Factor Scores

Score	Factor I	Factor II	Factor III	Factor IV	Factor V
-2.5					
-2.4					
-2.3					
-2.2		ENG-C			
-2.1					
-2			NIG-A		
-1.9				SCO-C, N-Z-B	
-1.8	NIG-C		IND-B	SCO-B	
-1.7			IND-A	SCO-A	USA-A
-1.6	NIG-B			N-Z-C	USA-B
-1.5	ENG-B	HUN-A			SWE-A
-1.4		NET-A, NET-C			
-1.3		ENG-B	USA-C, ITA-A		SCO-A, SWE-B
-1.2			THA-A, ITA-B		HUN-A
-1.1	USA-B, NET-C, NIG-A	NET-B, THA-C		ITA-A	CHI-A
-1	NET-B	IND-A			NET-A, ENG-A

		Table 3.6 (Cont'd.)			
Score	**Factor I**	**Factor II**	**Factor III**	**Factor IV**	**Factor V**
-0.9	HUN-A		IND-C, KEN-A, NIG-B		ITA-A
-0.8	SWE-C, USA-A	ITA-A		NET-B	IND-A
-0.7	NET-A			ENG-A, ITA-B	IND-C
-0.6	ENG-A, USA-A	ITA-B		NET-A	
-0.5		IND-B, SCO-C		IND-B	
-0.4	ENG-C	THA-B	USA-A		CHI-B
-0.3		IND-C	ENG-C, ITA-C	IND-A, IND-C	
-0.2	SCO-B, SCO-A		CHI-B	NET-C, NIG-A	
-0.1	KEN-B, KEN-C		HUN-A, NET-B		IND-B, SWE-C
0	SCO-C, ITA-A, IND-A	CHI-BC, ENG-A, USA-C	THA-B, SCO-A	ENG-C, SWE-A	ITA-B
0.1	KEN-A		NET-C	CHI-C	USA-C, THA-A, N-Z-B
0.2		USA-AB	USA-B, N-Z-C	ENG-B, USA-A	NET-B

Score	Factor I	Factor II	Factor III	Factor IV	Factor V
		Table 3.6 (Cont'd.)			
0.3	ITA-C, ITA-B, CHI-A	SWE-C, THA-A, N-Z-C	NET-A	NIG-B, SWE-B	NET-C
0.4		KEN-C, SCO-B		USA-A	
0.5			ENG-A, CHI-A	USA-C, NIG-C	SCO-C, ENG-B
0.6	IND-B	CHI-A, ITA-C, SCO-A	KEN-C, CHI-C	ITA-C, CHI-A, KEN-A	CHI-C
0.7				KEN-B	THA-C
0.8		N-Z-B	SCO-B		ITA-C, THA-B
0.9	SWE-A	KEN-B	NIG-C, N-Z-B		KEN-A
1	N-Z-B, SWE-B			KEN-C, CHI-B, THA-A	NIG-AB, KEN-B
1.1	CHI-C	SWE-B			SCO-B, NIG-C
1.2		SWE-A	SWE-A	SWE-C, THA-C	KEN-C
1.3	CHI-B	KEN-A		THA-B	
1.4	IND-C, THA-A, N-Z-C	NIG-C	THA-C, SCO-C, SWE-B		
1.5			SWE-C		N-Z-C

Score	Factor I	Factor II	Factor III	Factor IV	Factor V
		Table 3.6 (Cont'd.)			
1.6	THA-C		ENG-B		
1.7					
1.8					
1.9	THA-B	NIG-AB			
2.0					
2.1					
2.2					
2.3				HUN-A	
2.4					
2.5					
2.6					ENG-C

Missing Cases: FIN-A-B-C, AUS-A-B-C, HUN-B-C, N-Z-A, HAM-B

For Factor I, Academic Writing as a Humanistic Value, we observe that three populations of a given school system tend to appear as a group. Usually the three populations (curricula) are close to each other on the factor score scale, meaning that a clear differentiation of writing objectives between different age populations does not exist. Countries (school systems) do differentiate. Learning language and writing is a strongly emphasized objective in the curricula of Thailand, Chile, Indonesia (Populations B-C), New Zealand, and Sweden (Populations A-B). Least emphasis is given to this objective in England, Nigeria, The Netherlands, USA, and Hungary.

Personal Development, Factor II, is a highly emphasized objective of writing in Nigeria, Sweden, New Zealand, Chile, Kenya, and Finland (Populations A-B). (New Zealand, Population A and Finland, Populations A-B are included in this group on the basis of scale scores, which are not documented here.) Personality development has little or no emphasis in the curricula of Indonesia (Populations A-B), The Netherlands, England (Populations B-C), Hungary (Population A), and Thailand (Population C). Hamburg (Population B) and Hungary (Population C) are also placed in this group.

Writing for Practical Life, Factor III, is an emphasized objective especially in some European countries: England (B), Sweden (A-B-C), Scotland (B-C), and Hamburg (B). This objective is emphasized also in New Zealand (A-B), Thailand (C), and Nigeria (C). Least emphasis on this objective is found in Nigeria (A), Indonesia (A-B), Thailand (A), and Italy (A-B), Hungary (B-C), and Finland (A).

Correctness of Writing, Learning Stylistic Conventions, Factor IV, is emphasized in Hungary, Italy, Thailand, Kenya, Sweden (C), and Chile (A-B). Least emphasis is given in Scotland and New Zealand.

Academic Writing, Factor VII, is an important objective for older student populations (B-C). England, New Zealand, Hungary, Australia, Finland, Italy (C), and Nigeria and Kenya (A-B-C) are the highest scoring countries.

Summary

The description of teaching writing does not deviate very much in any essential point from the description of the general language curriculum. All three approaches, knowledge about writing, skills in writing, and personal growth, are well represented in the curricula. The knowledge of writing approach is less emphasized than the skills in writing and the personal growth approaches. In the personal growth approach, the differences between school systems (countries) are largest. New Zealand, Sweden, and Chile have the highest scores, and the scores are high. The Netherlands, England, and Hungary score lowest on this approach. The factor analysis and the resultant factor scale scores show one main factor, Academic Writing as a Humanistic Value, which distinguishes certain countries, but there is not the clear pattern of distinction that was found in the earlier analysis. The factors generally show the differing approaches and goals of writing in various systems, but the differences are not so great as to suggest that any one system has radically different goals from the others. In general, all of the countries have expressed goals of writing instruction that concur with various positions in the debate on approaches to composition instruction.

Table 3.7

Student Writing

Students write more than a page a week in:

	Mother Tongue	Foreign languages	Social Sciences	Natural Sciences	Mathematics	Religion	Total
AUS-A	yes	-	-	-	-	-	1
AUS-B	yes	yes	yes	-	-	yes	4
AUS-C	yes	yes	yes	yes	-	yes	5
CHI-A	yes	-	yes	yes	-	-	3
CHI-B	yes	yes	yes	yes	yes	-	5
CHI-C	yes	yes	yes	yes	yes	-	5
ENG-A	yes	yes	yes	yes	yes	-	5
ENG-B	yes	yes	yes	yes	yes	yes	6
ENG-C	yes	yes	yes	yes	yes	yes	6
HAM-B	yes	yes	yes	-	-	-	3
FIN-A	yes	-	-	-	-	-	1
FIN-B	yes	yes	-	-	-	-	2
FIN-C	yes	-	-	-	-	-	1
HUN-A	-	-	-	-	-	-	-
HUN-B	yes	yes	-	-	-	-	2
HUN-C	yes	yes	-	-	-	-	2
IND-A	yes	-	-	yes	yes	yes	4
IND-B	yes	-	yes	yes	yes	yes	5
IND-C	yes	-	yes	yes	yes	yes	5
ITA-A	yes	-	yes	-	yes	-	3
ITA-B	yes	yes	yes	-	yes	-	4
ITA-C	yes	yes	yes	-	yes	-	4
KEN-A	yes	-	yes	-	-	-	2
KEN-B	yes	-	yes	yes	-	yes	4
KEN-C	yes	-	yes	yes	-	yes	4
NET-A	-	-	-	-	-	-	-
NET-B	-	-	-	-	-	-	-
NET-C	-	-	-	-	-	-	-
NZ-A	yes	-	yes	yes	yes	-	4
NZ-B	yes	yes	yes	yes	yes	-	5
NZ-C	yes	yes	yes	yes	yes	-	5
NIG-A	yes	-	-	-	-	yes	2
NIG-B	yes	-	yes	yes	-	yes	4
NIG-C	yes	-	yes	yes	yes	yes	5
THA-A	yes	-	yes	yes	yes	yes	5
THA-B	yes	yes	yes	yes	yes	yes	6
THA-C	yes	yes	yes	yes	yes	yes	6
USA-A	yes	-	yes	-	-	-	2
USA-B	-	-	-	-	-	-	-
USA-C	yes	yes	yes	-	-	-	3
SWE-A	yes	-	-	-	-	-	2
SWE-B	-	-	-	-	-	-	-
SWE-C	yes	-	-	-	yes	-	2
SCO-A	yes	-	-	-	-	-	1
SCO-B	yes	-	yes	-	-	-	2
SCO-C	yes	-	yes	yes	-	-	3

Table 3.7 (Cont'd.)

	Number of writing Assignments		Typical length of papers.				
	per month	total	<250	250-500	500-1000	>1000	portion done as homework
AUS-A	-	-	3	2	1	1	0.1
AUS-B	-	-	3	3	1	1	0.5
AUS-C	0	0	1	3	3	2	0.75
CHI-A	6	15	3	2	2	2	0.75
CHI-B	6	24	3	2	2	2	0.75
CHI-C	5	24	2	3	3	2	0.75
ENG-A	-	-	-	-	-	-	-
ENG-B	-	-	-	-	-	-	-
ENG-C	-	-	-	-	-	-	-
HAM-B	3	12	2	2	2	2	0.9
FIN-A	-	-	3	2	2	-	-
FIN-B	-	-	-	-	-	-	-
FIN-C	-	-	3	2	2	3	-
HUN-A	1	1	3	2	1	1	0.75
HUN-B	1	1	3	3	2	1	0.5
HUN-C	1	1	2	3	3	1	0.75
IND-A	2	-	3	1	1	1	0.5
IND-B	2	-	2	2	1	1	0.5
IND-C	3	-	2	2	2	1	0.5
ITA-A	8	16	3	2	1	1	0.5
ITA-B	8	15	2	2	2	2	0.67
ITA-C	3	7	1	2	3	3	0.67
KEN-A	-	-	3	-	-	-	-
KEN-B	-	-	-	3	-	-	-
KEN-C	-	-	-	-	3	-	-
NET-A	-	-	-	-	-	-	-
NET-B	-	-	-	-	-	-	-
NET-C	-	-	-	-	-	-	-
NZ-A	-	-	3	2	-	-	0.5
NZ-B	-	-	2	3	2	2	0.5
NZ-C	-	-	2	3	2	2	0.5
NIG-A	4	2	3	1	1	1	0.25
NIG-B	5	5	2	3	1	1	0.5
NIG-C	8	6	2	2	2	2	0.75
THA-A	-	10	3	1	1	1	0.7
THA-B	-	16	3	2	2	2	0.7
THA-C	-	16	3	2	2	2	0.7
USA-A	4	6	3	2	2	1	0.1
USA-B	2	4	2	3	2	2	0.5
USA-C	2	4	2	2	3	2	0.6
SWE-A	-	-	3	3	2	2	0.1
SWE-B	-	-	2	3	2	2	0.1
SWE-C	1	4	2	3	3	2	0.25
SCO-A	2	-	3	2	1	1	-
SCO-B	3	-	2	2	3	1	-
SCO-C	4	-	2	3	2	1	-

Other Aspects of the Curriculum

Amount of Writing

The amount of writing in schools is not easy to study and can here be measured only indirectly. The curricula themselves do not give any exact figures for the amount of writing, but some information has been given in the curriculum questionnaire by National Committees or National Coordinators for the Writing Study.

Table 3.7 shows that students write "More than a page a week" in mother-tongue in most of the countries and for most of the populations. This amount of writing is also typical in foreign language teaching, social sciences, natural sciences, mathematics and religion in many of the countries. If these six subjects are considered, students in England, Thailand, New Zealand, Chile, and Indonesia write five to six compositions a week that are more than a page. This is true for almost all the populations in these countries. Very little writing is expected outside of mother-tongue in the curricula of Finland, Hungary, Sweden, and Scotland.

Some curricula contain information about or suggestions for the amount of writing assignments to be given either in Mother tongue or in other subjects (as well). This information may be written in curricula, or National Committees have rated and reported the "general praxis" of schools. In the mother-tongue, writing assignments are given eight times a month in Nigeria (Population C) and Italy (A and B), and six times in Chile (A and B). Countries which report that writing assignments are given also tend to report that writing assignments are given in other subjects too. The total number of writings may be very high if other subjects are also considered. Chile, for example, reports a total of 24 writing assignments per month for Populations B and C, and 15 for Population A in all relevant subjects. This means almost one assignment per day. Thailand (10 to 16 assignments), Italy (7 to 16 assignments) and Hamburg (12 assignments for Population B) also report high amounts of writing. Other countries indicate either very few assignments per month or do not give this kind of information.

Whether there is information about the number of assignments in curricula or not, students still write papers and use writing both in the mother-tongue and in other subjects. Table 3.7 includes information about the typical length of papers, and this information is much more complete than the information about the number of assignments. It is natural that younger populations write shorter pieces than older populations. Here it may be enough only to pick an observation from this list. In Finland, writing assignments occur infrequently for Population C; however, it is typical to write a thousand or more words, which means about four pages. This writing is done at school. For Population C in Italy, it is typical to write long papers frequently, but two thirds of them are done as homework. Writing as homework is also reported in Table 3.7 and the general picture is that most countries assign writing as homework. However, it is very seldom used in Finland and Sweden.

The curricula do not give any overall picture about the amount of writing of students in school. No coherent observations can be made in this respect based on the curriculum questionnaire. The question as such is important and interesting, however, and, in extra effort to highlight this activity, the teacher files were also consulted. The teacher files in the IEA Study of Written Composition contain variables measuring the amount of writing in the sample of classes in each country. This information is also incomplete because of the different levels of participation of countries and populations in the study. Most countries did not participate for all populations and, therefore, the actual amount of writing can be described only for some countries and populations. Table 3.8 contains information gathered from the teachers of the sampled classes; such information supplements that given in chapter 5.

Teachers were asked how many compositions of the length of one or more pages students have written during the last three months. Population A results show that Italian teachers report students writing 16.5 compositions on average. The smallest figure is for Sweden, 2.1., and students in Sweden do not write over four compositions in any school. The figures for other countries range from 5.4 to 8.5. Standard deviations seem in general to be quite large and the ranges are often surprisingly large. It is normal to find schools (or at least a school) where no compositions were written during the three months preceding the study as well as schools with 20 compositions reported in the same time period. This happens in several countries for Population A: Indonesia, Italy, New Zealand, Finland, and the USA. The given figures for Italy fit only a few schools. If Italy is not considered, the rest of the countries do not deviate from each other very much.

For Population B the average number of compositions varies from 2.4 to 11.7. Italy, England, Wales, and New Zealand, have the highest means, and The Netherlands and Sweden the lowest. There are countries where the range is quite narrow: Sweden (2-5), Finland (1-8), and The Netherlands (0-8). For the rest of the countries it is typical that schools vary considerably in the amount of compositions written in the preceding three months. For instance,the range for the USA is 0 to 20. Between schools there can be very great differences in the amount of writing in most of the countries. In Sweden, Finland, and The Netherlands the amount of writing is the most uniform and extreme differences do not appear.

Table 3.8

Amount of Written Compositions
(Information Provided by Teachers)

POP	N Comps past 3 mos.			Periods mo for comp			Min typical class comp			Hrs. out of cl comp term		
	x	s	Range	x	s	Range	x	s	Range	x	s	Range
IND-A	5.7	3.5	1 20	4.6	3.1	1 16	60	19.6	15 98	7	6.5	1 40
ITA-A	16.5	4.7	10 20	15.5	4.9	8 20	85.1	20.4	30 98	44.9	12.7	24 60
NZ-A	8.5	5.4	0 20	10.9	5.7	2 20	46.1	19.4	15 98	4.5	3.6	0 20
FIN-A	5.7	3.8	2 19	5.4	3.4	1 20	63.9	20.3	40 98	1.4	1.6	0 15
SWE-A	2.1	0.9	1 4	5.7	2.9	1 15	62.1	21.9	2 98	2.2	3.6	0 13
USA-A	5.4	4.5	0 20	6.9	4.8	0 20	43.3	17.7	15 98	9	9.4	0 48
CHI-B	5.3	3.5	0 18	5.3	3.5	0 16	38.8	13.5	15 90	13.8	9.7	0 48
ENG-B	7.8	3.5	2 20	8.3	3.9	2 20	62.4	21.2	20 98	13.5	10.6	0 60
FIN-B	3.1	1.1	1 8	3.9	2.3	1 20	78.1	17.9	40 98	0.7	0.8	0 4
HAM-B	4.2	2.5	0 12	4.2	2.5	0 12	90.9	10.2	45 98	1.7	1	1 5
HUN-B	5.2	2.9	2 14	4.4	3.2	0 20	59.8	21.3	25 90	6.5	4.5	0 21
ITA-B	11.7	5.3	2 20	11	4.8	2 20	96.2	9.5	18 96	43.3	13.5	10 60
NET-B	2.4	2.3	0 20	4.8	3.2	1 13 ?	3.1	1.3	1 8	3.8	3.1	1 15
NZ-B	6.7	4.4	0 20	5.6	3.2	1 15	34.4	14.3	6 98	5.1	5.4	0 40
NIG-B	4.3	2.4	1 12	6	4.7	1 16	37.6	6	9 45	12.3	8.4	1 30
SWE-B	3.4	0.7	2 5	3.6	2.1	1 15	79.9	19.6	40 98	4	4.7	0 23
USA-B	5.9	3.8	0 20	7.7	4.7	0 20	51.3	23.4	10 98	11	10.1	0 60
WAL-B	7.1	3.9	2 15	5.6	2.2	3 10	42.1	10.1	30 60	11.7	10.9	3 42
FIN-C	3.1	1.1	2 7	8.5	2.9	4 16	94.3	4.1	85 98	0.5	0.8	0 4
HUN-C	4.7	3.4	0 20	3.5	2.8	0 11	83.4	16.8	30 98	9.1	7.1	0 36
ITA-C	6.5	5.1	1 20	6.6	3.4	2 15	95.7	13.8	-98	31.7	15.1	8 60
SWE-C	3.6	1	2 5	3.6	2	1 10	86.9	17.3	30 98	5.2	4.9	0 20
THA-C	3.1	3.4	0 22	4.8	4.5	0 20	41.4	9.5	14 60	7.2	7.6	0 30
USA-C	8.1	4.6	2 20	9.1	5.3	2 20	48.9	18.6	2 98	12.6	12.3	2 60

Comment: many values are missing for ITA-A and ITA-B

The same holds for Finland and Sweden in Population C. Students write 2 to 4 compositions in three months and "extreme schools" do not appear. Thailand has a slightly larger range. In Italy, Hungary, and especially the USA, schools differ a lot regarding the number of compositions, with ranges between 0 and 20, and the frequency of writing is greater than average.

Table 3.8 also contains information about the number of class periods that is used for composition writing in a month, and the number of times students write a "typical" home composition in a term. In general, the amount of writing is small in Indonesia (Population A), Finland, Sweden, and Hamburg. Schools in these countries do not differ noticeably from each other. Also, homework is generally not given. There seems to be a uniform practice in the teaching of writing in these countries. Teachers in other countries report widely different amounts of writing in different schools, and the amount of writing in general is greater.

The amount of writing in the sample classes is very different in different schools, even within the same country. The most uniform practice is in Sweden and Finland, followed by The Netherlands, Hungary, and Hamburg; these countries have the smallest standard deviations--and the smallest means. Writing in school is clearly the teacher's decision in most countries, and sample classes are writing very different amounts of compositions in different countries, also often within the same country.

Types of Written Work Emphasized

A General Model of Written Discourse was developed for the IEA Writing Study. The model presents the theoretical bases of school writing (Vähäpassi, 1988). This model has been used in planning and selecting writing tasks used in the international study. The questionnaire listed 27 types of possible writing tasks in school writing, grouped into six larger groups under the headings Essay, Report, Letter, Factual, Personal, and Literary. The 27 types of tasks are classified according to the General Model of Written Discourse in Table 3.9. The model is used here to describe how these writing tasks, taken from the curriculum questionnaire, cover the theoretical model.

Looking at Table 3.9, one can see that the 27 writing tasks do not cover the model completely. Many empty cells appear for reproductive cognitive processing, and some uncovered cells can be found for higher cognitive processes as well. It is simply noted here that the tasks, as asked about in curriculum questionnaire, do not fully cover the theoretical model. The actual intention is to show how curricula in different countries cover the 27 tasks (Table 3.10). In order to give some perspective to these tasks, they are set in the theoretical model.

Table 3.9

Curricular Emphasis to Task Types, Population B

Process Purpose	Reproduce	Organize	Invent	
Learn		Abstract:CH,EN, FG,IN,NZ,SW Summary:AU,CH,EN FG,HN,NT,NZ,SW, TH,US Precis:CH,EN,NT,NZ ,SW,TH Notes:AU,CH,EN, FG,HN,IN,IT,NZ, SW,TH Lecture:CH,EN, FG,IN,NZ,SW,TH, Outline:CH,EN,FGHN ,NG,SW,TH,US		
Convey		Personal Letter: All except.FI,NT Journal;AU,CH, IT,NZ,SW,TH,US	Reflective Essay: AU,CH,EN,FG,IT, NT,NZ,SW,TH Personal Essay:AU,CH,EN, HN,IN,IT,NT,NZ, NG,SW,TH Expressive Comp.: AU,CH,EN,HN,IN, IT NT,NZ,SW,TH,US	Philosophic Essay: CH,TH Literary Essay: CH,EN, NZ,TH
Inform	Factual Ans: CH,EN,Hn,IN,NZ, NG,SW,TH,US	Documented Report:AU,CH,FG,IT, NT,SW,US Narrative: All except FI,NT Description: All except AU,FI Sci/Tech:CH,FG, TH,US Informal:CH,HN, IN,IT,NZ,TH		
Convince		Business Letter: CH,EN,FG,IN,NZ, NG,TH,US Polemical Letter:EN,FG,SW, US	Argument:CH,EN, FG,NT,NZ,SW,TH, US Persuasion:CH, EN,FG,NZ,SW,US	
Entertain			Story: AU,CH,EN,HN,IN, NZ,NG,SW,US Poem; AU,CH,EN,NZ,SW, TH, US Drama;CH, EN, NZ Aphorism:None	
Keep in Touch				

Table 3.10
Types of Written Work Emphasized

Essay

Population A

Statement	AUS	FIN	HUN	ITA	USA	NIG	SCO	SWE	IND	NET	ENG	NZ	THA	KEN	CHI	HAM	MEAN	SD
2. Personal	0	1	1	1	1	3	3	2	1	2	3	3	3	3	3		2	1.1
1. Reflective	0	0	0	0	0	0	0	2	1	1	2	2	1	3	2		0.9	1
4. Argumentative	0	0	0	0	0	0	0	0	1	1	1	1	2	2	2		0.7	0.8
5. Persuasive	0	0	0	0	0	0	0	0	1	1	1	2	0	3	2		0.7	1
6. Literary	0	0	0	0	1	0	0	0	1	0	0	0	1	1	3		0.5	0.8
3. Philosophic	0	0	0	0	0	0	0	0	0	0	0	0	1	0	1		0.1	0.4
Sum of scores	0	1	1	1	2	3	3	4	5	5	7	8	8	12	13			

Essay

Population B

Statement	HUN	AUS	IND	NIG	FIN	ITA	NET	USA	SCO	SWE	HAM	ENG	THA	NZ	KEN	CHI	MEAN	SD
2. Personal	2	2	2	3	1	3	2	1	3	2	1	2	2	3	3	3	2.2	0.8
1. Reflective	0	2	1	1	1	2	2	1	2	3	3	2	2	2	3	3	1.9	0.9
4. Argumentative	0	1	1	1	2	1	2	2	2	2	3	2	3	2	3	3	1.9	0.9
5. Persuasive	0	1	1	1	2	1	1	2	2	2	2	2	1	2	3	2	1.6	0.7
6. Literary	0	0	1	0	0	1	1	1	0	1	1	2	2	3	2	3	1.1	1
3. Philosophic	0	0	0	0	1	0	0	1	0	0	0	1	2	1	0	2	0.5	0.5
Sum of scores	2	6	6	6	7	8	8	8	9	10	10	11	12	13	14	16		

Table 3.10 (Cont'd.)

Essay — Population C

Statement	ENG	HUN	SWE	NET	FIN	IND	NIG	SCO	ITA	NZ	USA	KEN	THA	AUS	CHI	HAM	MEAN	SD
1. Reflective	0	1	2	3	3	1	3	3	3	3	2	3	3	3	3		2.4	0.9
4. Argumentative	1	1	2	2	3	3	3	3	2	2	3	3	3	3	3		2.4	0.7
2. Personal	0	2	2	1	3	2	3	2	3	2	3	3	2	3			2.3	0.9
5. Persuasive	1	1	2	2	2	2	3	2	3	3	3	2	3	3			2.2	0.7
6. Literary	3	3	1	1	1	3	1	0	3	3	3	3	3	2	3		2.2	1.1
3. Philosophic	0	1	1	1	2	1	2	1	2	2	2	1	3	2	3		1.6	0.8
Sum of Scores	5	8	10	11	12	12	13	13	15	15	15	16	16	16	18			

Report — Population A

Statement	AUS	NIG	IND	NET	THA	ENG	NZ	SCO	HUN	ITA	USA	CHI	SWE	FIN	KEN	HAM	MEAN	SD
2. Narrative	2	2	1	2	1	3	2	2	3	2	2	2	3	3	3		2.2	0.7
3. Descriptive	1	2	1	1	2	3	2	2	3	3	2	3	3	2	3		2.2	0.8
5. Informal	0	0	3	1	2		3	2	2	2	2	2	2	3	3		1.9	1
1. Documented	0	0	1	2	0	1	0		0	1	1	2	3	2	1		1	1
4. Scientific/Tech	0	0	0	0	1		0	1	0	0	1	2	0	2	2		0.6	0.8
Sum of Scores	3	4	6	6	6	7	7	7	8	8	8	11	11	12	12			

Report — Population B

Statement	AUS	ENG	NET	SCO	NIG	HAM	HUN	IND	NZ	USA	FIN	ITA	THA	SWE	KEN	CHI	MEAN	SD
3. Descriptive	1	3	2	2	3	2	3	2	2	2	2	3	3	3	3	3	2.4	0.6
2. Narrative	2	2	2	2	3	2	3	2	2	2	2	2	2	3	3	2	2.2	0.5
1. Documented	2	1		0	0	3	0	1	1	2	2	2	1	1	1	3	1.6	1
5. Informal	1		0	1	1	0	2	3	3	1	2	2	2	2	3	2	1.6	1
4. Scientific/Tech	0		3	1	1	2	0	1	1	2	2	1	2	2	2	3	1.5	0.9
Sum of Scores	6	6	7	6	8	9	9	9	9	10	10	10	11	12	12	13		

Table 3.10 (Cont'd.)

Report Population C

Statement	ENG	HUN	NET	NZ	AUS	SCO	SWE	FIN	NIG	USA	KEN	THA	IND	CHI	ITA	HAM	MEAN	SD
3. Descriptive	0	1	2	1	1	2	2	2	2	2	3	3	3	3	3		2	0.9
2. Narrative	0	1	1	1	1	2	2	1	2	2	3	3	3	2	3		1.8	0.9
4. Scientific/Tech	-	0	0	0	2	3	2	3	2	2	2	2	2	3	2		1.8	1.1
1. Documented	0	0	2	1	2	-	2	2	2	3	1	2	1	3	3		1.7	1
5. Informal	-	1	1	3	1	0	0	2	2	1	3	2	3	2	3		1.7	1.1
Sum of Scores	0	3	6	6	7	7	8	10	10	10	12	12	12	13	14			

The centers were asked to rate whether a topic is receiving no emphasis (0), minor (1), moderate (2), or major (3) emphasis in a country's curriculum in each of the three populations. These answers are listed in Table 3.10. The table is arranged by tasks (e.g., Essays), by populations, and by countries (centers). Within these classifications individual subtasks (e.g., Personal Essay), are arranged in descending order to give a quick overview of tasks and countries receiving low or high emphasis.

Essay, shortly defined as an extended piece of original writing usually more than 2 or 3 pages employing the writer's own ideas, is mainly recognized in the curricula of pre-university populations (Population 3). Reflective, argumentative, personal, persuasive, and literary essays are all receiving at least moderate or major emphasis at this level on average. Some countries are quite selective in emphasizing different types of essays as writing tasks, for example, England and Hungary emphasize only literary essays.

Personal, reflective and argumentative essays receive moderate emphasis in the curricula of Population B level, and some countries (Scotland, England, New Zealand, Nigeria, Thailand, Kenya, and Chile) use the personal essay as a type of writing also on Population A level.

Report is defined as a piece of writing of varying length usually based on observation or reading. Narrative and descriptive reporting are emphasized at least moderately in most of the countries, mainly at Population A and B levels. Some countries make clear selections between different types of reports as tasks in writing. Only the informal report receives major emphasis. New Zealand places moderate emphasis on descriptive and narrative report in Populations A and B. England makes a clear distinction among types of reports and among populations.

Letter, a piece of writing addressed to a single person either known or unknown, is an emphasized task in Populations A and B, provided that the letter is of a personal nature. A business letter receives emphasis at the Population B level in about half of the countries, and occasionally at the Population C level. The polemical letter is moderately emphasized at Population B level in Finland, England, Hamburg, Scotland, Sweden, the USA, and Kenya.

Factual writing includes abstract, summary, precis, notes (either from lecture or reading), outline, and answer. At Population A level, writing an answer is the only task receiving moderate or major emphasis in most of the countries. No other type of factual writing is generally used. Sweden is an exception, describing all types of factual writing as receiving at least moderate emphasis. At Population B level, writing an answer is still the most frequent type of factual writing. Summarizing, taking notes from reading, and outlining are types of factual writing used in the USA, New Zealand, England, Finland, Sweden, Thailand, Kenya, and Chile. Some countries make a clear differentiation in this respect. Notes (from lecture), precis or abstract are not taught at all in Hungary, but the rest of types of factual writing receive major emphasis.

At the pre-university level (Population C), abstract and precis are the most rare writing tasks. Notes (from reading), summary, outline, and answer are generally emphasized writing tasks.

Personal writing includes here either journal/diary or expressive writing, defined as "less than an essay." Expressive writing is emphasized at least moderately in all of the populations, and by most of the countries. Diary is used as a writing task in about a half of the countries at Population A level, and less in older populations.

From *literary types of writing*, story is most often used. Drama, poem, or aphorism are not taught at all in many of the countries, and only some countries give major emphasis, for example to poems.

Specific Subtopics in Teaching Writing

There have been discussions concerning the role of various subtopics in the composition curriculum (Hillocks, 1986). Some of them were examined as general policy options in the participating countries. Teaching grammar in connection with composition teaching may be recommended in mother-tongue curricula. Curricula can also direct the practice to language uses, spelling, and development of vocabulary. Curricula may also give advice or suggestions in several other topics closely connected with composition writing. Comparison or cause-effect, for example, may be taught as examples of different rhetorical types of paragraphs and essays. Other topics may include outlining, analysis of the audience, propaganda techniques, logical analysis, different meaning of words, rhetorical figures, (e.g., metaphors or personification), techniques of revising and editing, and ways of thinking about a topic before writing. These topics were listed in the curriculum questionnaire and the degree to which they are taught as separate topics was rated using a scale from 0-3. Zero indicated that the topic is not taught and/or that it is not important; 1 indicated that it is not taught except incidentally; 2, that it is taught as a separate topic in some classes; and 3, that it is taught in most classes.

Teaching grammar and the practice of language usages may adopt one or several of different types of conceptions about grammar. The use of traditional, structural, transformational, functional, or communicative grammar was asked separately. Table 3.11 gives the general image that if grammar is used at all in teaching writing, it is mainly the traditional conception of grammar. Countries where the (traditional) grammar is taught as a separate topic in most of the classes are Sweden, Hungary, Hamburg (for Population

B), and Finland. In these countries the traditional grammar is taught in all populations, and also used in practice of language usages. Other conceptions of grammar are seldom, if ever, mentioned in the curricula of these countries. Only incidental use of (traditional) grammar is reported by Australia; in Scotland traditional grammar is taught in some classes at Population B and C levels. Little or no attention is given to grammar in New Zealand. The United States of America reports a more varied use of different conceptions of grammar; functional and communicative grammar are taught as a separate topic in some classes at all three levels of populations. More varied use of different conceptions of grammar is reported by Chile, Kenya, Nigeria, and Thailand where structural, functional, and communicative grammar are reported also being taught as separate topics, often in most classes.

Spelling and vocabulary are important topics in practically all of the countries in teaching writing. These topics are especially important at Populations A and B level, where they are taught in most classes. Other important topics are the teaching of different meaning of words (although not in Australia and Indonesia). These topics are considered important for all population levels and in most of the countries.

Neglected topics are *analysis of the audience,* which is taught only in some countries and only in some classes. Also neglected are *Propaganda techniques,* which are taught in most classes only in some population in New Zealand and Sweden. *Techniques of revising and editing* is generally taught only in New Zealand and Kenya.

Topics like *different rhetorical types of paragraphs and essays, logical analysis, rhetorical figures* (e.g., metaphors, personification), *ways of thinking about a topic before writing,* and *outlining,* are naturally rated more important for Population C level than for the younger populations. In some of these topics the variation in the amount of teaching between countries may be quite large. Logical analysis of the writing and the use of outlining are examples of these.

Materials Used in Instruction

Different materials can be used as an aid in teaching writing and in actual writing. Table 3.12 lists these kind of materials and indicates the extent to which they are used in different school systems and populations. The dictionary and workbook are the most frequently used aids at Population A level. At Population B level, the most frequently used aid is collection of literary selections or other literary texts. Dictionaries and workbooks are also used. Collections of literary selections are important aids at Population C level.

Table 3.11

Specific Sub-topics in the Writing Curriculum

A. Grammar	AUS	CHI	ENG	FIN	HAM	HUN	IND	ITA	KEN	NET	NZ	NIG	SCO	SWE	THA	USA	MEAN	SD
Population A																		
1. Traditional	1	3	-	3		3	1	2	2	3	1	1	2	3	3	2	2.1	0.9
2. Structional	0	2	-	2		0	3	0	2	0	0	1	-	0	3	1	1.1	1.2
3. Transformational	0	0	-	0		0	0	0	1	0	0	0	-	0	0	1	0.2	0.4
4. Functional	0	3	-	-		0	0	0	3	0	0	3	-	0	0	2	0.9	1.4
5. Communicative	0	-	-	-		1	1	1	3	0	0	3	-	0	-	1	1	1.2
Population B																		
1. Traditional	1	2	-	3	3	3	1	3	2	2	2	1	1	3	3	2	2.1	0.8
2. Structional	0	3	-	1	2	0	3	1	2	0	0	1	-	0	3	1	1.2	1.2
3. Transformational	0	1	-	1	1	0	0	1	1	0	0	0	-	1	0	1	0.5	0.5
4. Functional	1	3	-	-	2	2	0	1	3	0	0	3	-	0	0	2	1.3	1.3
5. Communicative	0	-	-	-	1	1	1	1	3	-	0	3	-	0	-	1	1.1	1.1
Population C																		
1. Traditional	1	2	-	2	2	3	1	3	2	0	2	2	1	3	3	2	1.9	0.9
2. Structional	0	3	-	1	1	0	3	1	2	-	0	2	-	1	3	1	1.4	1.2
3. Transformational	0	1	-	1	1	0	0	1	1	-	0	0	-	2	0	1	0.6	0.7
4. Functional	0	3	-	-	-	1	0	1	3	-	0	3	-	2	0	2	1.4	1.3
5. Communicative	0	-	-	-	-	1	1	2	3	-	0	3	-	1	-	2	1.4	1.1

Table 3.11 (Cont'd.)

B Practice of lang. uses	AUS	CHI	ENG	FIN	HAM	HUN	IND	ITA	KEN	NET	NZ	NIG	SCO	SWE	THA	USA	MEAN	SD
Population A																		
1. Traditional	1	3	-	3		3	1	1	2	-	1	1	2	3	-	2	1.9	0.9
2. Structional	0	2	-	0		-	3	0	2	-	0	0	0	0	-	1	0.8	1.1
3. Transformational	0	0	-	0		-	0	0	1	-	0	0	0	0	-	1	0.2	0.4
4. Functional	0	3	-	2		-	0	0	3	-	0	3	3	0	-	1	1.2	1.4
5. Communicative	0	-	-	2		3	1	1	3	-	0	3	3	0	-	1	1.4	1.3
Population B																		
1. Traditional	1	2	-	3	3	3	1	2	2	-	1	1	2	3	-	2	2	0.8
2. Structional	0	3	-	1	-	-	3	1	2	-	0	0	-	0	-	1	1.1	1.2
3. Transformational	0	1	-	0	-	-	0	0	1	-	0	0	-	0	-	1	0.3	0.5
4. Functional	0	3	-	2	-	3	0	0	3	-	0	3	-	0	-	2	1.5	1.4
5. Communicative	0	-	-	2	-	3	1	1	3	-	0	3	-	0	-	1	1.4	1.3
Population C																		
1. Traditional	1	2	-	3		3	1	2	2	-	1	1	1	3	-	2	1.8	0.8
2. Structional	0	3	-	1		-	3	1	2	-	0	1	-	0	-	1	1.2	1.1
3. Transformational	0	1	-	-		-	0	0	1	-	0	0	-	1	-	1	0.4	0.5
4. Functional	0	3	-	-		-	0	0	3	-	0	3	-	2	-	2	1.4	1.4
5. Communicative	0	-	-	-		1	1	2	3	-	0	3	-	0	-	1	1.2	1.2

Table 3.12

Materials Used in Instruction in Writing: Pop A

	AUS	CHI	ENG	FIN	HAM	HUN	IND	ITA	KEN	NET	N-Z	NIG	SCO	SWE	THA	USA	MEAN	SD
A. Textbooks (Treat each separately even if combined in one volume)																		
1. Grammar	0	2	-	3		3	0	2	3	2	0	0	1	3	2	3	1.7	1.3
2. Workbook	0	3	1	3		3	0	1	3	2	0	3	1	3	3	3	1.9	1.3
3. Composition text	0	2	-	2		0	0	0	2	0	0	2	0	0	1	0	0.6	0.9
4. Lang. description	0	2	-	1		0	0	0	1	0	0	0	0	2	1	0	0.5	0.8
5. Dictionary	2	3	-	1		2	1	2	3	1	2	2	2	3	3	2	2.1	0.7
6. Reading (general)	1	3	1	2		3	0	3	2	0	0	2	2	2	1	1	1.5	1.1
7. Readings	0	1	1	2		0	0	0	2	0	0	2	1	1	0	1	0.7	0.8
8. Lit. selections	1	3	2	3		2	0	0	1	0	0	2	-	2	3	1	1.4	1.2
B. Other materials																		
1. Std's own writings	0	3	1	2		0	1	0	1	0	2	0	1	2	1	1	1	0.9
2. Media	2	3	1	1		1	0	1	2	0	2	0	3	3	3	1	1.4	1.1
3. Progr./comp. ass't	2	0	0	0		0	0	0	0	0	0	0	1	1	1	1	0.4	0.6
Population B																		
A. Textbooks (treat each separately even if combined in one volume)																		
1. Grammar	0	2	-	3		3	0	2	3	2	1	1	0	3	3	3	1.8	1.2
2. Workbook	1	2	1	3		3	0	2	3	2	1	3	1	3	3	3	2	1
3. Composition text	0	0	-	3		2	0	1	2	0	0	2	0	0	1	2	0.9	1
4. Lang. description	0	2	-	2		2	0	1	1	0	0	0	0	3	1	0	0.9	1
5. Dictionary	3	3	-			2	3	3	3	1	2	3	1	3	3	2	2.1	0.9
6. Readings (general)	1	3	1	2		1	0	3	3	2	2	3	1	2	1	2	1.8	0.9
7. Readings (topic)	1	2	1	2		0	0	2	2	1	1	2	1	1	0	1	1.1	0.8
8. Lit. selections	3	3	2	2		3	1	2	1	1	3	3	3	2	3	2	2.3	0.8
B. Other materials																		
1. Std's own writings	0	2	1	3		1	1	1	1	2	0	2	1	2	1	1	1.1	0.8
2. Media	2	3	1	1		0	2	2	2	2	0	2	1	3	3	1	1.5	1
3. Progr./comp. Ass't	0	0	0	1		0	0	0	0	0	0	0	0	1	1	1	0.3	0.4

3 = used frequently as primary material

2 = used frequently but not the primary material

1 = used occasionally

0 = used seldom, if ever

The use of different materials varies between countries. In some countries, like Sweden, Finland, Hungary, and the USA, and also in Italy, the use of many different types of materials is frequent. In countries like The Netherlands, Scotland, Australia, Hamburg, and New Zealand, only one or two types of the materials are in frequent use. A group of countries, composed of Chile, Kenya, Nigeria, and Thailand, reports rather wide use of several of the listed materials.

Programmed material or computer-assisted instruction is practically an unknown way of teaching writing. The use of media as an aid is important in Sweden for all populations, but used less frequently in Australia, Italy, New Zealand, Chile, Kenya, and Thailand, and for Population C in Nigeria. Students' own writings are used as materials for instruction in Finland quite frequently, and less frequently in New Zealand, Italy, and Sweden.

Standards of Writing

Curricula may or may not indicate standards of good writing. Ten countries (covering all populations) report having these standards; six countries do not have standards in their curricula. Of those countries having standards, seven also have more differentiated standards according to the type of writing. This global information was detailed by listing eleven possible standards of good writing and asking about their importance. Ten of these standards were subjected to factor analysis. A two-factor solution was found to lend itself to a fairly clear interpretation (Table 3.13). The first factor describes a dimension of correct, standard writing, the second factor describes personal, imaginative writing.

Standards of Writing, Factor Scores

Factor scores, based on the factoring of the ten standards of good writing, are given in Table 3.14 for the school systems and populations. Finland, The Netherlands, England, and Thailand do not have these scores, and they appear as missing values in the table.

Two observations can be made concerning Factor Scores I, "Correct, standard writing." School systems do not clearly differentiate their standards among populations. A country's three populations are in general quite close together on the scale. The only clear exception is Italy, which considers these standards to be the more important the older the students are. Secondly, we see that these standards are of more importance for the older than for the younger populations.

Table 3.13

Standards of Writing.
Rotated Factormatrix.

Item	I'	II'	Writing should...
2411	83	1	follow conventions of form.
2405	77	27	be logical.
2406	73	-27	be simple without metaphors or other devices.
2410	73	-5	be in accordance with tradition.
2403	60	-4	be clear and unambiguous.
2404	58	-19	be free of errors in grammar.
2408	-18	93	be original and individual.
2402	19	82	vary language for different purpose/audience.
2401	-5	78	express the writer's personality.
2409	-22	76	be imaginative.
Perc.	34	27	
Cum.	34	61	

Table 3.14

Standards of Writing. Factor Scores.

Correct, standard Writing		Imaginative, personal writing	
I'	CNT POP	II'	CNT POP
-2.8		-2.8	
-2.7		-2.7	NIG-A
-2.6		-2.6	
-2.5		-2.5	
-2.4		-2.4	
-2.3		-2.3	ITA-A
-2.2		-2.2	
-2.1		-2.1	
-2	ITA-A	-2	
-1.9		-1.9	
-1.8		-1.8	
-1.7	NZ-A	-1.7	
-1.6		-1.6	
-1.5		-1.5	
-1.4		-1.4	NIG-B
-1.3	NZ-B NZ-C	-1.3	
-1.2	IND-A IND-B	-1.2	
-1.1	AUS-A SCO-A	-1.1	IND-A IND-B ITA-B
-1		-1	
-0.9	AUS-C	-0.9	USA-B
-0.8	IND-C	-0.8	USA-A
-0.7	AUS-B	-0.7	
-0.6		-0.6	
-0.5		-0.5	USA-C HUN-A-B IND-C
-0.4	SCO-C	-0.4	
-0.3	SWE-A	-0.3	
-0.2		-0.2	HAM-B HUN-C
-0.1	CHI-A	-0.1	NIG-C
0	SCO-B	0	
0.1	ITA-B HAM-B	0.1	
0.2		0.2	AUS-B
0.3	HUN-B HUN-A	0.3	AUS-A
0.4	CHI-B CHI-C HUN-C	0.4	SCO-A
0.5	USA-A	0.5	SCO-C
0.6	USA-B	0.6	AUS-C CHI-A
0.7	SWE-C SWE-B	0.7	SWE-A KEN-A-B-C
0.8	USA-C	0.8	SWE-C SCO-B
0.9		0.9	NZ-A-B-C
1		1	
1.1		1.1	ITA-C SWE-B CHI-B-C
1.2	NIG-C KEN-A-B-C	1.2	
1.3		1.3	
1.4	ITA-C	1.4	
1.5	NIG-A	1.5	
1.6	NIG-B	1.6	
1.7		1.7	

(Missing Cases: FIN-A-B-C NET-A-B-C ENG-A-B-C THA-A-B-C)

For Factor Scores II, "Imaginative, personal writing," we can again find that school systems tend not to differentiate between their populations when applying these standards. Sweden, New Zealand, Scotland, Australia, Chile, and Kenya are countries scoring high on the factor of imaginative, personal writing. Italy again is the country that makes a clear differentiation between populations, Population A scoring low, and Population C scoring high. Nigeria scores low on imaginative writing standards, but was the highest scoring country stressing correct, standard writing. This may be the result of the fact that the language of instruction is not the mother-tongue of most students.

Ten out of sixteen countries report having standards of good writing. For these ten systems, a factor analysis of ten specified standards showed that there are basically only two dimensions. The first is "correct, standard writing," the second, "personal, imaginative writing." But it is easy to question the scope of the standards given for rating in the questionnaire.

Conclusion

The National Coordinators and the National Committees of the Study of Written Composition were obliged to take considerable trouble in providing answers to the questionnaire. The content of mother-tongue teaching is broad and complex, which does not make a first empirical try-out like the IEA study easy. A general problem is that there are curricula intended to cover many of the phenomena met here, and there are curricula giving only the most important principles in mother-tongue teaching. What is plausible is that important things are taken into account in mother-tongue teaching in all school systems. However, they are not documented in the same way in all systems.

This chapter limits itself to the official documents guiding the teaching of the mother-tongue supplemented by the teacher questionnaire. By the use of the questionnaire, an answer, or response, to a variable "measuring" the curricula, is provided. Without this, it would have been impossible to collect this amount of information about all of the curricula. It is also possible to think that the responses to the questions are best rationalized, if they are rationalized by experts in each of the countries taking part in the study. Despite these advantages, there are some shortcomings of the questionnaire method as opposed to a single team performing a document analysis. One of the shortcomings is the possible different way of using the rating scales. Another is that no external validating information is used. The data are trusted, but not without critical evaluation. In the full range of the IEA Study of Written Composition, more information is provided on different levels, from teachers and students. The information reported in this study is best interpreted by consulting the other chapters, particularly the next two.

Nonetheless, we can conclude that the theoretical constructs derived in the preliminary phase of the study, Kadar-Fulop, Pezeshkpour, and Purves (1982), stand up to empirical scrutiny. The results also support the research of van de Ven (1988) who, in exploring the curricular histories of mother-tongue education in the West, found remarkably similar patterns of tensions among the major thrusts of the curriculum. This finding is supported in the subsequent review of Applebee and Purves (1992). The remarkable fact is that the tensions among the curricular thrusts are also played out in countries which have different traditions of literacy instruction. In this study, only Thailand can claim to be outside of European influence, either directly or through colonial residue. Indonesia developed an independent language after the departure of the Dutch, but its language curriculum is clearly influenced by the West. The African and South American countries in this study are clearly in the postcolonial tradition. Thailand has a long history of literacy and its language teaching shows some reflection of its Buddhist heritage, but the curriculum can be said to reflect Western influence. Alternatively, one could argue that the curricular thrusts discussed and reported in this chapter are not simply Western but represent some of the universal issues on the mother-tongue and particularly the writing curriculum. That argument cannot be supported or refuted from this study because of the sample of countries participating and the method of collecting data; nonetheless it remains a question to be studied further.

4

The Community of Teachers in Written Composition

R. Elaine Degenhart, Kari Törmäkangas, and Alan C. Purves

In the previous chapter, the different national approaches to the mother-tongue curriculum and written composition were explored and compared. Most of the data came from the national curriculum questionnaires, but some came from data reported by the teachers themselves and were aggregated to present a picture of the consensus curriculum in the various systems in the study. In this chapter, we will turn to look at the teachers who were included in the study to give a sense of the communities of language and writing teaching. Again our main focus will be on the teachers in Population B, but some attention will also be paid to the teachers in Populations A and C. The chapter is divided into three sections: the first on the characteristics of the teaching force, the second on the results of a cluster analysis that was conducted to explore patterns of practice across the teachers in the various systems of education, and the third on the emphases of the teachers at Population B on various aspects of composition and its performance.

Characteristics of the Teachers

Chapter 3 included some discussion of the practices of teacher training in each of the participating systems. As we look at the typical teacher of the written composition classes studied, we find that they generally conform to the standards for training. Other aspects of the group are, however, also worth study.

Gender and Experience

One of the commonplaces in many parts of the world is that the mother-tongue teaching force is predominantly female. An examination of the figures for this study confirms that impression with some exceptions (Table

4.1). The major exception is to be found in Italy, where the percentage is low for all three populations. The other finding that is somewhat surprising is the relatively low proportion of female teachers for Population A in many of the participating systems. Swedish and American elementary teachers are predominantly female, but they appear to be the exception. In the United States, the proportion of female teachers drops as one looks across the three age groups. It is generally believed that this trend results from the greater prestige and salary awarded to teachers of the higher grades. Such appears to be the pattern in all systems that have figures for more than one age group, but one cannot assert a clear cause for the phenomenon.

Table 4.1

Characteristics of Teachers

Country	Number	% Female	Mean Yrs Exp
POP A			
FIN	61	36.2	18.3
IND	150	49.7	12.5
ITA	42	12.2	22.0
N-Z	98	48.4	14.1
SWE	48	68.8	16.7
USA	83	81.8	14.0
POP B			
CHI	100	60.0	11.9
ENG	58	51.7	13.5
FIN	104	79.8	16.6
HAM	71	41.1	11.3
HUN	100	78.0	17.3

Table 4.1 (Cont'd.)			
Country	Number	% Female	Mean Yrs Exp
ITA	100	20.0	15.4
NET	107	28.0	13.6
N-Z	103	52.4	12.1
NIG	95	41.9	10.8
SWE	72	66.7	16.4
USA	174	69.0	14.4
WAL	12	58.3	12.1
POP C			
FIN	57	77.2	20.6
HUN	77	71.4	15.6
ITA	51	27.7	19.6
SWE	75	60.6	16.5
THA	65	87.7	13.0
USA	99	68.5	16.6

In most of the systems the teachers are quite experienced, with the number of years ranging from nearly 11 in Nigeria (B) to 22 in Italy (A). It is clear that the teachers in the study are veterans, whether because of the within-school nomination of classes or because they are truly representative of the total population is not clear. Nor is it clear that the years of experience are uninterrupted; given the gender of the teachers, and the family leave policies in most systems, we suspect that the service is not continuous. It would appear that teaching in most of the systems in the study is a stable profession with a clear career pattern that encourages individuals to continue in the profession.

Workload and Teaching Conditions

One of the often expressed concerns of teachers of written composition involves their workload. In this study, information was gathered concerning class size of the taught class as well as general student load, the number of different groups taught, which suggests different class preparations, and the amount of classroom time per week. These data are summarized in Table 4.2. One result which stands out at first glance is that class size is larger in the developing nations regardless of population.

Table 4.2

Teaching Conditions

Country	Class Size	# St Grps	Hr Tch Wk	#Yrs w/Cl
POP A				
FIN	17.2	2.6	18.5	3.0
IND	38.1	1.9	5.4	2.3
ITA	19.9	19.8	29.7	3.5
N-Z	28.7	2.5	22.5	1.1
SWE	25.4	4.5	17.7	2.8
USA	27.3	4.2	20.6	1.1
Mean	26.1	5.9	19.1	2.3
POP B				
CHI	38.0	3.1	21.7	1.8
ENG	25.7	5.8	18.6	2.0
FIN	27.5	7.2	14.9	2.6
HAM	21.3	5.3	11.9	1.2
HUN	27.2	4.2	13.9	2.9

	Table 4.2 (Cont'd.)			
Country	Class Size	# St Grps	Hr Tch Wk	#Yrs w/Cl
ITA	20.4	22.3	30.8	2.2
NET	NR	NR	NR	1.6
N-Z	24.2	5.1	19.4	1.1
NIG	37.0	2.1	14.1	2.0
SWE	24.3	5.2	14.3	2.5
USA	26.5	3.9	20.7	1.1
WAL	24.8	6.3	17.3	2.4
Mean	27.0	6.4	18.0	2.0
POP C				
FIN	26.7	6.2	14.3	2.8
HUN	26.9	5.2	13.8	3.5
ITA	23.7	27.6	25.5	1.8
SWE	23.2	5.1	13.1	2.0
THA	41.1	7.3	11.0	1.8
USA	26.1	4.0	20.6	1.2
Mean	28.0	9.2	16.4	2.2

Within the industrialized countries there is variation at Population A, which is defined as the population with self-contained classrooms. It is clear, however, that composition teachers in some of the systems appear to have specialized roles, or at least work with different groups during the course of their week. Indonesian teachers appear to be most confined to a single group of students, and Italian teachers appear to work with a great variety of groups. At Population B, the class size in the industrialized nations is relatively stable, but the number of student groups again fluctuates. If one considers the combination of class size and number of groups, the total load of the teachers in Chile, Indonesia, and Nigeria may not be any greater than that of teachers in the industrialized nations.   The figures for Thailand at Population C, however, suggest a heavy student load.

In terms of instructional time, teachers at Population A appear to put in more classroom hours than do teachers at the other two populations. The amount of variability across systems is great for each of the populations, however, with those in some systems putting in twice as many hours as those in others.

Table 4.2 also points to one clear difference among the participating systems.   This concerns the assignment of teachers to cohorts of students rather than to grade levels. In New Zealand and the United States it is the practice to have the students move from teacher to teacher as they progress through the school.   Such is clearly not the case in Finland, Hungary, Italy, and Sweden, where students and teachers remain together for a period of two years or more. One clear matter of interest in this study concerns the relative efficacy of the two practices, each of which can be defended philosophically.

The workload of teachers is not confined to class time, of course, and for teachers of composition, one must consider what is called the paper load, the amount of time spent in marking. In chapter 3 the number and frequency of compositions was discussed, and one must see the load in the light of the frequency of writing assignments. The teachers reported their out-of-class load in terms of hours per week spent preparing for class and marking compositions and examinations (Table 4.3).

Table 4.3

Teachers' Amount of Work Outside Class

	Hours Preparation	Hours Marking
POP A		
FIN	1.3	1.6
IND	2.7	2.5
ITA	2.3	2.6
N-Z	1.4	1.8
SWE	1.5	1.5
USA	2.0	2.7
Mean	1.9	2.1

Table 4.3 (Cont'd.)		
	Hours Preparation	Hours Marking
POP B		
CHI	2.7	3.0
ENG	2.4	3.2
FIN	2.4	2.9
HAM	3.0	2.9
HUN	2.8	2.5
ITA	2.2	2.4
NET	2.3	2.7
N-Z	2.3	2.3
NIG	2.3	2.9
SWE	2.3	2.2
USA	2.9	3.4
WAL	3.2	3.9
Mean	2.6	2.9
POP C		
FIN	3.2	3.7
HUN	3.5	2.6
ITA	2.9	3.1
SWE	3.0	2.9
THA	2.5	3.2
USA	2.8	3.4
Mean	3.0	3.2

In all three populations, teachers report they spend more time marking than they do preparing lessons. The teachers of older students report spending more time in both than do teachers of younger students. This result appears to support the general ideas that primary teachers spend more time on classroom activities and that the amount of time marking is proportionate to the presumed length of the writing to be marked. What is noteworthy is the relative lack of extremes in time from any of the reporting groups; the pattern appears uniform.

Results of the Cluster Analysis of Teaching Practices

In the earlier chapters on writing in general and on the curriculum in particular, different orientations to writing instruction were identified. The general thrusts of knowledge, skills, growth, and values were discussed in chapter 3. When one looks at the orientation of teachers, these four categories must be modified, in part because such models do not fully accord with the practices of teachers. Recognizing that most teachers of mother-tongue, particularly those trained specifically in that field emerge from orientations towards the learning of the mother-tongue that are rooted in university curricula and thus their teaching reflects their training. In most of the countries in the study, university training in the mother-tongue focuses primarily on literature and secondarily on composition and rhetoric. We have earlier suggested that much scholarly attention to the teaching of writing is relatively new, and many university curricula had few if any courses in the subject. As a result, teachers in the schools may be relatively ignorant of the various issues and concerns in rhetoric and composition.

The recent history of the teaching of composition has suggested a much simpler division in orientation, one between teachers who focus on the text as produced by the student and those who focus on the means by which the student produces the text. Such a split is often referred to as a product/process split (Knoblauch & Brannon, 1984). The product teacher tends to focus on textual issues of content, organization, and style with greater or lesser attention to grammar, spelling, and handwriting. Within this group there may be a split between "liberal" and "conservative" approaches and views of text, but the focus of both groups would be on the text. The process approach is one that focuses on the gestation and birth of a text, which conceives of instruction as helping the student plan, draft, revise, and edit the text. The teacher may be more or less directive concerning this process and may use other students as mentors and editors or sounding boards. Throughout the process the text plays a part, but the explicit focus of instruction is on learning steps and procedures rather than forms.

To these two groups one should add a third type of mother-tongue teacher, one who comes out of the knowledge or heritage tradition as taught in the university but who has little knowledge of or interest in the teaching of composition. Literature is the focus, and students may write about literature or literary history, as a vehicle to something called literary understanding.

It was on the basis of this understanding of the approaches of teachers to the subject of composition that many of the questions were developed. The analysis of the results, however, did not begin with this theoretical orientation. Instead, certain responses to the questionnaire were selected on the basis of the theoretical approaches and then tested through factor and cluster analyses. Thirty-seven items were selected on the assumption that they would group teachers according to orientations that might be labelled process, product, grammar, and personal development. To these were added some variables that might further differentiate teaching styles: amount of writing assigned, hours spent marking papers, attention to the most able and least able students.

Table 4.4

Final Cluster Centers

Key Variable	Cluster 1	Cluster 2	Cluster 3	Cluster 4	Cluster 5
Data Coll	2.03	2.16	2.09	1.34	1.38
Cont Dev	2.01	2.55	2.27	1.51	1.61
Curr Led	1.58	1.61	1.60	1.93	1.97
Text Led	1.77	1.92	1.96	2.40	2.39
Syntax	2.17	2.50	1.96	1.39	1.90
Stc Comb	2.15	2.41	1.84	1.34	1.92
Topic Disc	1.80	2.70	2.66	1.05	1.69
Stu Disc	2.27	2.34	2.25	2.30	1.59
Hrs Mark	3.09	3.69	1.91	3.29	1.79
Most Able	2.06	2.01	1.94	2.10	1.35
Least Able	1.33	1.23	1.45	1.57	1.33

A cross-national cluster analysis was performed producing the five clusters (Table 4.4). The clusters can be labelled by the key variables that define them: Cluster 1 is marked by an emphasis on sentence combining and attention to marking papers; Cluster 2 is marked by attention to marking compositions and classroom exercises that emphasize both process and product; Cluster 3 can be defined as a prewriting focus; Cluster 4 as a curriculum and textbook dominated approach; and Cluster 5 by a focus on the most able students in the class and on the syllabus.

When the teachers in given systems of education are viewed in the light of these clusters and compared, we see rather striking differences in approach (Figures 4.1-4.5 and Table 4.5). Teachers in The Netherlands and Hungary appear to be most concerned with teaching syntactic development and they use sentence combining to achieve this goal. Teachers in the United States claim to use a variety of techniques that suggest an interest in both the processes related to writing and the product or the finished composition. The teachers in Nigeria, the United States, Italy, and Hungary all claim to be interested in emphasizing prewriting through discussion of the topic whether it be teacher- or student-initiated. In New Zealand, Hamburg, and Finland, teachers claim to teach according to the prescribed curriculum and the textbooks that are used. Finally, teachers in Sweden and The Netherlands combine this concern with a concern for the most able students in the class.

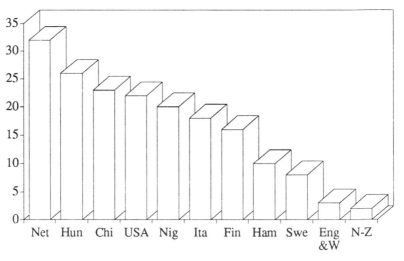

Figure 4.1: Cluster Scores Sentence Combining

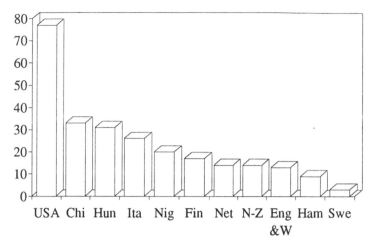

Figure 4.2: Cluster Score on Process/Product Teaching

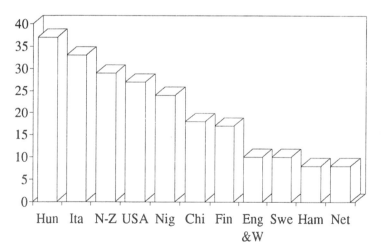

Figure 4.3: Cluster Scores for Pre-Writing Emphasis

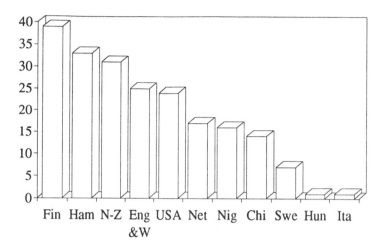

Figure 4.4: Cluster Scores for Curriculum and Text Emphasis

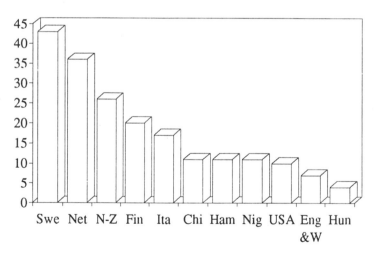

Figure 4.5: Cluster Score Most Able Focus

Table 4.5

Cluster Scores by Country

	Cluster						
	1	2	3	4	5	Total	Mean
CHI	23	33	18	14	11	99	9.3
ENG & WAL	3	13	10	25	7	58	5.5
FIN	16	17	17	39	20	109	10.3
HAM	10	9	8	33	11	71	6.7
HUN	26	31	37	1	4	99	9.3
ITA	18	26	33	1	17	95	8.9
NET	32	14	8	17	36	107	10.1
N-Z	2	14	29	31	26	102	9.6
NIG	20	20	24	16	11	102	9.6
SWE	8	3	10	7	43	91	8.6
USA	22	77	27	24	10	71	6.7
Total	180	257	221	208	196	160	15.1
Mean	16.9	24.2	20.8	19.6	18.5	1062	

Clearly, then, teachers in the various systems in the study differ as to the paramount concern influencing their various activities. The differences, however, are not marked by the ideological differences that appear in the literature surrounding composition teaching. As in other areas of the curriculum, the real concerns of teachers are more pragmatic than ideological.

Emphases of Writing Teachers in Relation to Outcomes

Here we will concentrate on the reported opportunity to learn some of the tasks that formed the basis of the writing assessment, together with discussion of teachers' emphases on the rating criteria. The focus is on Population B because that is the focus of the analysis in the later chapters of this volume.

Opportunity to Learn

The teachers were asked to give the number of assignments they had made during the year that could be labelled according to the task definitions used in the study. They were given the actual tasks to serve as examples. The results are given in Table 4.6, which also gives a picture of the amount of practice the students were given in written composition generally. One caution in interpreting this table is the figure for exposition; one suspects that the teachers saw the surface form of the task--a friendly letter--rather than the underlying structure and shaped their responses accordingly.

Table 4.6

Number of Assignments on Academic Topics
Population B

	Func tional	Sum- mary	Descrip- tion	Pers. Narr.	Refl. Essay	Argu- ment	Expos- ition	Open	TOTAL
CHI	6.89	8.70	2.40	1.96	2.11	1.39	0.97	1.02	25.44
ENG	8.26	2.09	1.73	4.47	2.83	3.11	0.95	-	23.44
FIN	3.50	2.67	2.74	4.86	4.36	1.90	0.79	1.32	22.14
HAM	1.98	-	-	0.74	0.66	2.00	0.09	-	5.47
HUN	3.94	2.23	1.08	2.90	1.14	0.81	1.13	-	13.23
ITA	15.92	10.71	7.46	4.79	5.72	3.56	3.26	3.89	55.31
NET	1.46	-	-	1.06	0.55	0.56	0.14	-	3.77
N-Z	8.36	-	1.73	4.58	3.85	3.84	1.20	-	23.56
NIG	11.18	3.27	3.33	2.51	2.43	2.39	2.43	1.59	29.13
SWE	7.62	4.58	2.26	4.78	1.63	1.83	0.37	1.22	24.29
USA	3.82	2.86	2.75	2.12	2.01	1.82	0.83	1.15	17.36
WAL	10.53	2.08	2.27	5.09	3.46	3.64	1.33	-	28.40
Mean	6.96	4.35	2.78	3.32	2.56	2.24	1.12	1.70	22.63

It is clear that Italian teachers assign significantly more functional and summary writing than do teachers in other systems. They also assign more writing generally--over ten times as much as teachers in The Netherlands (who may assign other kinds of tasks). These two types of writing are the most variable across the systems, although there is variation in the frequency of descriptive tasks and the open assignment as well. It is worth noting that summary, description, and the open topic are not assigned in some of the participating systems, or at least are not recognized. The more academic tasks of personal narrative, reflective essay, and argument tend to be assigned more uniformly across systems, with the first of these being somewhat more frequent than the other two.

What seems worthy of note is the relative infrequency of writing assignments of the sorts covered in the study in Hamburg and The Netherlands. As was noted in the preceding chapter, relatively few compositions are assigned in The Netherlands, but such is not reported in Hamburg. These two systems are not the only ones reporting less writing than the average; Hungarian and United States teachers also claim they do not assign these kinds of writing as frequently as do teachers in the other systems. It might be expected that the students would not perform as well on writing generally if we can credit the belief that "practice counts."

Criteria of Good Writing

A final aspect of the teacher questionnaire is directly related to the scoring scheme used in the study. The teachers were asked to rank the importance of the major criteria (content, structure, style and tone, and mechanics) as applied to each of the types of composition. Because the argumentative task will figure in subsequent analyses, we present the results of that ranking for the Population B teachers here (Table 4.7). It is clear that all of the systems except Hungary report each of the aspects as in the important range, and the Hungarian results may be attributed to a coding error.

Some system differences are of note. Nigerian and Chilean teachers rate mechanics high, and the Nigerian teachers rate it well above content. Several systems rate structure as high as content or higher, but none rank style and tone first or tied for first. The Finnish teachers do rate it second, which may help explain something of the results that will be reported in the the appendix on scoring (Appendix B). The ratings are extremely close, of course, but the range was not great (1-3); nonetheless these findings do suggest that the communities of teachers differ in ranking the qualities of good writing, and that uniformity of definition may be an illusion.

Table 4.7

Teachers' Rating of Score Aspects for Argument
Population B

	Content	Structure	Style	Mechanics
CHI	2.8	2.7	2.7	2.8
ENG	2.9	2.9	2.8	2.5
FIN	2.8	2.3	2.7	2.1
HAM	2.8	2.8	2.5	2.0
HUN	1.1	1.2	1.2	1.2
ITA	2.8	2.9	2.7	2.7
NET	2.8	2.6	2.7	2.4
N-Z	2.8	2.9	2.6	2.2
NIG	1.1	2.7	2.6	2.8
SWE	2.9	2.9	2.7	2.6
USA	2.9	2.9	2.7	2.6
WAL	2.3	2.8	2.5	2.1

Conclusion

What we have seen of the teachers, then, is that they are generally a group of experienced practitioners, mostly female, with varying working conditions. Internationally, the teachers share certain goals and aims, but the national and cultural differences are strong. They extend to the frequency and amount of writing assigned and to the criteria used for judging the quality of writing. These differences are clear to their students as we shall see in the next chapter.

5

Pupil Perception of Writing Instruction in Schools

Sauli Takala and R. Elaine Degenhart

In the preceding chapters, some data have been presented reflecting the reported opportunity to learn particular types of writing in the classroom and the teaching approaches and methods of instruction employed. The sources of these data are the Teacher Questionnaire and reported curriculum and examination items. This chapter will examine an aspect of the International Study of Written Composition that was designed to analyze what students have to say about writing as a school subject.

The data on which this chapter is based come from the writing task described in some detail in the first international report volume (see Bauer & Purves, 1988). The form of the assignment was a letter of advice to a younger student in which students write freely about their perceptions of writing instruction in their schools. When the idea for this task was discussed at the first International Study Committee meeting in 1981, the task was felt to be unusual and too unfamiliar to the students, and so it was not included in the first set of tasks piloted by National Centers. As experiences accumulated in the project, however, it became clear that researchers in the past have not asked students themselves about learning to write. It is possible that students receive very different messages about what is important than their teachers realize -- or intend. In order to examine this question, the original idea for a "letter of advice" task reemerged. (Since the decision about the task was made, the study of pupil conceptions, misconceptions and perceptions of specific school subjects has considerably increased throughout the world.)

This task was designed to serve two functions in the study. In addition to its function as a means of evaluating achievement in a particular type of writing, it was also intended to be "a composition about composition, thus providing information about what students in the various systems of education knew and thought about school writing" (Bauer & Purves, 1988, p. 100). The expectation was that such an exercise would complement and enhance various questionnaire data that would emerge from students and teachers. In particular, the task would provide "the students' perspectives on the criteria for good writing; how they perceived the school and the teacher, and what values the school and the teacher place on various aspects and textual features of writing" (p. 100). The task instructions were given as follows:

Letter of Advice to a Younger Student

Write a letter of advice to a student two years younger than you who is planning to attend your school and who has asked you to tell them how to write a composition that will be considered good by teachers in your school. Write a friendly letter and describe in it at least five specific hints as to what you think teachers in your school find important when they judge compositions.

The task was presented to all students in the sample population who were at the end of compulsory schooling, that is, that stage where the majority of the age cohort were still in school (Population B). It was also presented to half of the students in the pre-university year sample population (Population C). There was a specified audience, a slightly younger student, to whom the writer was to present specific information in a friendly manner from previous experience. Presumably the information to be given was such that the writer should be able to extract it from memory, although it would not have been information that had been specifically studied. The information was then coded for its content and analyzed in respect to national and international perspectives on the activity of writing and on the texts produced.

The development of a coding system that could be applied as uniformly and as quickly as possible by coders at all National Centers was a major task for the Steering Committee. The coding scheme was constructed on the basis of earlier conceptual work done in the project and was pilot tested and revised several times on the basis of comments from some of the participating National Centers. The final version of the coding scheme makes a distinction between the process of the writing product, and behavior tactics in class as major sources influencing success in getting good grades.

Content Coding

The theoretical basis for the coding scheme comes from the domain specification of the study (Purves, Soter, Takala, & Vahapassi, 1984; Vahapassi, 1988), which sets forth both cognitive and communicative dimensions of writing tasks. It also comes from the curriculum analysis reflected in the Teacher Questionnaire as set forth in Kadar-Fulop, Pezeshkpour, and Purves (1982). In addition, the scheme is partially derived from the scoring scheme of the study (Purves, Gorman, & Takala, 1988), which identified several dimensions that teachers and other raters attend to when scoring compositions (content, organization, style and tone, grammar, spelling and orthography, handwriting and neatness, and interest).

An examination of sample responses to the task indicated that most of the responses do indeed refer to these categories, although the students generally do not use terms like "reader" or "audience" but "teachers" or "they" when discussing what will be interesting. Interest on the part of the rater may, in fact, be considered the result of audience awareness on the part of the writer.

However, students added categories of their own as well. The compositions turned up two additional types of advice. The first of these concerned the processes involved in writing, which in great part refer to both the generally accepted stages of writing (planning, drafting, revising, and editing), and also to the cognitive operations underlying these processes as well as underlying the domain of writing itself. The students told how to succeed, not merely what success was. The second concerns what one might call tactics, and arises from the fact that many of the students interpret their teachers' judgments to refer to broader aspects of school work and behavior than composition. They believe that success in composition depends on other matters such as dress or behavior in class. The fact that they include advice on these broader aspects means that in order to report accurately, one should code these items even though they do not necessarily fit theoretically into the domain of composition.

From these considerations, then, three broad categories emerged for coding: Product, which includes content, organization, style and tone, and presentation (including grammar, spelling, and punctuation); Process, which includes consideration of audience, prewriting, writing, and postwriting; and Tactics, which includes behavior and personality. It was decided, however, that these categories were too general, and that a more specific coding scheme should be developed. From an examination of a sample of the National Centers' pilot test compositions, a final three-digit coding scheme was developed. The first digit indicates the general area (e.g., 1 for Content); the second indicates a subarea (e.g., 11 for Content/Information); and the third the specific topic within a subarea (111 for Content/Information/Keep to topic). The most specific level codes are cast in the form of sample statements. Table 5.1 lists the major and subcategory levels. The full scheme is given in Takala (1987).

Table 5.1.

Coding scheme for the major category and subcategory levels of coding.

1(00) CONTENT
           11(0) Information
           12(0) Approach to content
           13(0) Variety
           14(0) Details

2(00) ORGANIZATION
           21(0) Overall structure
           22(0) Introduction
           23(0) Body
           24(0) Paragraph level
           25(0) Conclusion

3(00) STYLE AND TONE
           31(0) Uniformity
           32(0) Clarity
           33(0) Elaboration
           34(0) Personality
           35(0) Lexical choice
           36(0) Syntactic choice
           37(0) Paragraph or discourse choice
           38(0) Set style of school/teacher

4(00) PRESENTATION
           41(0) Appearance
           42(0) Length/format
           43(0) Grammar
           44(0) Spelling and punctuation

5(00) PROCESS
           51(0) Selection of audience and preparation for it
           52(0) Selection of topic/task
           53(0) Advance preparation
           54(0) Planning
           55(0) Drafting
           56(0) Revision/editing
           57(0) Use of feedback
           58(0) Punctuality and time

6(00) TACTICS
             61(0) Dress/physical appearance
             62(0) Participation/behavior
             63(0) Attitude toward teacher
             64(0) Attitude with peers
             65(0) Honesty
             66(0) Time/use of resources

800 UNCLASSIFIABLE

An attempt was made to determine the relative importance of the items recommended by the students. However, pilot test experience showed that it greatly increased the level of inference and the coding time required. In a great number of cases it was virtually impossible to ascertain. For example, students might list several items as being "most important." For international purposes it was therefore decided simply to note the presence or absence of an item. Furthermore, many students listed more than the five items suggested. It was decided to record all of the items listed by each student.

The procedure required the coders to first mark the items listed by the student. These items were usually contained in a proposition, or "*t*-unit". Text that did not contain any advice about writing or classroom behavior was disregarded.

Although the *t*-unit was usually a good indicator of new advice, there were three major exceptions:

Take care of your spelling; a large number of spelling errors irritates the teacher.

Although this example contains two *t*-units, the second does not contain a piece of separate advice but gives the rationale or motive for the advice. The two propositions are coded as a single piece of advice.

Take care of your spelling and your grammar too.

This single *t*-unit contains two categories of advice. Therefore it would be coded as two separate pieces of advice rather than coding the whole proposition at a more general level.

Take care of your spelling. You really should check your spelling. Good spelling, is important in this school.

Here there are three *t*-units that say the same thing.   They are contained in a single unit of advice.   Although each could be coded, the coding would be redundant.

After identifying the items to be coded, the code number was entered on the code sheet provided.   An attempt was made to indicate as specific a subcategory as possible.   Raters were urged not to use code numbers that ended in zero unless the student's phrasing was ambiguous or the student gave a specific piece of advice not having a separate subcategory and the rater judged it to be so rare as not to deserve a new code number. Although illustrative samples were provided, raters were warned to evaluate the sense of what the student wrote since identical matches should not be expected.   In the international analysis, only the first two digits of the code are used.

Hello!

Well then here is a letter from me. You had asked me if I would write to you about that essay writing.

So let me start with that.   First of all you have to [sort out a title]*(1)* which really appeals to you.   When you have found that [start to think the whole story over first and make some notes]*(2)* (that is always easy for writing).   Personally [I usually write in the first person]*(3)* and [past tense]*(4)*. That is incredibly easy, because then you will never get confused between the present and the past tense. When you write in the first person it is also much easier to write and you don't get confused either. Do please [write stories which contain some   substance]*(5)*.   [Suspense   and   excitement   are   much appreciated]*(6)* at   our   school.   So   no   flannel   stories!   Well, furthermore [it is of course a question of good imagination]*(7)* and [spelling]*(8)*. Spelling especially counts very heavily in your total mark for the essay.   And ... also take into consideration that you should [write clearly]*(9)*.   I believe that this is just about the most important. Furthermore I hope that you will like it a bit at our school (it will be alright I think) and I'll see you in two weeks.

Greetings...

Figure 5.1.   Example of student composition marked for coding.

Figure 5.1 illustrates the coding process.   Nine different coded categories are found in this letter and are marked between brackets ([]).   The following annotation of the codes given illustrate the use of the system:

1. **52** This point has been categorized as process (5), selection of topic (2).

2. **54** This point has been categorized under those aspects which deal with the process (5) of planning (4) a composition.

3. **35** This point is categorized under that aspect of style and tone (3) which deals with the writer's use of the personal (5-lexical).

4. **37** This point is thought to refer to the writer's choice of syntactic structure rather than that of grammatical correctness, and is therefore categorized under the aspect of syntactic choice of style and tone (3-style and tone; 7-paragraph or discourse choice). This analysis is borne out by the writer's qualification of this point in the next sentence.

5. **11** The fifth point is categorized under that aspect of content (1) which deals with the amount of information (1) the writer includes in the composition.

6. **14** The sixth point is categorized under that aspect of content (1) which deals with the writer's expression of his/her personal experience in the composition (4-details).

7. **12** The seventh point is categorized under that aspect of content (1) which deals with the writer's use of his/her imagination in an essay (2-approach to content).

8. **44** The seventh point is categorized under that aspect of how the composition is presented (4) in terms of spelling (4-spelling and punctuation).

9. **80** The last point mentioned is categorized as "unclassifiable" as it is uncertain whether the writer is referring to that aspect of style and tone which deals with clarity, or that aspect of presentation which deals with handwriting neatness.

The Sample

The original proposal and planning of the IEA Study of Achievement in Written Composition included extensive background searches, questionnaire data and achievement scores on at least three actual compositions per student in the sample. The additional exercise of content coding for one of these compositions was not proposed until after many of the National Centers had secured and fixed their budgets for the project. Therefore, although this new activity was enthusiastically accepted by the members of the International Study Committee (i.e., representatives from each participating National Center), some were financially unable to do this coding.

For the centers that did participate, it was recommended that they code a sample of the Population B (final year of compulsory schooling) compositions. In this population, all pupils wrote this particular task, giving the largest available representation of the age group. Each center was asked to select from each classroom in the Population B international sample of 100 classrooms the compositions from the first rotation. (See Gorman, Purves, & Degenhart, 1988, Appendix A for an illustration of the task rotation system.) This would yield twelve compositions per classroom, or approximately 1200 compositions per country/system. For those countries who would find this number too burdensome, a minimum number of six compositions per classroom was recommended.

Nine of the twelve Population B countries completed the content coding exercise. In addition, this international analysis includes Thailand which only tested the pre-university students (Population C). Although similar in age, these students have a more academic background than their counterparts in Population B. Table 5.2 lists the countries/school systems participating in the exercise. With the exception of Wales, all centers coded at least 600 compositions.

Table 5.2.

Countries/school systems reporting the content coding of the letter of advice and the number of compositions coded for Population B (plus Thailand, Population C)

Country	No. of Compositions
Chile	600
England	1001
Finland	1670
Hamburg	2332
Italy	896
Netherlands	1252
New Zealand	1108
Sweden	663
Thailand (Pop C)	659
Wales	278

Reliability of Coding

To check the reliability of coding, double coding was recommended for at least every fifth paper. Raters were urged to strive for total agreement at the major category level (first digit); 85% agreement at the subcategory level (second digit); and 75% agreement at the item level (third digit). However, consistency at the item (third digit) level proved to be too difficult and the final analyses are based on only the major category and the subcategory levels.

Specific reliability information is available only from Finland, The Netherlands, and Sweden. Two coders were used in the Netherlands. Each rescored 30 of their own scripts for intracoder stability and 60 scripts from the other coder for intercoder agreement. Cohen's K was found to be .85, a fairly satisfactory level of agreement. In Sweden, 20 compositions were recoded both for Population B and for Population C. Coder agreement was computed as a percentage of agreement at three levels from the more general to the more specific: primary category (100-800), secondary category (110, 120, etc.), tertiary category (111, 112, etc.). The degree of agreement for the three categories was 96%, 88%, and 84% for Population B and 93%, 89%, and 87% for Population C, respectively. In Finland, 30 compositions were double-coded for Pop B. The percentage of agreement at the most detailed (three-digit) level was high: 95%.

Written information and talks with coders in England and Italy suggest that coding was done in a careful manner. In Italy, for example, teams were set up to check the applicability of the category system and to do the coding (for a detailed description, see Fabi & Pavan de Gregorio, 1988). Thus, even though all National Centers were not able to double code or check the reliability of coding statistically, we have no reason to suspect that their coding reliability differs considerably from the rest.

Main Results

Although the test instructions only asked for five items of advice from each student, the actual per student national averages were higher (see Table 5.11). The remaining tables in this chapter will report percentages based on the total number of coded items in each country, not the percentage of students mentioning a particular category. In many cases, especially at the major category level, students have included more than one item from a single category in their advice.

Only Population B compositions were used for this analysis, with the exception of Thailand where only the pre-university year (Population C) was tested. The Welsh-language schools are not included. The results are first reported using the main categories of the coding scheme to give an overview of the distribution of student advice (Table 5.3). Each category is then presented in greater detail.

Table 5.3 shows some uniform patterns across the nine countries reported. The numbers represent the percent of all coded advice that fall within each general category for each country. The categories are shown in descending order of frequency across countries, with presentation clearly being mentioned most often and tactics and unclassified the least.

Table 5.3

Percentage distributions of student advice in nine countries/school systems broken down by main categories of the coding scheme

Category	CHI	ENG	FRG	FIN	ITA	NET	N-Z	SWE	THA
Presentation	49.1	40.0	39.0	34.9	36.0	47.5	31.4	33.9	22.2
Content	9.6	15.0	23.2	20.6	24.0	9.2	20.5	14.1	12.3
Process	20.8	15.0	4.3	11.4	12.0	11.0	18.5	19.6	17.6
Organization	4.1	15.0	14.0	18.3	10.0	17.0	14.5	12.9	33.3
Style/tone	14.0	13.0	18.2	13.0	15.0	7.8	13.5	15.4	14.
Tactics	1.1	2.0	1.3	1.5	3.0	1.4	1.7	0.0	0.1
Unclassified	1.3	0.0	0.0	0.3	0.0	6.1	0.0	4.1	0.3

Students in all countries/school systems, with the exception of Thailand, most frequently mentioned points related to the presentation of composition: the general appearance, length/format, grammar, spelling, and punctuation. Least frequently mentioned was advice related to tactics or advice that could not be classified. Between these two extremes there is less agreement in the order of frequency. For example, when the rank order of the major categories is averaged across countries, content appears second in frequency. However, in Chile, The Netherlands, Sweden, and Thailand, content is ranked fourth or fifth. The differences between the averaged percentages of these four categories (content, process, organization, style/tone) are relatively small.

Presentation

Features related to presentation not only rank first in eight of the nine countries, but they account for a significant portion of the total advice given in each country. Almost half of the items coded in Chile (49.1%) and The Netherlands (47.5%) fall in this category. Even in Thailand, where this category was ranked second, 22.2% of the total responses are found here. Across countries the mention of spelling and punctuation is considerably greater than the remaining subcategories. The only exceptions are in Italy, where there is a stronger perceived emphasis on grammar (14.7%), and in Thailand, where unspecified national options are stronger (9.5%).

Table 5.4.

Percentage distribution of student advice within the presentation category, broken down by the main subcategories

	CHI	ENG	FRG	FIN	ITA	NET	N-Z	SWE	THA
Total %	49.1	40.0	39.0	34.9	36.0	47.5	31.4	33.9	22.2
Spelling/ Punctuation	26.0	19.0	18.9	13.1	10.7	21.5	16.1	17.4	4.7
Appearance	18.2	11.0	7.9	9.8	6.4	11.7	7.9	8.1	3.8
Length/format	4.6	8.0	5.8	9.5	4.2	8.6	5.5	6.4	3.0
Grammar	0.3	2.0	6.4	2.5	14.7	5.7	1.9	2.0	1.2
National options									9.5

In the national report for England and Wales, Gubb, Gorman and Price (1987) suggest two possible reasons for the prominence of presentation items among student advice. First, teachers' marking practices continually alert students to these easily marked and least time-consuming aspects of their compositions. It is likely that the red marks are more firmly planted in the students' memories than the less concrete oral discussions of the finer points of organization and style. As a result the students may be unintentionally led to overestimate the importance of this category.

The second point raised in the English report suggests that "the various aspects of presentation come easily to mind and can be listed without a great deal of thought" (p. 59). This point seems to be supported by the observation that poorer writers tend to concentrate more on presentation than do better writers, who tended to see presentational features as "servicing agents to the more substantive aspects of writing" (p. 59).

The examples from student compositions used throughout the remainder of this chapter are not meant to convey any representative sample of pupil advice, but simply to illustrate the way pupils phrase their advice. The original spelling, punctuation, and grammar have been preserved as much as possible, even in examples translated into English from other languages. The following excerpts illustrate how pupils phrased their advice on presentation. (The numbers in parentheses represent the subcategory level codes as shown in Table 5.1.)

> The purpose of my letter is to give you advice of here in the school regarding composition one of the details that is mostly taken into consideration is orthography, so I personally advise you that you prepare yourself. (440)

> That is enough but the most important thing in writing is to be neat. (410)

> Also when you write a story try to make it quite long about six pages. So this gets you better marks and teachers do not like short storys of about a page. (420)

Content

Presentation accounted for 37% of the student responses across countries. The next four categories together contain just under 60% of the remaining responses with less than one percentage point separating any pair.

As a result, there is no clear agreement of the order of importance (as interpreted by rank order) among countries for these four aspects. There is also a sharp drop in the number of responses in each category, with second-ranked content features accounting for only 16% of the total. Within countries, these responses ranged from 9.2% in the Netherlands to 24.0% in Italy (Table 5.5).

Table 5.5

Percentage distribution of student advice within the content category, broken down by the main subcategory

	CHI	ENG	FRG	FIN	ITA	NET	N-Z	SWE	THA
Total %	9.6	15.0	23.2	20.6	24.0	9.2	20.5	14.1	12.3
Information	4.4	3.0	8.1	12.5	7.4	6.6	6.5	4.2	6.4
Approach	4.4	5.0	4.1	4.0	6.8	1.2	11.8	5.6	3.5
Details	0.4	2.0	2.0	0.7	2.6	1.0	1.3	4.1	0.5
Variety	0.4	1.0	2.8	3.4	2.5	0.4	0.9	0.2	1.0
General (100)		4.0			4.7				
National options			6.2						0.9

Advice related to the information to be included in a composition dominated in most countries, and featured especially prominently in Finland (12.5%). This subcategory consisted of advice on the amount of information (relevant points only vs. everything), keeping to the topic, and the acceptability of fiction vs. only facts. Advice related to the general approach to the content was most frequent in New Zealand (11.8%). This would include originality and imagination, objectivity, and interest. In the main category of content, both Hamburg (FRG) and Thailand made use of national coding, while England and Italy found a number of items that did not fit the suggested subcategories and were coded on the most general level. The following examples illustrate the aspects of information, approach to content, and the use of details:

> If you want it can be fictitious that is to say unreal. (110)

> Make sure your essays are exciting. If your essay has lots of imagination it brightens up thirty boring essays so you'll get good marks for that. (120)

> She likes to read long composition which includes some background and advantural events of the writer. (140)

Process

The process category includes most of the prewriting activities of selection and planning as well as revision and use of feedback. Pupils' references to the processes of writing are noticeably fewer in Hamburg (4.3%) than in the other countries. For students in Chile (20.8%) and Sweden (19.6%), on the other hand, the process of writing was second only to presentation in the total number of responses. However, much of the advice in Chile (9.4%), and to a lesser extent in the Netherlands (2.4%), did not fit within the international subcategories.

With eight identified aspects to this category, the advice is spread fairly thinly without great differences between them. It is clear, however, that prewriting activities such as planning with the aid of lists, brainstorming sessions, drawing up outlines, and drafting are familiar concepts to pupils. Although the choice of topic is seen as important, the choice of audience is less so. Revision and editing of drafts does not seem to be prominent in the pupils' awareness.

> [S]start to think the whole story over first and make some notes (that is always easy for writing). (540)

> Firstly, when presented with some essay topics, it is important to select a topic which suits you best. (520)

> [G]o over what you have written several times and correct as many mistakes as you can. (560)

If it involves research do some (then at the end have a page showing what books you used, or information obtained and where did it come from). (550)

Table 5.6

Percentage distribution of student advice within the process category, broken down by the main subcategory

	CHI	ENG	FRG	FIN	ITA	NET	N-Z	SWE	THA
Total %	20.8	15.0	4.3	11.4	12.0	11.0	18.5	19.6	17.6
Planning	2.4	4.3	1.1	1.8	2.1	1.7	5.0	5.9	6.2
Topic/task choice	3.9	2.0	0.3	4.7	3.0	2.3	3.5	5.6	3.4
Revision/editing	1.3	3.0	1.0	1.8	3.9	1.2	4.7	4.9	0.8
Advance prep.	1.4	1.0	1.0	1.8	0.6	1.2	1.1	0.6	2.8
Drafting	0.9	2.0	0.4	0.1	1.9	1.1	2.0	2.1	1.3
Audience choice	1.1	2.0	0.4	0.4	0.2	0.7	1.1	0.2	1.3
Use of feedback	0.2	0.4	0.0	0.5	0.1	0.2	0.6	0.2	0.0
Punctuality & time	0.2	0.3	0.1	0.3	0.2	0.0	0.5	0.1	0.3
General (500)	9.4					2.6			
National options									1.5

Organization

References to organization in pupils' letters of advice ranged from 4.1% in Chile to 33.3% in Thailand. With the exception of these two extremes, the countries show a relatively uniform pattern with frequency of advice on aspects of organization ranking third or fourth among the six main categories and within a short range of 10% to 18% of the total responses.

It is interesting to note that in a preliminary analysis of student performance on the writing tasks, Chacon, Jury, and Carrasco (1989) concluded that Chilean students' written communication was "deficient in organization" (p. 27). The students did not report it as an important aspect for getting a good grade and their performance suggests that they are not conscious of it when they write.

At the other extreme, the students in Thailand considered organization to be the most important aspect with one third of the total responses falling in this category. In fact, organization and presentation together account for 55.5% of the total responses in the Thai sample. It should be remembered that the students in this sample were in the pre-university year and therefore a more select and academically oriented population than the other countries in this analysis. It should also be noted that almost half of the Thai responses (16.0%) were coded using national codes.

Table 5.7

Percentage distribution of student advice within the organization category, broken down by the main subcategory

	CHI	ENG	FRG	FIN	ITA	NET	N-Z	SWE	THA
Total %	4.1	15.0	14.0	18.3	10.0	17.0	14.5	12.9	33.3
Conclusion	0.5	2.0	2.8	3.0	2.4	2.8	3.7	3.1	5.4
Introduction	0.4	3.0	3.1	3.0	2.5	2.6	3.3	3.0	3.9
Paragraph level	0.8	5.0	1.0	5.7	0.2	0.7	4.2	4.5	1.7
Body	1.0	2.0	2.8	2.9	1.6	1.3	1.7	1.5	6.0
Overall structure	1.4	3.0	0.1	3.7	1.5	6.9	1.6	0.8	0.3
General (200)			4.2		1.8		2.7		
National options									16.0

The subcategories of organization are self-explanatory. It should be noted, however, that the overall structure refers to the ordering of ideas and information and should not be confused with matters of physical placement on the page which would be coded under presentation (format). Comments on conclusions, introductions and use of paragraphs are almost equally frequent across countries. Within countries, the paragraph level is mentioned either most frequently (England, Finland, New Zealand, and Sweden) or least frequently (Hamburg/FRG, Italy, the Netherlands, and Thailand).

> Second, a good composition should have an introduction to persuade readers to be interested in our composition. (220)

> They are also very keen on paragraphs - each one must begin with its theme sentence, which is like a mini-introduction to that paragraph. If you can't tell what a paragraph is going to be about by reading its theme sentence - then the theme sentence has failed!! (240)

> After allowing one paragraph for the introduction, you should then launch into the body of the essay. (230)

> And again as you've always or have often been told make sure it begins, carries, and finishes properly. (210)

> The most basic ingredient that they insist on is the general shape of the composition. It must have, in some form or other, a beginning, middle and end. They drum this idea into from the very first day! -You start your composition with a brief introduction, saying 'What you are going to say', followed by you actually saying it, and rounding it off with a nice conclusion saying what you have first said!

Style and Tone

Although aspects of style and tone are infrequently mentioned in The Netherlands (7.8%), this category appears to have the highest degree of agreement across countries. The number of responses is low, however, falling within a narrow range from 13% (England and Finland) to 15.4% (Sweden), with Hamburg at 18.2% only slightly higher than the others.

Table 5.8

Percentage distribution of student advice within the style and tone category, broken down by the main subcategory

	CHI	ENG	FRG	FIN	ITA	NET	N-Z	SWE	THA
Total %	14.0	13.0	18.2	13.0	15.0	7.8	13.5	15.4	14.2
Lexical choice	5.2	4.0	3.0	4.2	4.2	0.5	6.4	6.6	5.9
Clarity	5.5	2.0	4.2	3.1	3.5	0.7	2.2	0.5	0.9
Elaboration	0.8	1.0	2.0	0.7	2.6	2.6	1.2	1.0	1.8
Syntactic choice	0.8	1.0	2.4	1.3	2.1	0.1	1.1	5.3	0.2
Personality	1.1	1.0	0.0	1.4	0.6	0.4	1.8	0.6	0.1
Uniformity	0.4	1.0	0.3	0.8	0.1	0.4	0.6	0.2	0.3
Paragraph/ discourse choice	0.1	1.0	0.0	1.4	0.1	1.5	0.1	0.1	0.1
Set style	0.1	0.0	0.0	0.1	0.1	0.0	0.1	0.0	0.5
General		2.0	6.3		1.7	1.6		1.1	
National option									4.4

Pupils seem to understand style and tone mainly in terms of making lexical choices and using a rich and expressive vocabulary. This category presented difficulties for the raters as well since the general, unspecified sub-category was used in more than half of the countries. In Hamburg fully one third of the total advice given on style could not be placed within the international subcategories. Thailand also found it necessary to use national codes for almost one third of the Thai student responses pertaining to style and tone. When giving advice on aspects of this category, students were more likely to illustrate their point with examples, as can be seen in the following excerpts:

> I must tell you that many teaches like descriptions, especially if they are interesting. You should put descriptive adjectives into a sentence. I will give you an example. "The boy walked up the road." This is just a basic sentence with no details of how the boy walked and no descriptions of the road. This sentence could be composed as: "The miserable boy walked slowly up the steep road." Please remember this point, it is very important. (330)

> [You] should not make erroneous repititions of words, which make nothing more but to extend and make your composition boring. (350)

> Personally I usually write in the first person and past tense. That is increadibly easy, because then you will never get confused between the present and the past tense. When you write in the first person it is also much easier to write and you don't get confused either. (340)

> It is best to select your favourite style when writing, because you will probably do your favourite style best. (370)

Tactics

As mentioned earlier in this chapter, the category of tactics has no real basis in the theory of composition writing. Some students, interpreting the task instructions literally and in a broad sense, revealed that "to get a good grade" did not depend entirely, in their perception, on academic features. Advice of this nature does not constitute a large portion of responses in any country, but it does appear in all countries often enough to be noted. It is this category, more than any of the others, where the "unintended curriculum" of the classroom is revealed.

Table 5.9

Percentage distribution of student advice within the tactics category, broken down by the main subcategory

	CHI	ENG	FRG	FIN	ITA	NET	N-Z	SWE	THA
Total %	1.1	2.0	1.3	1.5	3.0	1.4	1.7	0.0	0.1
Participation/ behavior	0.3	1.0	0.6	0.9	1.1	0.3	1.1	0.0	0.0
Attitude w/teacher	0.1	0.4	0.6	0.3	0.4	0.7	0.2	0.0	0.0
Honesty	0.3	0.0	0.1	0.1	0.7	0.1	0.0	0.0	0.1
Dress/physical appearance	0.1	0.2	0.0	0.0	0.0	0.2	0.3	0.0	0.0
Time/use of resources	0.1	0.3	0.0	0.0	0.6	0.0	0.0	0.0	0.0
Attitude w/peers	0.0	0.0	0.0	0.0	0.1	0.0	0.1	0.0	0.0
General (600)	0.2	0.1			0.1	0.1			

Pupils are aware that the quality of their writing may not be the only factor that determines their marks. It pays to know what kind of behavior can also contribute to getting a good mark. Participation and classroom behavior are especially prominent in Finland and Hamburg. In The Netherlands and Hamburg the student's attitude toward the teacher is important. Honesty and the use of time and resources are mentioned in Italy. The almost total absence of references to tactics in Thailand (only honesty is mentioned) might be a result of the more select, academic sample of students.

When writing research essays never copy straight from a textbook, as the teacher can usually tell the difference between published material and the written work of a year eleven student. (650)

One important point is that you should dress yourself neatly because it can also help you. (610)

It is like most schools I suppose, the odd teacher likes this or that while others forbid it. You have to bend to fit the teachers attitude. (630)

Relationship of Performance and Student Perceptions

An interesting point to pursue is to study how the advice given by pupils is related to their own performance. To do this, students were divided into three groups according to their achievement on the writing tasks. (See Gorman, Purves, & Degenhart, 1988, for descriptions of the writing tasks and the scoring scheme.) For each country, the mean of the summed overall impression scores was used as the standard. Then the sum of each student's overall impression scores was compared to that mean. Students who scored one standard deviation or more below or above the country mean were assigned to the "poor writers" group or the "good writers" group, respectively. Students falling in between were classified as "average writers." Finally, the number of coded items of advice given by the students within each of these groups was averaged and the correlation with performance was calculated. The following table presents the results of this exercise. For each country, the average number of items of advice, the standard deviation, and the number of students for each ability group are given together with the correlation and significance level.

The data show two consistent trends in all countries. First, the total number of advice given showed a linear correlation with the level of performance. The good writers gave the most advice (on the average 7-9 items), average writers gave 5-6 items of advice and poor writers 3-4 items. Second, the variability of the amount of advice given was also linearly related to the level of performance: good writers varied most in terms of the number of advice and poor writers least.

When broken down by coded main category, the same pattern of a linear correlation between level of performance and the number and variability of advice was found. However, the strength of this correlation varies between categories. In the content, organization, and style/tone categories, the correlation was strong and uniform across countries ($p = <.00$ in all cases). The trend was the same in the presentation and process categories, that is, good writers always gave the most advice, but there was less agreement across countries. In the presentation category the differences were smaller (in Finland and Italy, $p = <.10$) and the linear variability was evident in only 4 out of 8 cases. In the process category, the *p*-values in Hamburg and Italy did not reach the level of significance (*p* = .17 and .16, respectively) and the variability in Italy was greater among the average writers than the good writers.

Table 5.10

Number of Total Advice on Writing Given by Poor, Average, and Good Writers: Population B

		Poor	Average	Good	Total	*F*	*p*
Chi	Mean	4.39	5.33	7.34	5.60	62.81	.00
	STD	1.46	1.82	2.54	2.13		
	N	70	417	113	600		
Eng	Mean	3.53	5.75	7.94	5.74	140.21	.00
	STD	2.11	2.38	2.59	2.69		
	N	163	653	161	977		
Ham	Mean	4.26	5.50	6.42	5.49	50.94	.00
	STD	1.76	2.00	2.13	2.08		
	N	156	801	196	1153		
Fin	Mean	4.44	6.51	9.10	6.61	208.33	.00
	STD	1.69	2.25	2.84	2.65		
	N	197	808	200	1205		
Ita	Mean	4.91	5.69	7.32	5.81	42.48	.00
	STD	1.86	2.04	2.38	2.18		
	N	116	553	114	783		
N-Z	Mean	3.53	5.72	7.66	5.58	143.71	.00
	STD	2.34	2.41	2.82	2.77		
	N	230	693	179	1102		
Tha	Mean	4.00	5.57	7.79	5.65	50.59	.00
	STD	2.04	2.68	3.34	2.90		
	N	107	449	98	654		
Wal	Mean	3.37	5.92	7.17	5.84	42.84	.00
	STD	1.78	1.81	2.24	2.17		
	N	33	182	53	270		

The tactics category diverges clearly from the pattern. Poor writers tended to give the most tactical advice, but statistically significant differences were found only in England, Hamburg, and Italy. The trend was also evident in Finland and New Zealand, but the differences were so small that they did not reach the level of statistical significance. No difference was found in Chile and Thailand. In Wales alone the good writers gave the most tactical advice, but the differences were not statistically significant.

The Dutch Analysis

Less proficient writers tended to emphasize classroom tactics, presentation, and writing process. By contrast, the more able pupils tended to refer to the importance of audience awareness, stylistic considerations, content, and organization.

The Dutch data were coded in a slightly different way from the international coding scheme. Even so, in their national analysis, Schoonen and DeGlopper (1987) found the same overall pattern as in the other countries. That is, in absolute terms, better writers gave more advice in general with an emphasis on all product categories as well as the prewriting and composing categories.

Table 5.11 shows the distribution of advice as percentages within each ability group. For example, even though the poor writers have been shown to give less advice in absolute numbers, a higher percentage of the advice they do give falls within the mechanics/grammar and presentation categories. Proportionally less advice from this group concerns organization. The better writers also acknowledge the importance of mechanics/grammar, but stress aspects of organization as well. There was very little difference between the three groups concerning style/tone and none for content and the writing process categories (prewriting, composing, and revision).

Spelling, punctuation, grammar, and handwriting were scored nationally and were not a part of the international data. However, Schoonen and DeGlopper analyzed these aspects of the Dutch pupils' performance in relation to the advice they gave in these categories. They discovered that there were no differences between poor, average, and good writers in their advice on grammar and handwriting relative to their performance. However, the pupils who were poor in punctuation gave much more advice on punctuation while it was the good spellers who gave somewhat more advice on the importance of spelling. There were no differences with regard to grammar.

Table 5.11

Relative frequencies (in %) of types of advice for poor, average and good writers (data from the Netherlands).

| | GENERAL MERIT | | | | | | | |
| | Poor | | Average | | Good | | | |
	M	SD	M	SD	M	SD	F	r
Mech. & Grammar	32	27	28	22	24	18	5.8	.00
Presentation	25	21	20	16	17	15	12.4	.00
Organization	13	18	22	20	25	18	19.6	.00
Style & Tone	10	17	9	14	13	15	3.8	.02
Content	10	17	10	14	10	13	0.2	.84
Prewriting	6	13	7	12	7	13	0.6	.58
Composing	2	6	2	5	2	5	1.0	.38
Revision	1	3	1	5	1	4	1.7	.19

Conclusion

This chapter has presented results from nine countries concerning the advice that students wrote to an imagined younger pupil who was coming to the writer's school and needed help in learning how to get good marks in writing in that school. There were some patterns which appeared consistent in all or most of the nine countries/school systems concerned.

Most pupils made reference to matters of presentation in their advice to a younger pupil, stressing the importance of correct spelling and punctuation, neat handwriting and clear lay-out as major determinants of their teachers' assessment of composition writing. The authors of the English national report point out, however, that while better writers tended to only catalogue the features of presentation in passing, their less competent classmates tended to make these aspects central items of advice. An interesting further study would be to explore the generalizability of this finding across the languages and cultures of this data set.

The differences between the amount of advice given for the aspects of content, process, organization, and style/tone are small. The data show that only the more proficient writers appear to be concerned with the latter two aspects especially. Comments and advice on classroom tactics tended to be given by the less competent writers.

The analyses reported here confirm the view that pupils are valuable sources of information about the teaching of composition in school. Although the task was "unusual and unfamiliar," as was suggested at the outset of this paper, students are conscious of what is expected of them and are able to write about their experiences.

6

A Comparative Perspective on the Performance of Students in Written Composition

Alan C. Purves

As was pointed out in the discussion of the scorer training in Volume I of this study (de Glopper, 1988), and again in Appendix A of this volume, the problems of implementing strictly controlled scoring across sites, times, and languages proved insurmountable given the funds available to the study and, perhaps, the intractable nature of the problem of comparative performance assessment. It seems clear from the national scoring reports and the analysis of the scoring sessions and results in chapter 6 that each system's scoring had its own integrity, and we can rely upon the reliability of the scores within in a given system of education. At the same time, it is true that the ways by which the scoring sessions were organized differed sufficiently so that we cannot assert that the scores mean precisely the same thing across all situations. In some systems scorers were assigned by task; in others they were assigned across tasks. For these reasons, it is impossible to give direct comparisons of student means in writing, or to say that the students in one system of education perform better in writing than do the students in another. As an example of the problem of direct comparability, Table 6.1 on the next page gives the percentage of the students in Population B receiving scores lower than 2, which might be assumed to be the equivalent of the percentage judged below a minimum competence level. The table shows a range across countries from nearly one fourth of the population to about one-fortieth of the population. This tenfold difference appears to result from the variation between national scoring teams in their application of the scale rather than from a true variation in the competence level of the students. In some systems, scorers appear reluctant to give a failing score, a finding that is paralleled in the reports of various national assessments. Such variation among systems makes international comparisons difficult.

That is not to say that the task of comparison must be foregone. We take for granted the integrity of the scoring of each center in the sense that each center's scoring was consistent across cases and populations. We also know that each scoring team used the same scoring scheme and we know that they used approximately, but not exactly, the same scale. Given these facts concerning the study we may compare the results of each center's scoring, but not thereby the performance of the students across systems of education within certain limitations. We can, for example, examine comparatively the perceived performance of students across tasks, the perceived growth of students in systems where more than one population was tested, and the perceived performance of selected groups who, we think, might bear similar relationships to each other internationally.

Table 6.1

Percentage of Population Scoring below 2: Population B

	Func-tional	Narra-tive	Argu-ment	Reflec-tive	Exposi-tion	Mean
Chile	10.9	11.0	16.0	10.3	12.8	12.2
England	4.4	3.0	7.4	11.1	8.3	6.8
Finland	12.0	6.4	15.2	14.4	20.3	13.7
Hamburg	2.2	0.7	2.3	2.5	3.5	2.2
Hungary	10.3	12.5	32.0	16.5	6.3	15.5
Italy	17.0	9.6	18.5	23.0	14.6	16.5
Netherlands	16.4	28.3	25.5	20.3	21.4	22.4
N. Zealand	5.8	6.6	7.6	18.0	13.0	10.2
Nigeria	7.1	9.1	24.2	31.3	18.5	18.0
Sweden	13.5	7.2	13.8	31.2	26.4	18.4
USA	2.0	1.1	2.1	3.7	2.9	2.4
Wales	5.5	10.6	6.5	11.2	11.9	9.1
Mean	8.9	8.8	14.3	16.1	13.3	12.3

In making these comparisons, we should remind ourselves and our readers that the writing the students have performed is the composition of drafts under limited time restrictions. These drafts have been rated by teams who, although experienced and trained, are nonetheless basing their judgments on culturally bound perceptions of quality--perhaps the only guide there is. Whether these perceptions of the quality of drafts reflect the true abilities of the populations is impossible to determine. The scores are the best indication of performance in written composition that assessment has yet devised, and such ratings are trusted in examinations of various sorts within systems of education. They should be examined in any between-system comparison, but not trusted to the point of saying that students in one system are better writers than students in another; the comparisons are among the perceptions of writing by teams of raters within a culture who are using a common scheme, but not a common metric.

Across-Task Performance

Since the students wrote in response to three tasks (a functional task, a common task, and a rotated task), one can examine the issue of consistency and patterns of performance. The consistency issue has been discussed to some extent in the previous chapter, but we will discuss the correlation of general impression scores between tasks for Population B here. The students wrote on a functional task (the scores are pooled), either the narrative, argumentative, or reflective task, and the expository task of writing a letter of advice concerning success in composition. The correlations appear in Table 6.2.

Two points arising from this table are worthy of note. The first is the variation across systems of the mean correlation coefficient. Some previous research, particularly with the United States National Assessment, had suggested that the correlations were stable around .25. That holds true in this study for the United States, but it is much higher in Sweden, Hungary, England, and Wales (which has a smaller number of students than other systems). What this variation suggests is that although there will always be task effects in any assessment of student writing, they may be mitigated by some other force--perhaps instruction. The second point is that the correlations of the rotated tasks are generally higher with exposition than with functional writing. Functional writing appears to be somewhat apart from the other tasks covered in the study. Whether it is intrinsically different or is situated differently in the curriculum is a point we shall return to in the next analysis.

Table 6.2

Correlation of General Impression Scores Between Tasks:
Population B

All Correlations are significant at the .001 or better

		Narrative	Argument	Reflection	Exposition	Mean
Chile	Functional	.18	.33	.31	.30	.33
	Exposition	.36	.43	.43		
England	Functional	.47	.48	.46	.52	.53
	Exposition	.56	.60	.59		
Finland	Functional	.38	.39	.44	.46	.47
	Exposition	.50	.49	.64		
Hamburg	Functional	.19	.31	.30	.30	.27
	Exposition	.21	.27	.30		
Hungary	Functional	.50	.43	.47	.58	.54
	Exposition	.62	.58	.61		
Italy	Functional	.33	.17	.24	.32	.35
	Exposition	.47	.41	.49		
Netherlands	Functional	.36	.41	.46	.38	.46
	Exposition	.50	.56	.56		
N Z	Functional	.28	.28	.31	.36	.35
	Exposition	.37	.39	.43		
Nigeria	Functional	.13	.21	.23	.21	.22
	Exposition	.17	.32	.28		
Sweden	Functional	.58	.58	.47	.52	.57
	Exposition	.59	.62	.60		
USA	Functional	.23	.21	.33	.27	.32
	Exposition	.37	.40	.41		
Wales	Functional	.64	.63	.46	.56	.61
	Exposition	.67	.63	.65		

In order to perform the analysis of score patterns across systems of education, the mean scores on overall impression were converted into standard scores in each population and in each system of education. Only those tasks were selected which were common across all of the systems in the population. For Population A, the tasks are the functional (FU), the narrative (NA) and the argument (AR). For Population B, they are the functional, the narrative, the argument, the reflective (RE), and the expository letter of advice (EX). For Population C, they are the functional, argumentative, reflective, and expository. The results of this analysis are to be seen in Figures 6.1, 6.2, and 6.3.

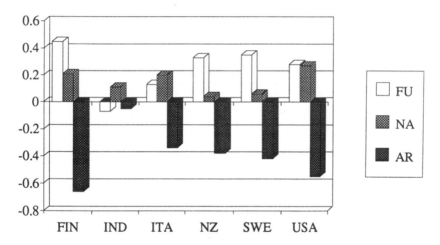

Figure 6.1: Within Country Relative Performance: Pop A

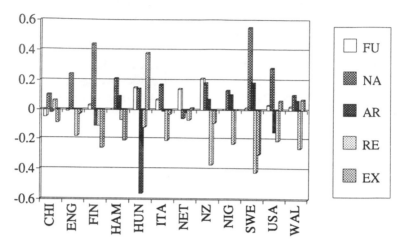

Figure 6.2: **Within Country Relative Performance: Pop B**

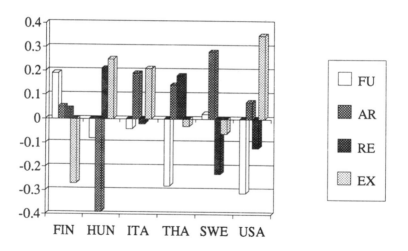

Figure 6.3: **Within Country Relative Performance: Pop C**

In Population A, two results are noteworthy. The first is the variation in spread of scores across systems. The performance of students in Indonesia appears to hover about the mean for all tasks, whereas in Finland there are wide variations across tasks. The spread in the United States, Sweden, and New Zealand is also great. One might infer that the Indonesian raters tended to be conservative in their scoring or that the students performed equally well in some objective sense; we cannot tell which interpretation is better. The standard deviations of scores for Indonesia average .84, somewhat less than the international mean across tasks, countries, and populations of .89, and considerably lower than the Population A mean of .93 (Table 6.3).

Table 6.3

Standard Deviations of Student Scores

| | Population A | | | |
	Functional	Narrative	Argument	Mean
FIN	1.15	0.92	0.88	0.98
IND	0.92	0.85	0.75	0.84
ITA	1.07	0.97	1.06	1.03
N-Z	1.21	1.03	1.07	1.10
SWE	0.96	0.82	0.70	0.83
USA	0.84	0.82	0.77	0.81
Mean	1.03	0.90	0.87	0.93

Table 6.3 (Cont'd.)

| | Population B | | | | | |
	Func- tional	Narra- tive	Argu- ment	Reflec- tive	Exposi- tion	Mean
CHI	0.83	0.94	0.98	0.92	0.88	0.91
ENG	0.91	0.89	1.01	0.98	0.98	0.95
FIN	1.02	1.00	1.00	1.00	1.04	1.01
HAM	0.77	0.78	0.85	0.82	0.83	0.81
HUN	0.96	0.92	0.74	0.86	0.87	0.87
ITA	0.97	0.91	1.05	0.92	0.89	0.95
NET	0.82	0.79	0.72	0.68	0.76	0.75
N-Z	1.04	1.05	1.06	1.04	1.11	1.06
NIG	0.74	0.70	1.16	1.04	0.95	0.92
SWE	0.96	1.07	0.89	0.88	0.90	0.94
USA	0.84	0.81	0.87	0.88	0.92	0.86
WAL	0.92	0.98	0.89	0.88	0.97	0.93
Mean	0.90	0.90	0.94	0.91	0.93	0.91

| | Population C | | | | |
	Functional	Argument	Reflective	Exposition	Mean
FIN	0.82	0.79	0.85	0.83	0.82
HUN	0.82	0.73	0.70	0.68	0.73
ITA	1.00	0.92	0.98	0.98	0.97
THA	0.66	0.72	0.71	0.75	0.71
SWE	0.94	0.97	1.00	0.94	0.96
USA	0.82	0.88	0.98	0.89	0.87
Mean	0.84	0.84	0.86	0.85	0.84

In Finland, however, it is clear that the raters perceived sharp differences in the average level of performance on functional as opposed to argumentative writing.   In all the systems, the lowest performance is on argumentative writing, a finding which is to be expected for this population since argument is infrequently taught and often seen as developmentally too advanced for the age group.

The other finding of note is the fluctuation among countries of the rank of narrative and functional writing.   In Indonesia and Italy the students do best on narratives; in the other systems they do best on functional writing (in the United States the two are scored almost the same).   It is clear from this finding that the common belief that narrative is "always easier" than other modes of writing for this age group is not supported by the data.

The results for Population B again deserve interpretation. First, the scores in Chile and the Netherlands are relatively homogeneous, and those in Hungary and Sweden are spread. The situation in Chile was reported as resulting from a tendency of the raters not to use the full scale; such was also the case in the Netherlands, where the standard deviation of scores is the lowest of any scoring group for the population (Table 6.3). In Hungary and Sweden, and to a lesser extent in the other countries, there would appear to be disparities among the tasks whether in terms of the amount of practice and familiarity of the students, or in terms of the scorers' perceptions. We would suspect the latter was a stronger contributor to the differences given the reports of students and teachers as well as the curriculum statements.

As in Population A, there are also differences among the countries as to the relative difficulty of specific tasks. Narration generally receives the higher scores, but there are exceptions in Hungary, where the expository receives the best scores, and The Netherlands and New Zealand where the functional receives the best scores.   There are greater differences with respect to the "most difficult" task, which in Chile is the functional; in Finland and Hamburg, the expository; in Hungary, the argument by a great margin, and in The Netherlands, the narrative. For the rest, the reflective composition receives the lowest scores, dramatically so in New Zealand. In most cases the relative rankings can again be accounted for by the emphasis in the curriculum.   This result is of importance to those who consider issues of writing pedagogy for this age group, for it tends to confound the argument that some writing tasks are developmentally "beyond" students of this age. Development appears to be contingent upon the curriculum and the argument becomes circular. Clearly the reflective composition is not taught to this age group in many systems of education, whereas it is taught in Hungary. Narrative is dropped from the Netherlands curriculum in favor of functional writing; the results are apparent in the scores given by raters in the system.

The results of this analysis for Population C show more clearly the effects of the curriculum (Figure 6.3). In three systems, Italy, Thailand, and the USA, the scores on functional writing are the lowest. Given the fact that the students are in a pre-university program, this could reflect a lack of practice and/or a lack of interest in the tasks, both of which cover a lack of functionality for the tasks. Only in Finland are the scores high, and there is no ready explanation for this, save the possibility that the students took the task seriously. The other highly rated tasks are exposition, argument, and reflection, each of which is the expected fare of the curriculum. One can also see that the reflective composition, which should be the staple in the curriculum for this age group, proves the most difficult task for students in Sweden and the United States. One may conjecture that exposure to this task is not as frequent as might be expected given the statements about the curriculum.

Another way of looking at these differences is by examining the standard deviations which indicate the spread of scores by task and system of education. These are given in Table 6.3. The mean standard deviation across all tasks, countries, and populations is .89, or just under one score point. The scores for Population C generally fall below that mean, which suggests more homogeneous performance on the part of the older students as compared to the younger ones; Population A has the highest standard deviation and Population B is close to the mean. One may interpret this result by asserting that the groups of younger students appear to be less similar, perhaps as a result of their scores resulting more from individual ability than from training; as the students get older individual variation gives way to a uniform standard of performance.

There are no clear patterns that emerge from the standard deviations for tasks; while those for systems may suggest something of the tendencies of the raters to use a more or less restricted scale, as we mentioned above.

Relating Performance to Opportunity to Learn

In other IEA studies, the issue of opportunity to learn (OTL) has loomed large in accounting for relative achievement, whether it is a curricular effect that takes place at the system level or an instructional effect that takes place at the classroom level. In the written composition study, the national curriculum questionnaire gave ratings to the various tasks (see chapter 3), and showed that they were all generally part of the curriculum.

In the main part of the study, the issue of OTL was approached through a task questionnaire to be filled out by each student after writing a given task. The questionnaire asked whether the student had had practice in the task, found the task easy, and was interested in the task, and also asked the student to give an estimate of performance. The students were additionally asked about the task type in general on the student questionnaire. In addition, the teachers were asked to give their rating of each task in terms of whether it had been taught in their class. Like many self-ratings, these attempts to triangulate upon OTL met with mixed success. To take the task questionnaire first, Table 6.4 shows the correlations of the four estimates with performance on an individual basis.

Table 6.4

Correlation of General Impression Score with Four Self-Estimates
By Student: Population B

Country	Issue	Func-tional	Nar-rative	Argu-ment	Refl.	Exp.
Chile	OTL	*.13	*.13	.03	*.15	*.06
	Ease	*.11	*.18	*.15	*.09	*.06
	Interest	-.01	.08	*.14	*.14	.03
	Self Test	-	-	-	-	-
England	OTL	.04	.04	*.23	*.25	.00
	Ease	.08	.04	.27	.13	*.18
	Interest	.02	.13	*.28	*.22	*.29
	Self Test	.05	.06	*.23	*.22	*.24
Finland	OTL	-.01	*.24	*.19	*.23	*.09
	Ease	*.15	*.19	*.23	.19	*.24
	Interest	*.19	*.30	*.35	*.39	*.35
	Self Test	.10	*.26	*.20	.14	*.21
Hamburg	OTL	.06	.10	.12	*.28	.06
	Ease	*.13	.15	.13	.21	*.15
	Interest	.10	.17	*.20	*.29	*.15
	Self Test	*.15	-.01	.13	.22	.12
Hungary	OTL	*.09	*.14	*.15	*.22	*.14
	Ease	*-.09	-.06	-.12	*-.13	*-.16
	Interest	*.12	*.19	*.25	*.30	*.22
	Self Test	-.03	-.01	-.01	.03	.05

Table 6.4 (Cont'd.)						
Country	Issue	Func- tional	Nar- rative	Argu- ment	Refl.	Exp.
Italy	OTL	*.08	*.12	-.07	*.18	.04
	Ease	*.18	.02	.05	.08	*.11
	Interest	-.01	.04	.09	.12	.06
	Self Test	.13	-	-	-	-
Nether- lands	OTL	.05	.13	.00	.08	.01
	Ease	*.20	.20	.08	.17	*.15
	Interest	-.07	.16	.22	*.38	*.19
	Self Test	-.03	.20	.08	.16	.04
New Zealand	OTL	.03	.09	*.21	*.34	.00
	Ease	*.17	.08	*.18	*.29	*.17
	Interest	*.09	*.18	*.27	*.28	*.27
	Self Test	*.13	*.12	*.22	*.22	*.28
Nigeria	OTL	-.03	.04	-.01	.01	*.08
	Ease	.00	.04	.01	.01	*.07
	Interest	.02	.12	.12	.01	.03
	Self Test	-.02	-.02	-.01	.00	.00
Sweden	OTL	*.14	*.27	.23	.03	.03
	Ease	*.27	*.33	.16	*.29	*.28
	Interest	*.33	*.43	*.35	*.43	*.42
	Self Test	-	-	-	-	-
USA	OTL	.06	.07	*.20	*.17	*.17
	Ease	*.13	.07	*.14	.09	*.15
	Interest	*.09	*.12	*.28	*.24	*.18
	Self Test	-	-	*.25	*.13	-.05
Wales	OTL	-.03	.15	.08	-.06	
	Ease	*.24	.34	.10	.21	
	Interest	.08	.37	.11	*.25	
	Self Test	.12	.19	.00	.20	

*P = .001 or better

What is striking about these results is how poor the students are at predicting their own performance. Although many of the correlations are statistically significant, they are not particularly high. Students in Finland and New Zealand appear to be the best predictors, those in Hamburg, The Netherlands, and Wales the worst. No one of the estimates appears to be a better predictor than any of the others, although Interest seems to be somewhat stronger. Why this should be remains somewhat a matter of conjecture. Cross-nationally, the students seem to estimate their performance in the more academic tasks of argument and reflection better than they do the other tasks. This may because they are more sure of the standards in those tasks than in narrative and functional writing.

When the students are asked about OTL in the questionnaire (where they are asked concerning the task type, not the particular composition), we find that at the system level their responses become excellent predictors of group performance (Table 6.5). Here we can compare them with the teachers' estimates of OTL, and with the exception of Chile, England, and Hamburg, the student estimates of OTL are better predictors than the teachers'. In Italy and The Netherlands, the teachers' estimates bear a negative relationship with performance.

More important than claiming who is the best predictor is the finding that in some systems, notably Finland, Hungary, Italy, New Zealand, Nigeria, Sweden, the United States, and Wales, the students' report on prior instruction gives a good indication of their relative performance on the tasks. This appears to confirm the general point that student performance is related to instruction, perhaps more than to something external to instruction like "ability."

Performance of Selected Groups

In this section we will examine three issues that are worthy of discussion cross-nationally: first, the degree to which there is a bias in the school system favoring certain schools; second, whether the bias is related to school location or to student background; and third, the effects of gender on performance.

To take up the issue of bias, we will first examine the differences among schools. This is reported in Appendix 1, but we will examine the issue a bit more fully here. Table 6.6 gives the standard deviations of school means by country and task for Population B. The average deviation is just over half a score point on a five-point scale. The variation is less on the functional tasks than on the academic tasks, perhaps because they are emphasized more in the less academic schools and less in the more academic ones. The systems with the most homogeneous performance across schools are Sweden, Hamburg, Hungary, and the United States. Those with the greatest disparity are Wales, England, and New Zealand. It would seem that there are clearly school effects on writing performance in all the participating systems, but whether these are related to the nature of the schools, the type of students, or some combination cannot be determined without causal analysis.

Table 6.5

Rank Orders within Country of Overall Impression Score, Student Rating of OTL, and Teacher Rating of OTL

		Fu	Na	Ar	Re	Ex	Rho w/ sc.
CHI	Rated Score	2	1	3	2	5	
	Student OTL	1	2	5	3	4	.20
	Teacher OTL	4	2	3	1	5	.70
ENG	Rated Score	3	1	2	5	4	
	Student OTL	2	1	4	3	5	.50
	Teacher OTL	4	1	2	3	5	.55
FIN	Rated Score	2	1	3	3	5	
	Student OTL	2	1	5	3	4	.82
	Teacher OTL	5	1	3	2	4	.45
HAM	Rated Score	3	1	2	4	5	
	Student OTL	1	2	5	4	3	.10
	Teacher OTL	4	2	1	3	5	.80
HUN	Rated Score	2	3	5	4	1	
	Student OTL	1	3	4	5	2	.80
	Teacher OTL	4	1	5	3	2	.50
ITA	Rated Score	2	1	3	5	4	
	Student OTL	2	1	5	3	4	.60
	Teacher OTL	5	2	3	1	4	-.30

		Fu	Na	Ar	Re	Ex	Rho w/ sc.
	Table 6.5 (Cont'd.)						
NET	Rated Score	1	4	3	5	2	
	Student OTL	1	2	5	4	3	.50
	Teacher OTL	4	1	2	3	5	-.75
N-Z	Rated Score	1	2	3	5	4	
	Student OTL	2	1	4	3	5	.60
	Teacher OTL	4	1	3	2	5	.25
NIG	Rated Score	3	1	2	5	3	
	Student OTL	2	1	4	5	3	.67
	Teacher OTL	5	1	4	3	2	.35
SWE	Rated Score	3	1	2	5	4	
	Student OTL	2	1	4	5	3	.70
	Teacher OTL	4	1	2	3	5	.70
USA	Rated Score	3	1	4	5	2	
	Student OTL	2	1	3	5	4	.70
	Teacher OTL	5	1	3	2	4	.10
WAL	Rated Score	4	1	3	5	2	
	Student OTL	2	1	3	5	4	.60
	Teacher OTL	4	1	2	3	5	.30

Table 6.6

Standard Deviation of School Mean Scores by Task: Population B

	Func- tional	Narra- tive	Argu- ment	Reflec- tive	Exposi- tion	Mean
CHI	.35	.57	.57	.54	.54	.51
ENG	.51	.69	.73	.73	.75	.68
FIN	.38	.52	.66	.63	.49	.54
HAM	.33	.44	.41	.46	.63	.45
HUN	.43	.50	.44	.47	.45	.46
ITA	.40	.47	.74	.53	.43	.51
NET	.45	.55	.56	.49	.51	.51
N-Z	.47	.63	.63	.69	.64	.61
NIG	.39	.31	.66	.70	.54	.52
SWE	.30	.50	.49	.46	.39	.43
USA	.33	.48	.52	.54	.54	.48
WAL	.57	.83	.63	.63	.80	.69
Mean	.41	.54	.59	.57	.56	.53

One possible source of the disparity is often claimed to be school location. In this study, the schools were asked in detail about the area from which they drew their students and in which they were physically located. The results were scaled from urban to rural and the correlation with individual student performance is reported in Table 6.7. In most cases the students in urban settings performed better than those in rural settings, most notably in Wales, but is also significantly in Chile, Hungary, and Sweden (negligibly in the USA, Finland, and England. School location is of course problematic, for although one might expect higher literacy with greater urbanization, there has come to be a curvelinear relationship in countries where the inner city schools form a counter example to the prevailing wisdom. Such seems to be the case in England and the USA; the Finnish case may have other causes.

Table 6.7

Correlation of School Locale with General Impression Score:
Population B (A negative correlation favors urban areas)

	Func- tional	Narra- tive	Argu- ment	Reflec- tion	Exposi- tion
CHI	*-.06	*-.11	*-.17	*-.13	*-.11
ENG	.04	-.01	.07	.06	.05
FIN	-.09	-.01	-.01	-.05	-.02
HAM	-	-	-	-	-
HUN	*-.12	-.08	-.04	-.11	*-.13
ITA	.02	*-.11	-.09	.02	-.04
NET	-	-	-	-	-
N-Z	.04	-.04	-.06	-.09	-.04
NIG	*-.15	-.08	-.05	-.06	-.07
SWE	*-.10	*-.14	*-.16	-.11	*-.14
USA	.02	.03	.03	-.04	-.02
WAL	*-.29	-.26	* -.31	-.40	-.41

* Significance >.001

Another view of social bias would focus on the home conditions of
the students, particularly their home literacy. One measure of this is the
number of books in the home which gives some indication of the availability
of literacy, and perhaps its encouragement. In order to highlight this
possibility, we present the difference in scores of the extremes of the
distribution (Table 6.8). The results show that books in the home are an
important predictor of achievement in Hungary (where the difference is two
thirds of a score point), Italy and, England. It is a significant predictor,
although less dramatically so, in Chile, New Zealand, and the United States.
In Nigeria there is little difference if any, perhaps because of the selectivity of
the system, which may be on other bases than home literacy (Akinnaso, 1991).
It is also noteworthy that the higher differences occur in the Argument and
Reflective tasks, which may represent the more academic, and thus "bookish."

Table 6.8

Difference of General Impression Mean Score of Students with
Fewer than 10 Books in the Home and Those with 26 or More: Pop B

	Func-tional	Narra-tive	Argu-ment	Reflec-tive	Exposi-tion	Mean
CHI	*.24	*.26	*.35	*.42	*.30	.31
ENG	*.47	.37	*.55	*.57	*.62	.51
FIN	*.32	.17	.20	.31	*.34	.27
HAM	*.27	.33	.30	*.44	*.27	.32
HUN	*.78	*.33	*.74	*.65	*.83	.67
ITA	*.39	.52	.59	*.67	*.44	.54
NET	.22	.16	*.58	.31	.23	.30
N-Z	*.57	*.56	*.55	.50	.40	.52
NIG	.07	.02	.27	.30	*.26	.18
SWE	-	-	-	-	-	-
USA	*.36	*.52	*.47	*.40	*.44	.44
WAL	.36	.81	.56	.03	.03	.41

* t-test   sig. >.001

The final issue concerning bias is that of gender. Earlier IEA studies have shown that in science and mathematics, boys tend to outperform girls, whereas in literature, girls outperform boys (Walker, 1976). At the same time there were few gender differences in reading. The question then arises as to whether writing is more like reading in being gender neutral or more like literature in favoring girls. Some national studies have tended to support the latter view, but an international perspective might demonstrate some surprises. The results of the written composition study on this matter are revealed in Table 6.9. They show that there is a widespread gender bias favoring girls that cuts across languages, cultures, and stages of economic development. In some countries, particularly Sweden, Finland, and Italy, the difference favoring girls increases with age to Population B and drops again for Population C. In New Zealand, there is no difference and barely a difference in the United States. One can expect gender bias to increase with age, perhaps, since such is the case with respect to mathematics, science, and literature. Why there should be a decline for the pre-university population is a matter for speculation and further inquiry. One cause might be in the greater selectivity of the population. The least interested and competent drop out from the sample, thus rendering the boys and girls who stay more equal than would have been the case were more in school.

Table 6.9

Difference in Scores of Boys and Girls--Overall Impression
Positive Numbers Indicate Girls Score Better than Boys

	Population A			
	Functional	Narrative	Argument	Mean
FIN	.37*	.44*	.36	.39
IND	.19*	.22*	.05	.15
ITA	.23	.6	.19	.19
N-Z	.30*	.45*	.46*	.40
SWE	.65*	.49*	.39*	.51
USA	.14	.09	.18	.19

Table 6.9 (Cont'd.)

Population B

	Func-tional	Narra-tive	Argu-ment	Reflec-tive	Exposi-tion	Mean
CHI	.16	.26	.16*	.35	.25	.24
ENG	.38	.33	.25*	.25*	.46	.33
FIN	.71	.34	.37	.65	.88	.59
HAM	.32	.14*	.14*	.14*	.40	.23
HUN	.52	.48	.26	.63	.57	.49
ITA	.31	.39	.43	.35	.41	.38
NET	.39	.43	.20*	.34	.42	.36
N-Z	.51	.17*	.33	.58	.40	.40
NIG	.11	.04*	.17*	.19*	.04*	.11
SWE	.71	.90	.61	.67	.65	.71
USA	.25	.12*	.20	.34	.30	.24
WAL	.44	.59*	.41*	.47	.64	.51
Mean	.42	.45	.37	.49	.49	.38

Population C

	Functional	Argument	Reflective	Exposition	Mean
FIN	.38*	.26*	.54*	.65*	.46
HUN	.33*	-.06*	.12*	.30*	.17
ITA	.26	.36*	.40*	.20	.31
SWE	.51*	.29*	.44*	.29*	.38
THA	.01	.17*	.09*	.15	.11
USA	.17	.14	.13	.24	.17

*= t-test   sig. <.001

Growth in Writing Performance

The examination of the standard deviations reported earlier in this chapter suggests some generalizations concerning growth in writing performance across all systems. The older students tend to be more similar to each other than do the younger ones, a finding we might expect given the role of schooling in most systems of education to make students more similar in performance. When we examine growth more particularly in those systems which tested two or three populations, we find a number of results of note (Figures 6.4-6.8). In Finland and Italy the students in Population A outperform those of Population B in Narrative. This result was hypothesized in certain systems, given the fact that narrative is the form most frequently taught the younger children, and it receives less and less emphasis as the grades progress. It is surprising, in fact, that in the other systems, the level of performance in narrative improves for the older students.

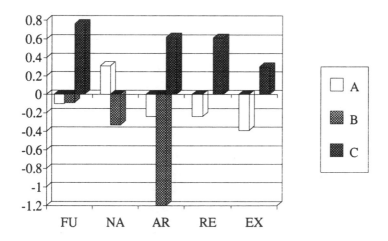

Figure 6.4: Growth in Performance: Finland

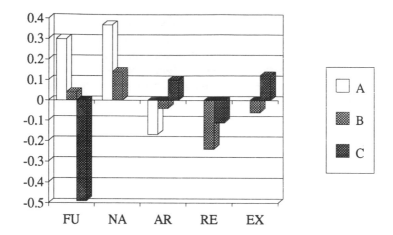

Figure 6.5: Growth in Performance: Italy

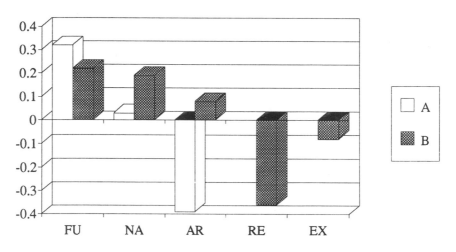

Figure 6.6: Growth in Performance: New Zealand

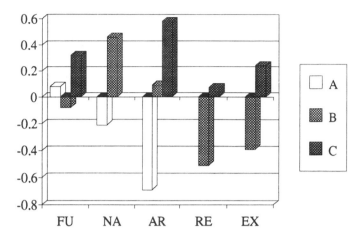

Figure 6.7: Growth in Performance: Sweden

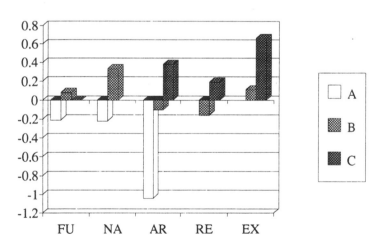

Figure 6.8: Growth in Performance: USA

The second finding of note is that in Italy and New Zealand the younger students also perform better on functional tasks than do the older ones. This may be the result of emphasis in instruction; it may be that the older students saw the tasks as childish and so did not treat them seriously; or it may result from a greater stringency on the part of the rating teams as they scored the tasks for the older students (one should remember that there was little overlap of specific tasks in this category between the two populations).

Summary

The limited comparisons of student performance that we have undertaken in this chapter do indeed shed some light on the state of composition in various educational systems of the world. It appears clear that there is a broad similarity in the performance of students from different cultures; in no system did students find any task impossible or too easy. At the same time there exist differences as to the breadth of student achievement. In some systems students tend to be more flexible than in others in that their performance across tasks is more even. It further appears clear that students do get better in their writing as they get older--or at least that scorers rate them higher. It also appears the case that girls perform better than boys.

The international variation within this broad picture suggests that there is an effect of the school and curriculum and its influence on the practice of students. Students do less well on tasks that they have not practiced or have not practiced recently. There do not appear to be universal dimensions regarding the difficulty of particular task types; ease or difficulty appears to depend upon practice and exposure. Students in rural areas tend to perform less well, as do students from homes where there is a lower manifestation of literacy activity. None of these findings is particularly unexpected given the results of prior surveys. At this point in the analysis we can conclude that students will do better in writing if they come from the right sort of home and go to an appropriate school where they are given practice in writing. If they are girls, they will probably be more successful than if they are boys. The following chapters will explore the relationship of achievement to these and other variables in greater detail.

7

Factors Predicting Writing Performance

Ruth Schick, Mary E. DeMasi, and Michael S. Green

Nations continue to be concerned with the performance of their educational systems and to compare them to the educational systems of other countries. Writing ability, as one consequence of formal education, is an area particularly difficult to assess in a comparative, cross-cultural framework because it is an expression of a culture. Writing represents values, tastes, preferences, traditions, history, and practices which are specific to cultural contexts. While direct comparisons are difficult as the preceding chapters have shown, the study allows for the first cross-national comparison of the prediction of writing performance based on comparable data sets.

The purpose of this analysis was to examine the factors associated with writing performance across the countries which participated in the IEA study. The three questions which guided the study were:

1) How well does a single model with similar measures of concepts predict performance in different countries?

2) For each country, how do the factors within the model differ in importance relative to writing performance?

3) Looking across countries, how does the relative importance of factors differ in the model?

The Model

The production function model of educational achievement is the theoretical model that guided this study (Brown & Saks, 1975; Murnane, 1975). This model, typically used by economists, was selected for this study because it provides a comprehensive strategy for examining the relationships among writing performance and home, classroom, school, and community characteristics.

The production function model for educational achievement examines student performance as a product of a set of inputs and input mixes or interactions (Hanushek, 1989). These inputs are typically viewed as: (a) student characteristics, such as home background, socioeconomic status, ethnic and cultural characteristics of the family, and parent and student attitudes about school and literacy skills, (b) teacher and classroom characteristics, such as teaching experience and training, class size, peer mix, and instructional approaches; and (c) school characteristics, such as school resources, urban/rural location, and level of community involvement in education. Achievement is most often viewed in terms of the achievement of individual students, but it may also be analyzed at the classroom, school, or regional level. The IEA writing data, by providing information on student home, teacher, and school characteristics, enables the production function model to examine the similarities and differences in the factors associated with writing performance across countries. Figure 7.1 depicts the general production function model.

The IEA writing composition study focuses specifically on performance in a language arts subject area. Therefore, the general production function model for this study was modified to place special emphasis on variables that relate to language use, communication, and literacy in the home. The specific model used in this study is represented in Figure 7.2. It was supposed that greater family interaction, and in particular greater family emphasis on discussions involving books, school and formally correct language usage, is associated with better performance in writing in school.

Method

This analysis identifies the common factors that explain writing achievement in ten countries. Analyses were restricted to Population B, students at the end of compulsory education. The measure of writing performance was students' persuasive argument essays.

A combination of factor analyses and hierarchical regression was used. Factor analyses were used to collapse the numerous variables into meaningful constructs. Hierarchical regression analyses, traditionally used in the production function model, were used to allow for controlled entry of the factors for home, class, and school (Hanushek, 1989). The inputs into the final regression equations represent a series of research decisions which weighed the integrity of the theoretical model against national differences in the availability and quality of the data.

Factor Analyses

Variables representing concepts presented in the production function model were selected from the student, teacher, and school questionnaires. An insufficient number of items were available to conduct factor analyses on school level data. Countries with significant amounts of missing data include

Germany, Hungary, and The Netherlands. Variables which are missing more than 15% of the data or show no variance were excluded for each system.

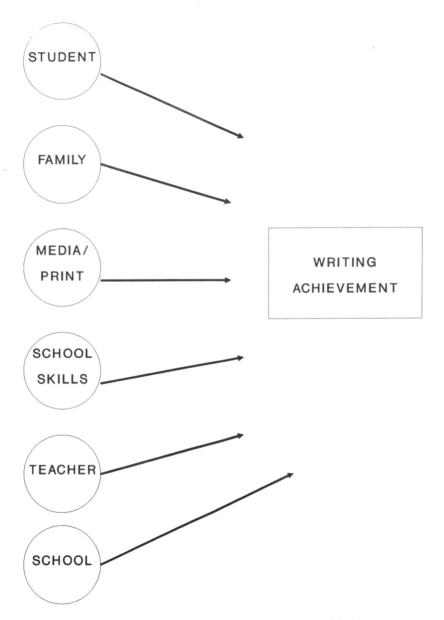

Figure 7.1: General Production Function Model

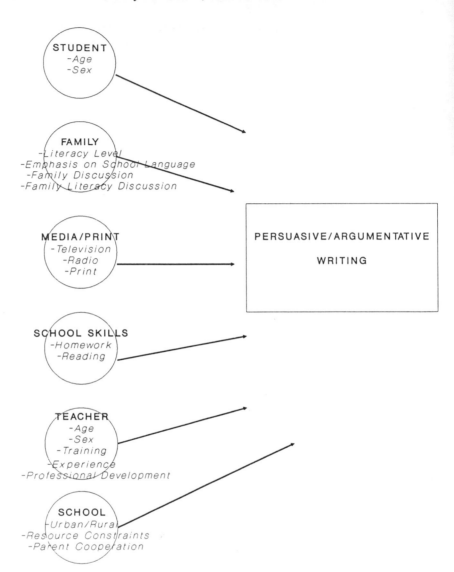

Figure 7.2: IEA Production Function Model

Separate factor analyses were performed for student and teacher variables. A principal components extraction and varimax rotation were used to identify factors in each country. The principal components extraction was used to allow differences in factor formation to emerge for each country. Interpretation of the factors was based upon variables with loadings of .50 or greater.

Regression Analyses

The dependent variable used in this study was students' performance on the persuasive writing task. Independent variables were entered into the regression equation hierarchically. The order in which blocks were entered is: student characteristics, family characteristics, school related skills, teacher characteristics and school characteristics.

Dependent Variable

The dependent variable used for the study is constructed as the sum of the overall impression score and the analytical subscores for the persuasive argument writing task. The constructed scale has the advantage over the simple overall impression score of expanding the potential range of variability for the dependent variable from a possible 4-point scale to a 17-point scale. Another advantage of the constructed scale is the increased reliability over the simple 4-point scale. Correlations ranging from .87 to .93 ($p = .001$) existed between each of the subscores and the overall impression scores for all countries.

Independent Variables

The regression analyses incorporated the factor scores from the factors described above as well as several individual variables. The variables entered singly were students' age and sex, teachers' age, sex, and years of teaching experience, teacher reported resource shortages, extent of community and parental support for the schools, and urban/rural location of schools. These variables do not fit conceptually within the factor analyses given the design of this analysis and the availability of data on classroom and school characteristics. Therefore, these variables are entered singly into the regression equation.

The "obstacles to progress" indicator began conceptually as a scale based on six variables, however, it was reduced to single variables for each country due to missing data. The "obstacles to progress" indicator for Chile, Finland, Germany, and Sweden refers to "shortage of time in class." For England, Hungary, Italy, The Netherlands, Nigeria, New Zealand and the United States, the indicator is "student absences from class."

Results

Factor Analyses

Factors which emerged for both student and teacher data are remarkably similar across all countries. The factor analyses on student questionnaire data result in the formation of four to nine factors across countries (Table 7.1). Differences in the number of student factors is largely attributable to differences in the number of variables entered into each factor analysis. The factor analyses on teacher data resulted in two factors, except for Hungary where missing data made it impossible to calculate factors.

For the student factor analyses, the first factor, defined as "family literacy level," typically incorporates parents' type of education, the number of books in the home, and students' desire for further education.

The second factor, named "family discussion," groups variables which indicate the frequency of family dialogue between parents and children on topics such as family plans, current news events, and general conversation. For Chile and Finland, this factor also includes variables which measure the frequency with which families discuss books and listen to each other tell stories. In Italy, The Netherlands, New Zealand, Sweden, and the United States, these latter variables form a separate factor referred to as "family literacy discussion."

Families differ in the emphasis they place on using standard language, or "school language." The fourth factor "school language emphasis" is formed by three variables: (a) parents' emphasis on their children's use of standard speech, (b) parents' emphasis on proper writing, and (c) the importance students themselves place on speaking in the manner expected of them in school. In Chile and Italy, an inverse loading exists in the importance in which students, as compared to parents, place on use of formally correct language.

Table 7.1
Factor Loadings by Country

(Student and Family Factors)

Factor Name	Variable	CHI	ENG	FIN	HAM	HUN	ITA	NET	N-Z	NIG	SWE	USA
Family Literacy Level	Father's Education	.8523	.7255	.8598	.7157	.8381	.8284	.7992	.7936	.8600	.8678	.7935
	Mother's Education	.8355	.6722	.8414	.6468	.8253	----	.7147	.7683	.8577	.8585	.7550
	Number of Books in the Home	.6724	.4331	----	----	.5842	.4707	.4896	----	----	.5154	.5105
	Years More Education Desired (Stud)	.5109	.5041	----	----	.7676	.7197	.5694	.6792	----	----	.5110
	Time Spent Reading - Fun	----	----	----	----	.4401	----	----	----	----	----	----
	Import Parents Place on Sch Lang	----	----	----	.6727	----	----	----	----	----	----	----
Family Discussion	Frequency of:											
	Discuss Family News	.7162	.8044	.6718	----	----	.7900	.7093	.7457	.7428	.7817	.8426
	Discuss General News	.7017	.6346	.7139	----	----	.6432	.5389	----	----	.6926	.5833
	Radio/TV Together	.6838	----	.7690	----	----	----	----	.5295	----	.5154	----
	Discuss Books	.6609	----	.4981	----	----	----	----	----	----	----	----
	Discuss School or Work	.6384	.8096	.6829	----	----	.6829	.6226	.6584	.5875	.7864	.7779
	Read Books Together	.5200	----	.6854	----	----	----	----	----	----	----	----
	Tell Stories Aloud	.6384	.5292	.5392	----	----	----	----	.7254	.7518	----	.7653
	Discuss Plans	----	----	----	----	----	.6522	----				
Family Literary Discussion	Frequency of:											
	Read Books Together	----	----	----	----	----	.5800	----	----	.7992	.7236	.6184
	Tell Stories Aloud	----	----	----	----	----	.6712	----	----	.7577	.7064	.6847
	Discuss Books	----	----	----	----	----	.7094	.6696	.7516	.6362	.6148	.7795
	Radio/TV Together	----	----	----	----	----	----	.7388	----	----	----	.6268
	Discuss General News	----	----	----	----	----	----		.6053	----	----	----
Emphasis on School Language	Import Parents Place on Sch Lang	.7544	.4584	----	----	----	.7364	.8248	----	----	.7542	.6908
	Import Parents Place on Spelling	----	.7714	.6467	.6467	----	----	.6346	----	----	.7336	.7295
	Import Students Place on Sch Lang	-.6855	.6008	.6977	.6977	----	-.7809	----	----	----	.5316	----

Table 7.1 (Cont'd.)

(Student and Family Factors. Continued)

Factor Name	Variable	CHI	ENG	FIN	HAM	HUN	ITA	NET	N-Z	NIG	SWE	USA
Television & Comics	Student Time Spent on:											
	TV - Nonschool Days	.8780	-.7987	.7083	.8707	.8639	.8517	.8296	.8782	.6920	.6993	.8664
	TV - School Days	.8760	-.7864	.7846	.8765	.8782	.8584	.8685	.7953	.7630	.7582	.8275
	Reading Comics	---	---	.6839	---	---	---	---	---	---	.5743	---
	Radio - School Days	---	---	---	---	---	---	---	---	.5686	---	---
Radio	Student Time Spent on:											
	Radio - Nonschool Days	.9183	.8684	.8541	.8636	.5316	.8972	.8608	---	---	.8259	.9365
	Radio - School Days	.9219	.8453	.8366	.8668	---	.9060	.8470	---	---	.8260	.9414
	Reading - Fun	---	---	---	---	---	---	---	---	---	---	---
	Student Frequency - Trips to Library	---	---	---	---	.7373	---	---	---	---	---	---
Print	Number Newspapers at Home	.7028	.7237	-.8028	---	.5066	---	---	---	.7345	.6480	---
	Number Magazines at Home	.5842	.8038	.6989	---	.6750	---	---	---	---	---	---
	Student Rating of Self as Writer	---	---	---	---	-.5623	---	---	---	---	---	---
	Import Parents Place on Spelling	---	---	---	---	---	---	---	---	-.6453	-.6767	---
	Number of Books in the Home	---	---	---	---	---	---	---	---	.4995	---	---
Homework	Time Spent on:											
	Homework - All	.7396	.6861	.8593	.7396	---	.8162	.7944	.8098	---	.6865	.7211
	Homework - Writing/All Subj	.6289	.7000	.5919	.6289	---	.4361	.4361	.8044	---	.7757	.7013
	Homework - Reading/All Subj	---	---	.8109	---	---	.5467	.5467	---	---	.4489	---
	Years More Education Desired (Stud)	---	.5535	---	---	---	---	---	---	---	---	---
Reading	Time Spent on:											
	Homework - Reading/All Subj	.6945	---	---	---	---	---	---	.5745	.8024	---	.5520
	Homework - Writing/All Subj	---	---	---	---	---	---	---	---	.6394	---	---
	Reading Comics	---	.7352	.8088	---	---	---	---	---	---	---	---
	Reading - Fun	.7779	.5064	.6633	---	---	---	---	.7464	.7019	---	.6397
	Student Frequency - Trips to Library	.7721	---	.5284	---	---	---	---	.5463	---	---	.7764
	Number of Books in Home	---	---	---	---	---	---	---	---	---	---	---

(Teacher Factors)

Table 7.1 (Cont'd.)

Factor Name	Variable	CHI	ENG	FIN	HAM	HUN	ITA	NET	N-Z	NIG	SWE	USA
Teacher Training	Amount of Training in:											
	Writing Processes	.7228	.5920	.7209	.6751	----	.7211	.6744	.7066	.7365	.7376	.6037
	Writing Subskills	.6432	----	.6813	.5003	----	.7148	.6110	.6304	.7035	.7779	.6037
	Writing Functions	.7218	.6903	.6991	.5260	----	.8587	.5936	.6956	.8487	.7392	.6797
	Diagnosing Problems	.5250	----	----	.5081	----	----	.6341	----	----	----	.5241
	Teach Stu w/ Lang Problems	----	----	----	----	----	----	.5459	----	----	----	----
	Motivating Students	.6506	.6431	.6572	----	----	.7850	.6188	.6052	----	.7077	.6856
	Evaluating Compositions	.6913	.7534	.6039	.7251	----	----	.6643	.7627	----	.6547	.6925
	Giving Feedback to Students	.6980	.6918	.5731	.6845	----	.6902	.8124	.7543	----	.6813	.6672
	Own Writing	.5848	----	----	----	----	----	----	----	.6132	.5175	.5194
	Study of Language	----	.5622	----	----	----	----	----	.6033	.5224	.6570	----
	Study of Literature	----	.5542	.5026	----	----	----	----	----	----	.6314	----
Professional Development	Frequency with which Teachers:											
	Read About Teaching	----	.5985	----	.5142	----	----	----	.6049	----	.4978	.5157
	Read About Mother Tongue	----	.5950	----	----	----	----	.5874	----	.5272	.6147	.5193
	Take TV/Radio Courses. M. T.	----	----	----	----	----	----	----	.5473	.5646	----	----
	Partic in Professionl Meetings	.6648	.6096	.5611	.6120	----	.6080	.5840	.5869	----	----	.6133
	Teach Model Classes	.7129	.6715	.5859	.5535	----	.5471	----	.5795	.7678	.4864	----
	Act as Professional Advisor	.7068	.7320	.6671	----	----	.6761	.5818	.6586	.6662	----	.6548
	Activ in Professionl Meeting	.6847	.6192	.7605	.5583	----	.7954	----	.7646	.7893	.5767	.7167
	Contribut to Profess Journal	.5356	----	.6424	----	----	----	----	.6647	.7325	----	----
	Design Curric/ Externl Use	.5284	----	----	.6856	----	.7161	----	.5348	.6798	.7382	.5240
	Partic in Teach Experiments	.7018	----	----	----	----	----	----	.6121	.6505	----	.5261
	Act as Educational Expert	----	----	----	----	----	.7161	.5905	.6500	.6965	----	.6251
	Member Mother Tongue Assn	----	----	----	----	----	----	----	----	----	----	----
	Officer Teachers' Organization	----	----	----	----	----	.5001	----	.6207	.5029	----	.6196

The fifth, sixth, and seventh factors represent common forms of media: print, television and radio. One might expect the amount of parental education to load consistently with the amount of print found in the home. However, in this study, the number of books in the home often loads with parental education. In almost all countries, television and radio form distinct factors. In some countries, pleasure reading is associated with television and radio. Newspapers and magazines form their own factor which typically does not show a high loading for any reading measures or number of books in the home. In Finland, newspapers and books load together as a factor with inverse signs while in Sweden, magazines and newspapers load onto the same factor, also with opposite signs. This particular variation suggests national differences in availability, cost, and relative popularity of different forms of text.

Reading comics tends to vary across countries, loading sometimes on the media or sometimes on the reading factor. In Finland, Germany, and Sweden, the amount of time students spend on reading comics loads with the amount of television they watch. For Hungary, amount of radio listening and pleasure reading load on a single factor. The final student factors, "homework" and "reading," vary somewhat across countries in terms of the variables which load together. These factors include measures of total amounts of homework for all subjects as well as time spent doing reading or writing as part of homework. The factors also include how often students go to the library, the amount of time they spend on pleasure reading, and the amount of time they spend reading comics. In Finland, the "reading" factor includes number of books in the home.

The factor analyses for teacher level variables include only variables indicating (a) the amount and types of professional activities teachers engage in, and (b) the number of courses taken on methods related to teaching writing. Two factors, named "teacher training" and "professional development" result. The loadings of variables on these factors affirm the distinction between training variables and professional development variables which was suggested in the teacher questionnaire. However, within each factor the order and strength of variable loadings differ across countries. These differences in teacher factors suggest differences in availability of, as well as incentives for, various types of professional activities for teachers across nations.

Though the factors which emerge from the factor analyses look extremely similar across countries, they explain considerably different amounts of variance across countries.

Regression Analyses

The amount of variance in student writing performance explained by the model varies dramatically across countries from .1496 ($p = .001$) in the United States to .3622 ($p = .001$) in Sweden. (The regression model could not be applied to the Nigerian data due to the number of cases eliminated by the listwise deletions.) The R^2, F value, and significance level of F are presented in Table 7.2.

In hierarchical regression it is only possible to meaningfully interpret the contribution of the block of variables entered last. The research hypothesis, based on the production function model, emphasizes variables subject to policy intervention. Therefore in these analyses, school and teacher characteristics, those variables presumed to be most directly influenced by policy intervention are entered last. Blocks of teacher and school variables contribute marginally to the amount of variance explained in all the countries at this point of entry. Only in Finland, New Zealand, and Sweden do these blocks continue to account for any notable amount of variance in performance. In Finland and New Zealand, teacher characteristics account for about 4% of the variance in performance, while school characteristics are not related to performance at this point of entry. In Sweden, teacher characteristics do not predict variation in student performance, but school characteristics predict approximately 4% of the variation.

One difficulty with hierarchical regression is the interpretation of the R^2 contribution of each block. It is impossible to determine the indirect relationships between the independent variables and the dependent variables. This ambiguity can be resolved using regression techniques by changing the order in which blocks are entered and analyzing changes in the R^2 contribution of all the blocks. It can also be clarified through use of analytic methods such as path models which can account for indirect effects of independent variables. The partial least squares (PLS) analyses presented in the next chapter provide an example of this type of approach. However, hierarchical regression is used here as preliminary analysis.

Table 7.2 presents the R^2 contribution of each block entered into the model. It is crucial to note that these R^2 contributions can only be read as the R^2 contribution of the block *at that point of entry*, having controlled for all variables entered earlier. Thus, the R^2 values presented in Table 2 give tentative indications of the predictive value of the blocks included in the model. At the final point of entry, teacher and school characteristics contribute less than 1% to approximately 7% of the variance in student writing performance. Further analyses that examine indirect relations are necessary to validate these results.

Table 7.2
Hierarchical Regression Results by Country

		CHI	ENG	FIN	HAM	HUN	ITA	NET	N-Z	SWE	USA
Student Block	R^2ch	.0497	.0216	.0271	.0439	.0473	.0784	.0507	.0374	.1074	.0210
	F ch	11.14	2.10	2.83	4.16	9.18	6.55	5.52	6.97	15.71	4.76
	a	.000	.125	.061	.017	.000	.002	.005	.001	.000	.009
Family Block	R^2ch	.1019	.1206	.0342	.0930	.2216	.1366	.1663	.0486	.0626	.0875
	F ch	16.93	8.81	2.43	6.39	111.82	6.53	10.78	6.31	4.84	10.80
	a	.000	.000	.066	.000	.000	.000	.000	.000	.001	.000
Media Block	R^2ch	.0318	.0871	.1531	.0250	.0220	.0157	.0225	.0125	.1261	.0317
	F ch	5.45	6.97	12.79	2.63	5.69	1.51	2.98	4.91	15.17	8.08
	a	.001	.000	.000	.075	.004	.225	.053	.027	.000	.000
School Skills Block	R^2ch	.0008	.0505	.0289	.0148	.0424	.0260	.0192	.0319	.0155	.0041
	F ch	.20	4.24	3.72	.78	11.62	2.55	2.58	6.47	5.68	1.04
	a	.816	.006	.026	.542	.000	.082	.079	.002	.018	.353
Teacher Block	R^2ch	.0156	.0236	.0367	.0069	.0022	.0149	.0293	.0350	.0105	.0010
	F ch	2.02	1.51	2.43	.48	.61	.73	2.01	3.66	.97	.13
	a	.090	.201	.049	.700	.543	.577	.095	.006	.427	.972
School Block	R^2ch	.0139	.0693	.0055	....	.0041	.0099	.0007	.0192	.0400	.0043
	F ch	2.42	6.44	.480	....	1.11	.64	.10	2.72	5.15	.72
	a	.065	.000	.697	....	.331	.590	.104	.045	.002	.539
Total Variance Explained	R^2	.2138	.3726	.2856	.1836	.3396	.2815	.2887	.1845	.3622	.1496
	F	6.57	5.77	4.15	2.72	16.87	3.20	4.90	5.22	8.22	4.44
	a	.000	.000	.000	.001	.000	.000	.000	.000	.000	.000

How is it that teacher characteristics do not help explain students' writing achievement? It is counter-intuitive to believe that teachers do not make a difference in students' performance yet these findings continue to appear in the literature (Fuller, 1987). Other studies which have employed regression techniques to analyze multilevel data have also shown that survey data on teacher characteristics do not provide good indicators of the teacher-student interactions which affect student achievement. In addition, when mixing student and classroom levels of analyses, variance at the teacher level is artificially suppressed. That is, the assumption that a teacher interacts in the same way with all students in the classroom is imposed. As Bidwell & Kasarda (1980) emphasize, it is desirable to have direct measures of student utilization of teacher resources.

The small contribution of teacher characteristics to student performance in the current analyses may also be a feature of small amounts of variation in the measures used to indicate teacher characteristics. In the U.S. there is little variation in teacher characteristics according to the formal indicators of teacher qualifications and training. Variables which themselves have little variance cannot show strong relationships to other variables. Here, teacher characteristics cannot show a strong relationship to student performance.

It appears, then, that statistical and measurement features may be responsible for the small contribution of teacher characteristics to explaining student performance. More sensitive measures which combine self-reporting with classroom observations are needed.

School variables, like the teacher characteristics, explain a disappointing amount of variance in student performance. Closer examination of data indicates the need to gather more complex, reliable measures of school quality.

Block one, gender and age, reveals that girls consistently outperform boys in persuasive writing across countries. This finding is consistent with other cross-cultural studies on language (Heyneman, 1989). A variety of explanations for this phenomenon are possible. Sociolinguistic research suggests that sex differences in language ability are often indications of socially based differences in girls' and boys' activities, and cannot be assumed to have physiological bases (Philip & Reynolds, 1987; Smith 1985). Models of oral and written language use are gender typed and vary with different and often gender-typed activities (Coates & Cameron, 1988). In Sweden, where student gender made a considerable contribution to explaining student performance, descriptive analyses showed a large difference between boys' and girls' activities. Whereas boys tend to read comics during their leisure time, girls are more likely to write in diaries or compose letters to pen pals (Lofgren & Schick, in press).

Hence, the association of language with sex differences is an association among gender, communication, and activity (Philip & Reynolds, 1987; Sherzer, 1987; Smith 1985). In addition the similarity of sex and performance findings across countries suggests that formal educational systems share certain gender-typing characteristics which are responsible for producing similar gender-related differences in writing performance.

The importance of the second block, family characteristics, to the overall model is consistent with the results of previous research which emphasize the contribution of family characteristics to student academic success (Heyneman, 1989; Purves, 1973). Not surprisingly, this block is important in explaining student achievement across countries. Since parents' educational level is a common proxy for socioeconomic status, these findings are to be expected (Heyneman, 1989). Frequency of family discussion also has a strong relationship to writing performance. Family discussion is valued in many cultures and is a meaningful contributor to student writing achievement for all of the countries in this study.

The emphasis that students and adults place on the use of standard, or "school" language does not contribute to students' writing performance. It is possible that the indicators used to measure the importance which families place on using standard language are not good measures of students' language experiences at home. It may also be that such an emphasis is class-related. Indicators of family discussions on the other hand, which do show a strong relationship with student performance are probably better measures of the student's home language experiences.

Large differences across countries in the amount of variance contributed to student writing by the family characteristics block suggest differences in the adequacy of the measures used to tap variations in family characteristics in different countries.

The block that represents print and media is not available in many countries. Where available, this block tends to have an inconsistent relationship to student writing. In Hungary and Chile, the presence of print in the home is negatively related to writing achievement. The block is extremely important for both Finland and Sweden, perhaps due to the print factor that had an inverse loading of variables. Deliberate decisions made regarding what type of print is made available within the home may influence its use. In other countries where print may be more accessible and relatively inexpensive, consumers may indiscriminately purchase reading material and read it more casually. This study suggests that differences in use of print in various countries are caused by price, distribution, and tastes, and affect differences in students' socialization to the use and production of texts.

Summary

The Written Composition study provides information on a wide number of variables related to mother tongue education. Some variables are excellent indicators of certain types of factors affecting writing performance, namely family literacy, family discussions, availability of print, and use of media in the home. A number of the indicators, however--most notably those relating to homework and reading, and to class, teacher and school characteristics--do not appear to measure those areas adequately to show an association with student performance.

Reflections on both the characteristics of the data set and the analyses conducted are useful in interpreting the results. The relative strength of home characteristics, and weakness of association between homework, teacher and school characteristics, and performance should be interpreted in light of not only the substantive questions they were designed to inform, but also the methodological constraints which limit the results.

The substantive results study are shaped by the finding that three of the six blocks entered into the regression analysis show little relationship to the dependent variable. In essence, this results less from the actual lack of the importance of these characteristics than from issues related to between-student analyses. The negative findings however, can also be suggestive. For instance, the lack of relationship between gender and performance in most countries may represent the fact that males and females generally do not differ in their ability to communicate in writing; this may contrast with typical spoken language. Other analyses of this IEA data set have shown that gender differences in writing performance tend to be smallest in the area of persuasive writing. These findings are consistent with those results.

8

Exploring the Causal Background of Achievement in Argument Writing

Rainer H. Lehmann and Kari Törmäkangas

The earlier chapters of this book have demonstrated that the IEA Study of Achievement in Written Composition has produced a wealth of detailed knowledge on the various cultures of school writing. It also has been shown that the assessment of writing achievement within the given writing cultures has been fairly successful in most instances, as judged by the current state of the art. Since it is not possible to compare the achievement measures across countries, the task for this chapter can only be to explore some country-specific relationships among and between the known background factors and the nationally rated quality of the student compositions.

This purpose requires a conceptual framework that models these relationships in such a way as to compare the ways in which the model works out in the specific educational systems. Because of cost and space in the volume, the analyses can be performed only with a small portion of the data. Building upon the work of the previous chapter, we selected the argumentative essays as the example to study, and the actual computations will be confined to six educational systems in Population B. The systems (Chile, Hamburg, Hungary, The Netherlands, and the United States) represent a geographic range, a linguistic range, and an educational range as based on the analysis of curriculum and instruction.

Structural Comparisons - Some Initial Caveats

The analyses reported in chapter 6 and Appendix 2 suggest that there were substantial differences among the national juries with respect to the characteristics which implicitly define the "quality of school writing": Some juries appear to have concentrated on content characteristics and others seem to have been concerned primarily with the appropriateness and correctness of style and grammar. By analyzing the convergent validity coefficients (the average correlation for each rating aspect across tasks) in conjunction with the intertask correlations, we find that the rated quality of student compositions is much more stable across assignments in the case of style-based judgments than in that of content-based judgments. That is to say that "Quality and

Scope of Content" is predominantly a text-specific characteristic (related rather indirectly to more general student abilities and associated with an unexpected amount of chance variation), while "Style" and "Grammar" refer primarily to those characteristics of performance that are manifested across texts in a more stable manner. If this interpretation is correct, the emphasis given content over style by national juries has serious implications for structural comparisons performed at the student level.

In chapter 7 it was noted that there were substantial differences between countries in terms of the explained variance (R2) of performance as reported from the student-level multiple regression analyses. If the hypothesis just given holds, it is to be expected that the effect-sizes (the R2s for individual variables, variable blocks, and the model as a whole) will be related to the national rating style as measured by the observed convergent validity coefficients. The higher the average convergent validity for a given national set of essay ratings, the higher will be the expected effect sizes, because high convergent validities imply low levels of chance variation at the student level. Figure 8.1. demonstrates graphically that the implication holds remarkably well for the ten countries whose argumentative task data were available for this analysis.

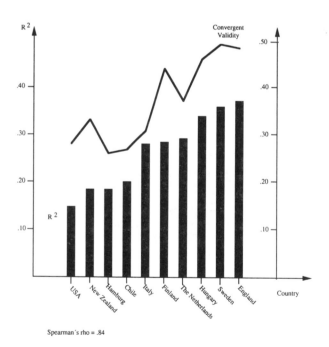

Figure 8.1: Rating Style and Effect Sizes: Multiple R Square in Regression Model and Convergent Validity by Country

The overall explained variances for the entire models were taken from chapter 7. They are represented by the bars and measured on the right-hand scale. The convergent validities were obtained as averages from the international core tasks only and the actual values refer to the left-hand scale (note that they are slightly different from the more complete, but less comparable values listed in Table 6 of Appendix 2). The rank-order correlation between explained variance and convergent validity (Spearman's rho = .84) expresses numerically this strong confirmation of the above hypothesis.

The case for insisting that effect sizes are incomparable across countries due to the culture-specific "meaning" of the scores can be made even stronger by studying the rank-order correlations for the various stages in which the multiple regression model is built up in chapter 7 (Fig. 8.2).

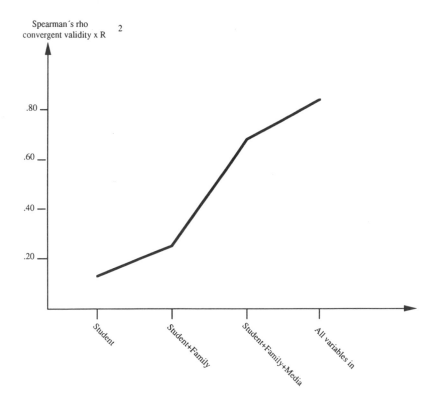

Figure 8.2: Rating Style and Effect Sizes: Across-Country Correlations between Convergent Validity Coefficients and Multiple R Square in Regression Model by Blocks in the Equation

It is seen clearly that the influence of rating style on the explanatory power of the model is cumulative: the more student-level variables are entered into the model, the more pronounced is the dependency of the explained variance (multiple R2) on the national jury's tendency to concentrate on student rather than text properties. Not only are the ratings of writing achievement as such incomparable across countries, but the same applies to the effect sizes also, because system-specific effects are inseparably confounded with the consequences emerging from the national juries' rating styles.

This assertion does not imply, however, that it is futile to investigate the determinants of scores on persuasive writing tasks comparatively. Even though the effect sizes cannot be directly compared internationally, they are useful indicators of the relative importance of certain determinants within a country on writing achievement as perceived by the national jury.

The General Model

Some of the earlier IEA work has been criticized for not taking properly into account the interrelationships among the various predictors of achievement (Pedhazur, 1982). Therefore, the results reported in chapter 7 have to be taken one step further by considering to what extent the influence of background variables can be regarded as unique (or "direct") and to what extent it is mediated by intervening variables. This can be done by applying path-analytic techniques (Blalock, 1985) and, more specifically, such methods which allow one to combine several indicators ("manifest variables") into blocks or constructs ("latent variables"). Writing achievement scores as measured by the four manifest rating variables (Overall Impression, Content, Organization, and Style) is an example of a latent variable.

However problematic direct comparisons may be in the international framework, it is obviously desirable to have a general pattern across the "national" path models so as to explore specific national differences. In developing such a pattern, the findings from the previous chapter are helpful, since the screening and grouping of background variables provide valuable information as to which variables are likely to form coherent constructs and which constructs are likely to be good predictors of writing achievement.

Thus, Tables 8.1 and 8.2 were first searched for variable blocks which appeared promising and which could be framed into a general model of causal relationships with an unambiguous quasi-temporal sequence. Given the generally low explanatory power and the highly country-specific nature of teacher, class, and school variables, as well as the well-known problems of separating student level from class/school level effects, it was deemed appropriate to disregard these variables, except "program type" in selective school systems. What emerged from this procedure, then, was a system of interrelationships - or hypothesized effects - which is displayed graphically in Figure 8.3.

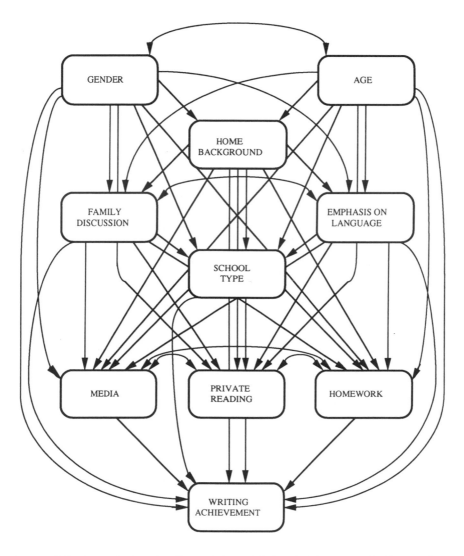

Figure 8.3: Hypothetical PLS Model Explaining Achievement in Persuasive Writing (Task 6)

In this diagram of the so-called "inner model," one-arrowed lines (or "paths") stand for direct causal relationships and double-arrowed lines represent correlations where for theoretical reasons no causal relationship can be established. The model as a whole is "recursive"; that is, it does not include any simultaneous effects between two or more variables in both directions. It also allows one to decompose the correlations between the latent variables into direct causal effects, indirect causal effects (computed from the product, or sum of products, of the direct effects involved), and noncausal effects which occur wherever the simple correlations must also to be considered. The direct causal effects are expressed as path coefficients, that is, standardized regression coefficients as they were also used in Table 8.2.

For the specification of the "outer model" (the allocation of manifest variables to each of the ten constructs considered in the inner model) the information proceeding from chapter 7 was again used. Those variables were selected which appeared to form coherent factors in most of the countries. These will become apparent later in the chapter. For each of the models to be discussed, the correlation matrix for all students who had taken the argumentative task and all manifest variables included in the outer model were computed. On the basis of these (unweighted) matrices, the latent variables could be determined iteratively according to the Partial Least Squares (PLS) algorithm developed by Hermann Wold (1982). This particular approach is recommended as an efficient and comparatively robust method for exploratory analyses of the present type. Although techniques exist to estimate the standard errors (and thus the statistical significance) of the reported coefficients, no such intentions are pursued in this chapter. All that can be done here is a very first exploration of causal relationships.

One more technical remark is in order. As the diagram shows, the initial inner model is quite complex, yet it cannot be taken for granted that all of the initially selected manifest variables will render a substantial contribution to the linear combinations which constitute the respective latent constructs. They will not act the same way in every system, in part because the variables represent different realities in different contexts; that is why the analysis must be replicated. Thus, general procedural rules had to be established to arrive at a more parsimonious path specification and at easily interpretable construct definitions for each country-specific model. These rules had the aim to start from identical specifications for all national data sets analyzed and then develop (by way of a common set of decision rules, listed below) simplified versions which could display the essential information without including misleading and/or uninterpretable chance effects.

The respective decision rules were:

(1) The outer model was to be simplified first. Any manifest variable with a communality < .10 with the other variables in the same block was

deleted from the model.

(2) Manifest variables with a change of sign from the expected/intended direction were excluded.

(3) In case of multicollinearity > .70 occurring within an "inward" (or regression mode) block, the specification mode was changed to "outward" (or principal component approach).

(4) Only then was the inner model revised. Any path associated with a path coefficient < .10 was deleted from the specification.

(5) With respect to the definite solution thus developed, checks were performed on the basis of the matrix of differences between the initial and the reproduced latent variable correlation matrix to make sure that no substantial effect had been eliminated erroneously during the iterative course of deleting single paths.

The computer program used in this process was PLSPATH, Version A (Schieber, 1983).

Before the individual country results are discussed, we should explain the selection of these particular countries. The six countries cover as much diversity in background as possible within the limitations allowed for this component of the international analyses. Thus, two data sets were chosen which refer to highly selective school systems in Western Europe (The Netherlands and Hamburg, Germany), but which nevertheless display significant differences. Finland provides an interesting contrast in that it changed its school system to a comprehensive scheme some time ago, but within a general political framework which is not too different from the two countries mentioned first. Hungary, on the other hand, has had a strongly centralized "general," or unitary, school system since the immediate postwar period, mainly for egalitarian principles inherent in the then dominant political system. The United States of America was included because in this high-income country, comprehensive schooling has had a long tradition while at the same time, differences between the local school systems are considerable, with socioeconomic stratification as a heavy contributing factor. Chile, finally, was selected, because it provides an example of a low-income country with great social disparities and a strong influence of private/church schooling in the population investigated.

The Netherlands - Institutional Selectivity at Work

The measurement model as applied to The Netherlands (Table 8.1) requires very little comment. Since it is the first to be discussed, however, it provides an opportunity to justify some of the general decisions made for the PLS-analysis of the data.

Table 8.1

Outer PLS Model Explaining Achievement in Persuasive Writing
(*N* = 414 Studnets from The Netherlands

Latent Variable Manifest Variables	Weight	Loading
Gender (male = 1; female = 2)	1.0000	-
Age	1.0000	-
Home Background Mother's Education Father's Education Number of Books in the Home Years of Further Study Planned	 .1640 .4303 .3112 .6019	 - - - -
Family Discussion Discuss General Matters Talk about Family Matters Talk about Work and School	 .5721 .2580 .5178	 - - -
Emphasis on School Language Student's Own Emphasis Importance of Adults on Spelling Expectations of Adults at Home	 - - -	 .3914 .9699 .5109
School Type (junior vocational = 1; senior grammar = 5)	1.0000	-
Media Hours Listening to Radio (workdays) Hours Listening to Radio (holidays) Newspapers (time spent reading) Magazines (time spent reading)	 - - - -	 .8267 .8048 .5759 .5499
Private Reading (time spent)	1.0000	-

Table 8.1 (Cont'd.)		
Latent Variable Manifest Variables	**Weight**	**Loading**
Homework		
All Homework	.4371	-
Reading Homework	.6432	-
Writing Homework	.4547	-
Writing Achievement		
Overall Impression	-	.9532
Quality and Scope of Content	-	.8893
Structure and Organization	-	.9086
Appropriateness of Tone and Style	-	.9139

The Home Background construct has satisfactory properties from a measurement point of view, but it is dominated (as are five of the six countries studied) by the indicator referring to the students' plans for further study. Since these may depend on the students' prior educational biographies (with Age as a proxy for success where grade repetition occurs and Gender standing for possible selection effects in terms of career expectations), it is advisable to model these relationships by considering Home Background as a dependent variable, in spite of its exogenous constituents.

The Family Discussion block is also consistent with its original specification. It is quite clear, however, that the variable referring to conversations about family matters is less distinctive with respect to antecedents and consequences than the other two indicators. Similarly, Emphasis on School Language retains all three manifest variables initially entered, although it had to be respecified as an "outward" block because of multicollinearity problems with the dominant indicator, "emphasis by adults on spelling."

A pivotal variable in the Dutch data set is School Type, which encompasses a hierarchy of five different programs ranging from Junior Vocational Schools to Senior Grammar Schools. Although initially seen as categories, they, in fact, form a hierarchy, which has been retained for the analysis.

The Media construct was originally composed of seven manifest variables. The print media (comics, newspapers, and magazines), however, were not related to the electronic media group, so that only the four variables referring to the latter were retained (again with a respecification to the outward mode as a consequence of the multicollinearity encountered). It seems that students are readers or viewers.

Private Reading was a single-variable construct to begin with, and the Homework construct is only mildly dominated by the reading component. The Writing Achievement block, finally, displays a very clear factorial structure with high loadings on all four constituents. As always, the Overall Impression score is the leading variable, but it is also apparent that the Dutch marking team has been guided by a rating style which was not strongly content-oriented.

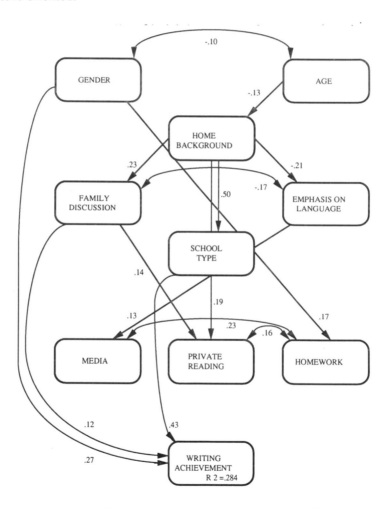

Figure 8.4: Inner PLS Model Explaining Achievement in Persuasive Writing (*N*=414 Students from The Netherlands)

Figure 8.4 depicts the interrelationships among the constructs for the Dutch participants in the IEA study. The two strongest causal effects in this model refer to the salient characteristic of the Dutch school system - its selectivity. This can be seen in the hierarchical array of the five different secondary programs, the access to which is governed by Primary School recommendations and the receiving school's entry requirements, as well as aptitude testing (cf. Nijhof & Streumer, 1988). Thus, School Type is the single most effective predictor of achievement in persuasive writing. At the same time, however, the price for the effective streaming of students appears to be an even stronger social bias in favor of those who come from better educated homes and who themselves have higher educational aspirations. It may be argued, of course, that some of these aspirations are also a product (rather than an antecedent) of the school program attended, but even so, it is clear that socioeconomic background differences are transformed into achievement differences by selection mechanisms associated with the type of school attended. It is also probable that the curricula differ so as to exacerbate the differences in achievement,

Another system-related effect can be inferred from the model as it stands. The Dutch Primary School's practice of having grade repetition based on norm-referenced testing is reflected by the negative sign in the relationship between Age (as a proxy for grade repetition) and Home Background, and possibly also in the negative correlation with Gender. Boys from less literate homes are held back in primary school and then placed in the "lower streams" and are rated as poorer writers. Since this practice tends to create more homogeneous learner groups over time which are then funneled into the various streams of the school system, the effects of age on School Type and Writing Achievement are only indirect.

The analysis shows a complex pattern of relationships between Home Background and its adjacent constructs. Obviously, this construct stands for a stimulating environment (effect on Family Discussion of $p = .23$) which encourages reading (direct $p = .19$) and ultimately also writing achievement (indirect effects mediated by Family Discussion (.03) and School Type (.21). Emphasis on Language, on the other hand, appears almost as a "remedial" phenomenon. It occurs in lower status, less discussion-minded families and it is accompanied by relatively high levels of radio and TV consumption. However, none of the three blocks referring to the students' own current activities (Media, Private Reading, Homework) contributes to the explanation of Writing Achievement, and they are also quite independent of the School Type variable.

As for the influence of gender on Writing Achievement, the girls' responses have confirmed in several ways prior expectations, or rather stereotypes. Female students appear to proceed through the system somewhat more smoothly (correlation with Age: - .10), and they say that they spend more time on homework and on private reading (p = .17). It is quite remarkable how well girls perform on the persuasive writing task (p = .27), but this phenomenon cannot be explained on the basis of the present data, although we speculate on it in chapters 6 and 7.

In summary, then, the Dutch data highlight the effects and mechanisms of an effectively managed, selective school system at work. The allocation of students to the existing school types is clearly at the center of any explanation of achievement differences among the students.

Hamburg, Germany - Institutional Selectivity at Odds

Very much like The Netherlands, Hamburg has a school system which is highly differentiated. At the grade level being tested (Grade 11, which is the latest point at which everybody receives at least some formal schooling), there are five different types of academic schooling and three levels and/or fields of vocational education (recoded to the simple distinction between academic [low code] and vocational [high code]). Only full time vocational classes were tested, so that roughly one half of the age cohort was excluded from the target population (the prevalent form of vocational education is a "dual system" of apprenticeship and part-time schooling). Even so, aggregate statistics show that the higher strata of the society send their children (usually at the end of Grade 4) almost without exception to academic programs while the lower strata tend to get them into academic programs if possible and will regard the vocational track as "second choice," with little distinction between part-time and full-time programs. The crucial point is that the initial tracking decision is made by the parents, although the secondary school can decide to keep or reject the student at the end of Grade 6, at the earliest. The basis for the latter decision is not provided by tests, but depends on the teachers' judgements alone.

These contextual characteristics have to be borne in mind when comparing the Dutch findings with those from Hamburg. With the exception of missing data on Family Discussion and a different specification mode for the Homework construct, the two outer models are fairly similar (Table 8.2). It will be noted, though, that the loadings on Writing Achievement indicate that the Hamburg jury has been guided primarily by content aspects. Thus, a relatively low explained variance in the criterion variable is to be expected, as is indeed the case ($R2$ = .064).

Table 8.2

Outer PLS Model Explaining Achievement in Persuasive Writing
(N = 434 Students from Hamburg)

Latent Variable Manifest Variables	Weight	Loading
Gender (male = 1; female = 2)	1.0000	-
Age	1.0000	-
Home Background Mother's Education Father's Education Number of Books in the Home Years of Further Study Planned	.1591 .3441 .2219 .6771	- - - -
Emphasis on School Language Student's Own Emphasis Expectations of Adults at Home	.6143 .5537	- -
School Type (academic = 1; vocational = 2)	1.0000	-
Media Hours Listening to Radio (workdays) Hours Listening to Radio (holidays) Newspapers (time spent reading) Magazines (time spent reading)	- - - -	.6930 .7781 .7055 .7070
Private Reading (time spent)	1.0000	-
Homework All Homework Reading Homework	- -	.9606 .9493
Writing Achievement Overall Impression Quality and Scope of Content Structure and Organization Appropriateness of Tone and Style	- - - -	.9743 .9406 .9383 .9276

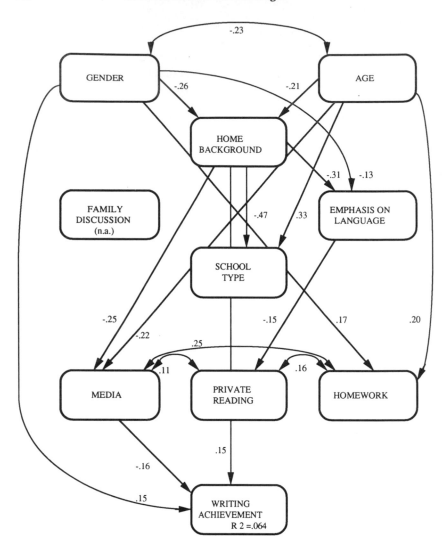

Figure 8.5: Inner PLS Model Explaining Achievement in Persuasive Writing
(*N*=434 Students from Hamburg)

The similarities between the Hamburg model and the Dutch model are manifold. Age again manifests its connotations of grade repetition and slower-paced education, but these effects are noticeably stronger than in The Netherlands. It is particularly important to note that the Hamburg system tends to channel the faster students into the academic programs, while the participants in vocational tracks have spent well over the minimum time required to reach the respective grade ($p = .33$).

Gender is also associated with some effects which were encountered in the Dutch sample and these, too, are more pronounced in the Hamburg case. In accordance with other research, female students move faster--and more successfully--through the system ($r = -.23$), and they give more emphasis to school-related matters ($p = .17$), if the homework variables may be taken as indicators for such attitudinal differences. Interestingly, they also report being confronted less frequently with problems regarding the schools' standards of language ($p = -.13$). While girls do not appear to be discriminated against directly in the allocation to the more prestigious tracks, there is (unlike the situation in The Netherlands) a remarkable tendency of gender-specific self-selection involved. The influence of gender on the Home Background construct ($p = -.26$) almost entirely results from the lower educational aspirations of girls, an effect which is still seen in university enrollment figures, for instance, but which was particularly strong during a period of severe youth unemployment in the mid-eighties.

The most salient points of comparison between the Dutch and Hamburg models, however, refer to the Home Background and the School Type constructs on the one hand, and the Writing Achievement block on the other. The liberal system in Hamburg of respecting parents' decisions as to their children's educational careers does not appear to reduce the social selectivity as compared with the Dutch situation. This is all the more remarkable given that the majority of youth preparing for blue collar jobs were not even included in the Hamburg sample. At the same time, School Type in Hamburg is not an effective filter to separate groups of students with clearly superior levels of achievement in persuasive writing. Instead, educationally favorable aspects of the home make a difference ($p = .15$), independent of the type of program attended. Yet given the different "career values" of academic and vocational school-leaving certificates, the absence of a direct correspondence between School Type and writing scores does raise serious policy questions about why Hamburg should differ from The Netherlands.

It is known from the Hamburg national report that writing scores in Hamburg are related to School Type, if the scores are based on academic writing assignments. Further, an education policy favoring discussion of controversial issues in all types of schools may have helped to diminish school type differences in this particular form of writing. In chapter 3 it has been pointed out that in The Netherlands there is a generally low amount of writing compositions, with little variance between schools, and in Hamburg there is more practice in writing throughout the system.

Finland - Social Selectivity Persisting

Finland is a particularly interesting country to study, because it abolished its traditional bipartite school system in the 1972 reform in favor of a comprehensive scheme (cf. Leimu, 1988, pp. 261f). It is also somewhat unique in that female students are strongly overrepresented in the group that completes the matriculation exams at the end of secondary school (63%) and still noticeably so at the lower university degree levels (53%), while falling behind only when the licentiate and the doctorate is considered (20%; Leimu, 1988, pp. 262f). In contrast to The Netherlands and Hamburg, grade repetition occurs extremely rarely (below 1%). It may be interesting to note that the apparent advantage of female students in the matriculation examinations corresponds well with Leimu's observation of a certain language bias in this examination (p. 266). This rather sketchy context description may provide some background against which to interpret the findings of the Finnish data.

The findings show the predominance of social background factors, even when the differentiating effects of a selective school organization are removed. To begin, the unusually high internal homogeneity of the Home Background construct shows how closely the parent's educational backgrounds are related to home environments favorable to learning (number of books) and the students' own plans in terms of further study. Also, a high incidence of family discussions ($p = .23$) and the rare occurrence (and perhaps perceived necessity) of insisting on correct language ($p = -.17$) point in this direction, and both of these factors are related to persuasive writing achievement. The same holds true for the relationship between Home Background and Private Reading ($p = .22$), even though the latter could not be demonstrated to affect positively performance in argument.

The key point, then, is that Home Background functions as a factor separating more successful students from the rest ($p = .30$). Of course, most of the caveats applying to the contrasts between the Dutch and the German data could also be repeated here, the most important of these being that the present measure of writing achievement cannot possibly be taken for the whole of learning outcomes. Nevertheless, it is quite convincing to see that the introduction of comprehensive schooling does not appear to lead, per se, to the elimination of, or complete compensation for, educational disadvantages associated with the Home Background variables.

Table 8.3

Outer PLS Model Explaining Achievement in Persuasive Writing
(N = 350 Students from Finland)

Latent Variable Manifest Variables	Weight	Loading
Gender (male = 1; female = 2)	-	-
Home Background Mother's Education Father's Education Number of Books in the Home Years of Further Study Planned	- - - -	.7138 .6943 .6573 .7369
Family Discussion Discuss General Matters Talk about Family Matters	- -	.7723 .9371
Emphasis on School Language Student's Own Emphasis Expectations of Adults at Home	.3032 .9422	- -
Private Reading (time spent)	1.0000	-
Writing Achievement Overall Impression Quality and Scope of Content Structure and Organization Appropriateness of Tone and Style	- - - -	.9740 .9221 .9473 .9338

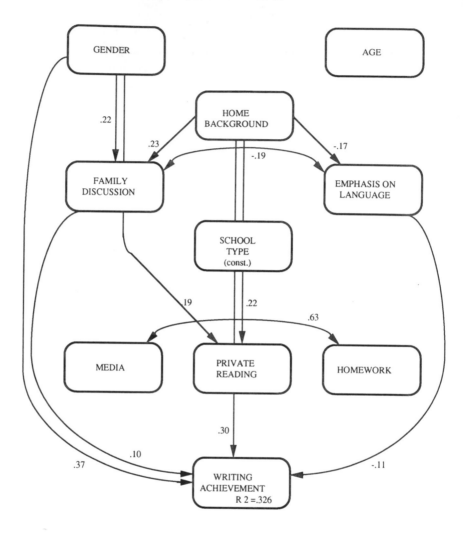

Figure 8.6: Inner PLS Model Explaining Achievement in Persuasive Writing
(*N*=350 Students from Finland)

That the Finnish model is not just happenstance can be demonstrated by the absence of any age (i.e., grade repetition) effect, in contrast with the Dutch and German results and by the prominent role of gender. It was mentioned above that female students are much more successful in the Finnish secondary school system than their male peers. Even bearing in mind that it is hazardous to compare effect sizes across countries in this study, one notes that the superiority of the female students' performance comes out remarkably clearly in the model (p = .37). It seems, then, that a possible general advantage of girls over boys in writing (cf. chapter 7) might be reinforced in Finland by the reported emphasis on language and writing in secondary schools. Obviously, success rates in school certification that we have cited add to the credibility of this interpretation, but do not explain it. The causal analysis, however, appears to have identified a rather critical point here which would certainly merit a more in-depth investigation.

Hungary - Social Mobility Still Unattained

At the time of the data collection (1985), Hungary was still a Peoples Republic with an (officially) unchallenged Marxist-Leninist philosophy, not only of state and society, but also of education. Whereas some of its fundamental aims (e.g., personality development and its emphasis on cultural values as well as productive skills) are certainly broad enough to be shared by educators worldwide, it is Hungary's early and pronounced insistence on promoting social mobility which distinguishes this country from the others included in this study (cf. Bathory, 1988, p. 339). Thus, the Hungarian sample was tested at a period when roughly forty years of determined efforts to compensate for the inequality of home backgrounds should have shown definite effects.

The present data do not provide an opportunity to investigate changes over time, and again, cross-national comparisons are to be made only with utmost care. However, Hungary does resemble The Netherlands and Finland in terms of its rating style and the overall variance explained by the model, so that, very tentatively, some inferences may be drawn. Thus, it is more than coincidence that, in the two countries with a centralized comprehensive, or "general," school system, the Home Background block is highly homogeneous, indicating the strong family influence on educational aspirations which, for Hungary, is also confirmed by external evidence (Bathory, 1988, p. 344).

It is also noteworthy that in the Hungarian case the Media construct is constituted by "newspapers" and "magazines" as opposed to the electronic media prevalent in most other countries. Apparently the positive effects of "serious" print media are easily overridden in the measurement model by the

combined negative influences of a merely entertaining "youth press" and
parallel radio and TV programs consumed by adolescents. Of course, the very
meaning of the construct changes, as do the signs of the respective path
coefficients. While the distracting "background entertainment" function of
radio/TV consumption is quite clear in some of the other countries (most
notably, Finland and the USA, where the positive correlations with Homework
are high, but likewise in The Netherlands and Hamburg), the specific situation
of Hungary and Chile in the mid-eighties appears to have favored the
educationally beneficial effects of reading newspapers and magazines.

Table 8.4

Outer PLS Model Explaining Achievement in Persuasive Writing
(N = 575 Students from Hungary)

Latent Variable Manifest Variables	Weight	Loading
Gender (male = 1; female = 2)	1.0000	-
Age	1.0000	-
Home Background Mother's Education Father's Education Number of Books in the Home Years of Further Study Planned	- - - -	.8801 .8031 .6449 .8232
Media Newspapers (time spent reading) Magazines (time spent reading)	.5729 .6768	- -
Private Reading (time spent)	1.0000	-
Homework All Homework Reading Homework	.8889 .3755	- -
Writing Achievement Overall Impression Quality and Scope of Content Structure and Organization Appropriateness of Tone and Style	- - - -	.9327 .9085 .9137 .9383

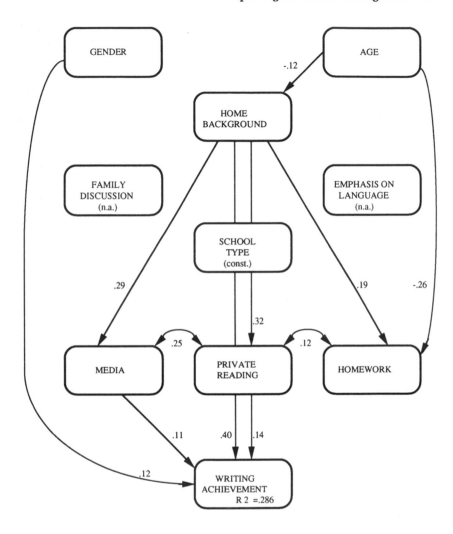

Figure 8.7: Inner PLS Model Explaining Achievement in Persuasive Writing
(*N*=575 Students from Hungary)

It is of primary concern, however, to analyze the effects associated with high achievement levels within the country. The positive influence attributed here to the print media is only one among several and, indeed, small (p = .11). By far the dominant direct influence in Hungary is exerted by the Home Background variables (p = .40), and it is augmented by the indirect contributions of the home through Media (.03) and Private Reading (.05). Although a gender effect is present (p = .12), it is unrelated to any other effect covered by the model.

A discrepancy between the publicly stated aims of minimizing the influence of the students' home backgrounds and the reality of family aspirations, then, functions as the primary explanation of those writing achievement differences which exist within the country. Even the phenomenon of grade repetition is tied noticeably to social factors (p = -.12), an effect which is underlined by the relationships of Homework with Home Background and Age, although homework (assigned and completed) is not demonstrated to be associated directly with a stronger performance in persuasive writing.

The model as a whole, even in this rather rudimentary form, does seem to have revealed important, albeit somewhat grossly sketched, features of the context in which Hungarian writing education takes place. The differences between the expected and attained results of an egalitarian educational policy are, indeed, striking and should be subjected to broader and more in-depth research.

The United States of America - Opportunities Constrained

The American set of ratings of compositions, like the German one, belongs into the group of countries where a content-oriented rating style was employed by the national jury. This can be inferred from the loadings in the Writing Achievement construct, and it is also reflected by the low R2 value for explained variance in the criterion block.

Given this restriction, it is all the more remarkable how strongly the Home Background construct makes itself felt. Apart from the gender effect which is present so uniformly in almost all countries studied (with the exception of Chile, where it fell below the exclusion criterion), Home Background is again the key determinant of achievement in persuasive writing. It is related to factors slowing down educational careers (p = -.11) and to the discussion climate in the family (p = .21), as well as to the students' consumption of "non-TV" media (p = .10). Above all, however, the size of the direct effect on writing achievement (p = .28) demonstrates once more that factors associated with the home are the crucial elements in fostering the ability to produce convincing persuasive texts.

Table 8.5

Outer PLS Model Explaining Achievement in Persuasive Writing
(N = 1230 Students from the Uniter States of America)

Latent Variable Manifest Variables	Weight	Loading
Gender (male = 1; female = 2)	1.0000	-
Age	1.0000	-
Home Background Mother's Education Father's Education Number of Books in the Home Years of Further Study Planned	.3797 .1191 .3328 .5611	- - - -
Family Discussion Discuss General Matters Talk about Family Matters Talk about Work and School	.5094 .1129 .5877	- - -
Emphasis on School Language Importance of Adults on Spelling	1.0000	-
Media Hours Listening to Radio (workdays) Hours Listening to Radio (holidays) Newspapers (time spent reading) Magazines (time spent reading)	- - - -	.7357 .6634 .7743 .7652
Homework All Homework	1.0000	-
Writing Achievement Overall Impression Quality and Scope of Content Structure and Organization Appropriateness of Tone and Style	- - - -	.9549 .9245 .9023 .8852

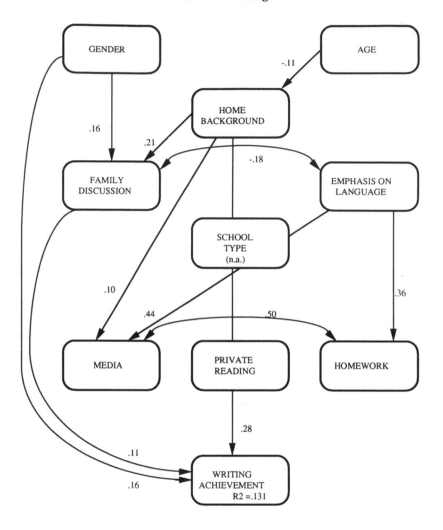

Figure 8.8: Inner PLS Model Explaining Achievement in Persuasive Writing (N=1230 Students from the USA)

Unfortunately, the present data set does not allow more thorough study of just what factors are at work through and beyond the four indicators in the construct. Likewise, there is no indication (apart from the Family Discussion block, with its potential emphasis on political awareness and work ethics) of how the nourishing effects of home background operate in the writing culture of American schools. The most obvious deficiency of the model in this respect is the absence of variables which would permit us to trace the students into different types of schools (public vs. private/parochial; inner-city vs. suburban vs. rural), since these are suggested by earlier research to have a significant intervening function. But even if such relationships could be mapped (undoubtedly, future investigations should and will take up this point), the conclusion is inevitable that in the United States, just as in all the other countries studied here, the individual students' opportunities to reach a high level of achievement in persuasive writing are constrained by social factors, notably the home.

It is true that there have been great efforts to change this - not only the early introduction of comprehensive schooling, but also the provision of compensatory programs such as Head Start.   Yet in the mid-eighties and among the variables measured, it was still the home background itself, rather than directly alterable measures such as the amount of reading or homework, which accounts for most of the difference between more or less successful writers.

Chile - Traditional Patterns Still Strong

Like most Latin American countries, Chile has retained in its school system certain characteristics which have strong historical roots, namely the pronounced engagement of the Roman Catholic Church at the secondary level (Rodriguez, 1988, p. 194) or, more generally, the provision of private schools that cater to students who, on the average, come from well-to-do families. Scarcity of public funds for education leads to the expectation that this pattern will be reflected once again by effects in the model which point towards strong social and institutional selection effects. As will be seen, this is indeed the case.

Before the various paths of influence are traced, it should be mentioned that Chile, too, has worked with a national jury of raters whose rating style was content-oriented. Therefore, the effect sizes with respect to writing achievement are generally rather low (cf. the block structure for Writing Achievement in Table 8.6 and the value for R2 in Figure 8.15).

Table 8.6

Outer PLS Model Explaining Achievement in Persuasive Writing
(*N* = 1102 Students from Chile)

Latent Variable Manifest Variables	Weight	Loading
Gender (male = 1; female = 2)	1.0000	-
Age	1.0000	-
Home Background Mother's Education Father's Education Number of Books in the Home Years of Further Study Planned	.2846 .2814 .4442 .3388	- - - -
Family Discussion Discuss General Matters Talk about Family Matters Talk about Work and School	.7859 .1704 .2258	- - -
Emphasis on School Language Importance of Adults on Spelling Expectations of Adults at Home	.9195 .1957	- -
School Type (public = 1; private = 5)	1.0000	-
Media Newspapers (time spent reading) Magazines (time spent reading)	.4164 .7550	- -
Private Reading (time spent)	1.0000	-
Homework All Homework Reading Homework	.8150 .4675	- -

Table 6 (Cont'd.)		
Latent Variable Manifest Variables	**Weight**	**Loading**
Writing Achievement		
Overall Impression	-	.9451
Quality and Scope of Content	-	.9411
Structure and Organization	-	.9166
Appropriateness of Tone and Style	-	.9201

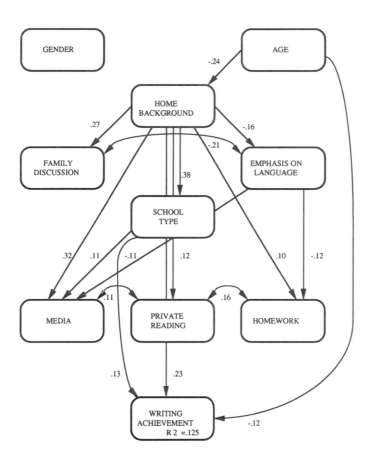

Figure 8.9: PLS Model Explaining Achievement in Persuasive Writing
(*N*=1102 Students from Chile)

Other characteristics of the Chilean situation include the homogeneity of the Home Background construct, which seems to occur regularly when strong social selection effects are suspected, and the prevalence of "serious" print media which makes Chile appear somewhat similar to Hungary. When looking at the inner model for the Chilean data, it is apparent how traditional stratification is at the heart of measured causes of achievement differences and how it is operating through several mechanisms at the same time. For instance, the high incidence of grade repetition in Chile (Rodriguez, 1988, p. 194) is clearly related to social factors (p = -.24), even though it also has an independent direct effect on writing achievement. The Family Discussion construct seems to indicate that the families with better educated parents do provide a more stimulating environment (p = .27) and the same seems to be reflected in the relationship between Home Background and Media (p = .32). Effects which are related more directly to conventional educational activities are those on Private Reading (p = .12), Homework (p = .10) and (remedial) Emphasis on School Language (correct spelling; p = -.16), none of which could be shown to have an impact on performance in this task, though.

The most important way in which the home determines achievement is in the selection of a private (usually Catholic) school (p = .38) which can be expected to produce better learning results (p = .13), but there is a strong residual (direct) effect (p = .23) which stands for all the more subtle (and unmeasured) mechanisms which might explain why children from better educated homes are more successful in writing persuasive texts. As mentioned before, this effect size is not directly comparable to findings from other countries, but it does indicate that in Chile, too, the educational opportunities provided by the home are probably as effective as any of the other countries investigated.

It may be worth commenting on the absence of a gender effect; the expected superiority of female students could not be demonstrated. Given that the Chilean girls are not discriminated against in terms of other measures in the model (cf. the enrollment figures given by Rodriguez, 1988, p. 194), there is much room for speculation on this point. But it might be worthwhile to pursue the hypothesis that since the society supports male cultural and political domination, such a situation will tend to diminish rather than increase writing achievement differences in favor of the female students.

Summary and Conclusions

To use a musical metaphor, this chapter has consisted of variations on a theme: the persistent influence of Home Background on Writing Achievement. The models discussed were able to capture some characteristic country patterns, but even so, this social influence was dominant, no matter what the institutional structure of the school system was.

Less extensively discussed, although almost equally present in all the data analyzed, was the superior performance of girls in persuasive writing. As in the case of Home Background, no clear between-country differences could be identified with respect to this gender effect (with the possible exception of Chile), and again, any assertions as to changes over time are prevented by the design of the study.

It has to be emphasized, however, that the findings thus summarized cannot be taken as universal and that they do not even provide definite explanations. In the case of home influence, the aspect of social selection has been stressed, but this is not equivalent to saying that any covariance between Home Background and achievement would automatically indicate   social injustice and discrimination. Nothing is assumed here as to the distribution of abilities of students--or their parents--within and between social strata. Similarly, there are no fixed assumptions as to a particular mechanism of transforming privileges of background into achievement, although there were some indications of certain educationally beneficial resources and practices in the homes. All one can say for sure is that student performance levels in persuasive writing do correspond (to some extent and in a remarkably consistent way) to the existing social stratification. In some countries this stratification becomes "institutionalized" in tracking.

The same holds true for any reference to the average superiority of female writers. Except for occasional effects suggesting that girls' behavior is somewhat more adapted to school expectation in writing, there is nothing in the data analyzed which would facilitate an answer to the question why girls are seen as writing, on average, more convincing essays. It is known from some of the country reports that, for instance, out-of-school writing habits may be an element in a more comprehensive explanation, but of course a rather long list of covariates would have to be tested before an explanatory synthesis could even be attempted.

So this series of case study analyses has but led to the conclusion that a much closer scrutiny of the cultures of school writing is required to reveal the processes underlying the surface findings discussed here. Yet at the same time, this analysis of survey data in a contrastive fashion has shown features in the homes and schools of the different countries and systems that deserve further research. Such is generally the aim of any survey study--the pointing to variables and anomalies that need to be investigated in a more detailed fashion.

9

Conclusion

Alan C. Purves

The IEA Written Composition Study has been an arduous and complex undertaking. What was envisaged as a fairly quick and straightforward endeavor has lasted longer than anyone dreamed and has proved to have been both a failure and a success. The failure is quite simply that what was thought to have been comparable (the rated performance of groups of students in different systems and languages) has proved impossible to achieve. This volume speaks at many points to the limits of the endeavor.

Rhetorical Communities Revisited

From this failure, however, we have learned several things about the assessment of writing and perhaps about performance assessment generally. The main lesson we have learned is that the original concept of a rhetorical community which we discussed at the beginning of this volume is clearly substantiated. The findings of the curriculum and teacher questionnaires, from the results of the scoring, and from the exploratory analyses that we have conducted, all support the idea that the construct that we call written composition must be seen in a cultural context and not considered a general cognitive capacity or activity. Even the consensus on goals and aims in writing instruction masks a variation both in ideology of the teachers and in instructional practices. However superficially similar the kinds of tasks assigned, the approaches to instruction, and the ways by which performance is judged are subject to national interpretation which is only partially a matter of language difference.

We have found that when asked about their perceptions of school writing, students across the systems in the study have in common a sense of the importance of the product and of the surface features of the product. Yet beneath that commonality, there exists national variation in the perception of what is valued. As reported in the first volume of this study, we have found that good compositions from different countries share common qualities of handling of content and appropriateness of style, but that such qualities have their national or local characteristics in organization, use of detail, and other aspects of rhetoric. We find in the report of the scoring that the international framework setting standards of good writing is interpreted differently in different systems of education. These standards are also applied more or less stringently in judging the actual compositions. All of these findings suggest that performance in writing is a part of a culture and that schools tend to foster rhetorical communities.

Students appear to learn to adapt to and become members of a rhetorical community that shares a number of assumptions and beliefs, only some of which are explicit. We have made some of those assumptions explicit; they concern the kinds of writing valued, the approach to the activity of composition that is desired, the relative importance of convention and individualism, the models of text and text practices that are considered appropriate in the school. Across the systems of education, the terms relating to written composition and its judgment are easily shared; the nuances and values given those terms are a part of the national culture that makes such sharing superficial at best.

Learning such a lesson has raised for several of us the question of whether the assumptions within systems are as commonly held as our more global analysis suggests. There is variation within the academic writing community in several systems and that is reflected in part by the variance within country of many of our findings. We suspect that writing is not as unitary a construct as many national assessments and writing researchers would have it. Such clearly are the implications of most of the volume. We should beware talking too facilely about concepts like writing performance or writing ability. They are task dependent and culture dependent as well. We cannot say that someone is a better writer than someone else. All we can say is at this particular time we think person a wrote a good composition on this topic.

The Issue of Gender

A second issue keeps recurring through various aspects of the study. That is the issue of the differential treatment of boys and girls in the school system, in writing instruction and in the rating of writing performance. It is clear that although the genders start school in demographically proportionate fashion, they do not end up the same way in many systems of education. The proportion of females who remain in the system through either the end of compulsory schooling or the pre-university year varies from system to system. This would appear to be the result of tracking or streaming.

Within the world of school lies the world of mother-tongue and composition teaching. In most of the systems in this study, that world is populated by women, particularly at the primary and lower secondary levels.

It was also the case that in most systems the rating teams were predominantly female (although we did not identify the raters by gender). The rating teams in many systems indicated that they could identify the gender of the writers (usually by handwriting). In this milieu, the most successful students are girls, and gender by itself or in combination with certain home variables is the most powerful predictor of successful performance, particularly on the more "academic" tasks.

The Effect of Home and School

The third finding common to both the regression analyses and the causal analyses is that what goes on in school does not account for the differences in ratings of student writing. Such a result appears to be paradoxical and to deny the first conclusion. We know that written composition is primarily a school subject. People in the systems in this study learn to read and write in school. We also see that certain features of curriculum and construction appear to divide teachers within as well as between systems. We see that "poorer" writers share certain beliefs about writing instruction distinct from those shared by "good" writers.

Despite what we know, we find that instructional variables do not appear to account for much in distinguishing the composition ranked high from that ranked low. What seems to make the difference is what goes on in the home. The study did not examine the difference among classes except cursorily; the analyses were at the student level because of the fact that class effects could easily be school effects or program effects, since there was only one class per school. When one considers all the students in the one hundred classrooms in each system at Population B, the distinctions in rating are not related to what goes on in the classrooms. It may be that the classrooms within a system are more similar than different. The teacher and curriculum analyses suggest that this is the case. It may be that on any given task, individual variability is simply greater than group variability. The intraclass correlations suggest that such is the case. What goes on in the classroom may make a difference; it probably does.

The analyses showed that the fact of school makes a difference. The location of the school may make a difference in some countries. In countries like The Netherlands, tracking clearly shows up in the rated performance of the students. It has a less clear effect in other systems, but the school is there. What emerges, however, is that for writing, as for many other schools subjects, the reinforcement of the home of the values of writing and participation in a "scribal culture" (Purves, 1990) appears in the rated performance of the students. The schools exist within an ethos of particular forms of literacy which is a part of the historically literate culture of a country; when children come from families that participate in that ethos, they tend to be seen as "good" writers.

Summary

Like many other IEA studies, the Study of Written Composition both fails and succeeds as a survey. The study points to the problems of survey studies and to the vulnerability of surveys of performance. The study parallels and highlights what the 1980s have brought to the measurement world concerning both the importance of performance assessment and its pitfalls. Those involved with the study have become all too aware that direct or performance assessment is not a panacea; that it is not simply performance but rated performance, and the pitfalls lie in the rating.

The study has, however, illuminated some issues in the teaching and learning of composition. In particular it suggests, as have other IEA studies, that simple comparisons only highlight the need for cautious studies of the nature of the school and the classroom to unearth what goes on to make for effective instruction. It does highlight the fact that the institution of the school serves not only to educate a portion of the population, but to sort the student population as well. It suggests that in many countries of the world there needs to be further exploration of how best to teach those students who are not in the academic tracks. It calls into question the system of tracking itself. It also suggests that teachers should probe more deeply into their beliefs and practices as teachers of writing to all kinds of students to see whether they are in fact helping them succeed.

References

Akinnaso, F.N. (1991). Literacy and individual consciousness. In E. Jennings & A.C. Purves (Eds.), *Literate systems and individual lives*. Albany: State University of New York Press.

Applebee, A.N., Langer, J.A., & Mullis, J.V.S. (1986). *The writing report card: Writing achievement in American schools* (Report No. 15-W-02). Princeton, NJ: Educational Testing Service.

Applebee, A.N., & Purves, A.C. (1992). Literature and the English language arts. In P. Jackson, (Ed.), *Handbook of curriculum research*. New York: Macmillan.

Báthory, Z. (1988). Hungary. In T.N. Postlethwaite (Ed.), *International encyclopedia of comparative education and national systems of education* (pp. 338-345). Oxford: Pergamon Press.

Bauer, B., & Purves, A.C. (1988). A letter about success in writing. In T.P. Gorman, A.C. Purves, & R.E. Degenhart (Eds.), *The international writing tasks and scoring scales. International study of achievement in writing: Volume 1*. Oxford: Pergamon Press.

Bidwell, C.E., & Kasarda, J.D. (1980). Conceptualizing and measuring the effects of school and schooling. *American Journal of Education*, 401-430.

Blalock, H.M. (1985). *Causal models in the social sciences*, 2nd Ed. New York: Aldine.

Breland, H.M. (1983). *The direct assessment of writing skill: A measurement review* (College Board Report No. 83-6; ETS RR No. 83-32). Princeton, NJ: Educational Testing Service.

Brown, B.W., & Saks, D.H. (1975). The production and distribution of cognitive skills within schools. *Journal of Political Economy*, *83*, 571-593.

Campbell, D.T., & Fiske, D.W. (1959). Convergent and discriminant validation by multitrait - multimethod matrix. *Psychology Bulletin*, *56*, 81-105.

Chacon, E., Jury, M., & Carrasco, V. (1987). *Some general considerations and preliminary results of the IEA written composition study in Chile*. Santiago: Universidad de Chile.

Coates, J. and Cameron, D. (Eds.). (1988). *Women in their speech communities: New perspectives on language and sex*. New York: Longman.

Coffman, W.E. (1966). On the validity of essay tests of achievement. *Journal of Education Measurement, 3*, 151-156.

Delpit, L.D. (1988). The silenced dialogue: Power and pedagogy in educating other people's children. *Harvard Educational Review, 58*(3), 280-298.

Diah, M. (1982). *National language policy and the writing curriculum in Indonesia: A case study*. Unpublished dissertation, Urbana, IL.

Diederich, P.B. (1966). How to measure growth in writing ability. *English Journal, 55*, 435-449.

Diederich, P.B., French, J.W., & Carlton, S.T. (1961). *Factors in judgments of writing ability* (Research Bulletin RB 61-15). Princeton, NJ: Educational Testing Service.

Fabi, A., & Paven de Gregorio, G. (1988). La prova 9: risultati di una ricerca sui contenuti in una prova di consigli sulla scrittura [Test 9: Research findings: The content of suggestions on writing]. *Ricerca Educativa, 5*(2-3), 137-178 (English abstract, 249).

Fuller, B. (1987). What school factors raise achievement in the third world? *Review of Educational Research, 57*(3), 255-292.

Gaur, A. (1985). *A history of writing*. New York: Scribner's.

Goody, J. (1977). *The domestication of the savage mind*. Cambridge, England: Cambridge University Press.

Goody, J. (1986). *The logic of writing and the organization of society*. Cambridge, England: Cambridge University Press.

Goody, J. (1987). *The interface between the written and the oral.* Cambridge, England: Cambridge University Press.

Gorman, T.P., Purves, A.C., & Degenhart, R.E. (Eds.). (1988). *The international writing tasks and scoring scales. International study of achievement in writing: Volume 1.* Oxford: Pergamon Press.

Gosling, G.W.H. (1966). *Marking English composition.* Hawthorn, Victoria: Austrialina Council of Education Research.

Gubb, J., Gorman, T., & Price, E. (1987). *The study of written composition in England and Wales.* Windsor, England: NFER-Nelson.

Hairston, M. (1986). Different products, different processes: A theory about writing. *College Composition and Communication, 37,* 442-452.

Hanushek, E.A. (1986). The economics of schooling: Production and efficiency in public schools. *Journal of Economic Literature, 24*(3), 1141-1177.

Hanushek, E.A. (1989). The impact of differential expenditures on school performance. *Educational Researcher, 18*(4), 45-51.

Heath, S.B. (1983). *Ways with words.* New York: Cambridge University Press.

Heyneman, S.P. (1989). Commentary: Multilevel methods for analyzing school effects in developing countries. *Comparative Education Review, 33*(4), 498-504.

Heymeman, S.P., & Loxley, W.A. (1983a). The distribution of primary school quality within high- and low-income countries. *American Journal of Sociology, 88*(6), 1162-1195.

Heyneman, S.P., & Loxley, W.A. (1983b). The effect of primary school quality on academic achievement across twenty-nine high- and low-income countries. *American Journal of Sociology, 88*(6), 1162-1195.

Hillocks, G. (1986). *Research on written composition: New directions for teaching.* Urbana, IL: National Conference on Research in English.

Kadar-Fulop, J. (1988). Culture, writing, curriculum. In A.C. Purves (Ed.), *Writing across languages and cultures: Issues in contrastive rhetoric* (pp. 25-50). Newbury Park, CA.

Kadar-Fulop, J., Pezeshkpour, P., & Purves, A.C. (1982). Perspectives on the curriculum in written composition.

Kish, L. (1965). *Survey sampling.* New York: John Wiley & Sons.

Knoblauch, C.H., & Brannon, L. (1984). *Rhetorical tradition and the teaching of writing.* Montclair, NJ: Boynton.

Leimu, K. (1988). Art. "Finland". In T.N. Postlethwaite, (Ed.), *International encyclopedia of comparative education and national systems of education.* Oxford: Pergamon Press.

Lofgren, H., & Schick, R. (in press). *Relationships between pupils' sociocultural background, sex, attitudes, and writing achievement.*

Markova, A.K. (1979). *The teaching and mastery of language.* London: Croom Helm.

Marsh, H.W. (1988). Multitrait-multimethod analysis. In J.P. Keeves (Ed.), *Educational research, methodology, and measurement. An international handbook* (pp. 570-580). Oxford: Pergamon Press.

Murnane, R.J. (1975). *Impact of school resources on the learning of inner city children.* Cambridge, MA: Ballinger.

Nijohf, W.S., & Streumer, S.N. (1988). Art. "Netherlands". In T.N. Postlethwaite (Ed.), *International encyclopedia of comparative education and national systems of education* (pp. 498-506). Oxford: Pergamon Press.

Peaker, G.F. (1975). *An empirical study of education in twenty-one countries: Technical report.* Stockholm: Almqvist & Wiksell.

Pedhazur, E.J. (1982). *Multiple regression in behavior research.* New York: Holt, Rhinehart, & Winston.

Philips, S.U., & Reynolds, A. (1987). The interaction of variable syntax and discourse structure in women's and men's speech. In S.U. Philips, S. Steele, & C. Tanz (Eds.), *Language, gender and sex in comparative perspective*. New York: Cambridge University Press.

Purves, A.C. (1973). *Literature education in ten countries*. New York: John Wiley and Sons.

Purves, A.C. (1987). The organization of raters in marking writing assessments. In R.E. Degenhart (Ed.), *Assessment of student writing in an international context. IFER publication series B: Theory into practice, vol. 9* (pp. 107-113). Jyväskylä: Institute for Educational Research.

Purves, A.C. (1990). *The scribal society: An essay on literacy and schooling in a technological age*. White Plains, NY: Longman.

Purves, A.C., Gorman, T.P., & Takala, S. (1988). The development of the scoring scheme and scales. In T.P. Gorman, A.C. Purves, & R.E. Degenhart (Eds.), *The international writing tasks and scoring scales. International study of achievement in writing* (Vol. 1) (pp. 41-58). Oxford: Pergamon Press.

Purves, A.C., Hansson, G., & Foshay, A.W. (1973). *Literature education in ten countries: An empirical study. International studies in evaluation*. Stockholm: Almqvist and Wiksell.

Purves, A.C., & Purves, W.C. (1986). Viewpoints: Cultures, text models, and the activity of writing. *Research in the Teaching of English, 20*(2), 174-197.

Purves, A.C., Soter, A., Takala, S., & Vahapassi, A. (1984). Towards a domain-referenced system for classifying composition assignments. *Research in the Teaching of English, 18*(4), 385-416.

Purves, A.C., & Takala, S. (Eds.). (1982). *An international perspective on the evaluation of written composition. Evaluation in education* (Vol. 5, number 3) (pp. 247-264). Oxford: Pergamon Press.

Quellmalz, E.S., Capell, F.J., & Chou, C. (1982). Effects of discourse and response mode on the measurement of writing competence. *Journal of Education Measurement, 19*(4), 241-258.

Rodriguez, C. (1988). Chile. In T.N. Postlethwaite (Ed.), *International encyclopedia of comparative education and national systems of education* (pp. 192-197). Oxford: Pergamon Press.

Rossi, P.H., Wright, J.D., & Anderson, A.B. (1983). *Handbook of survey research*. Orlando: Academic Press.

Saari, H. (1991). *Writing curricula in sixteen countries: International study in written composition* (Report #42). Jyväskylä, Finland: Institute for Educational Research.

Schieber, N. (1983). *PLSPATH*. Hamburg: University of Hamburg.

Schoonen, R., & DeGlopper, K. (1987). *Writing performance and knowledge about writing*. Unpublished manuscript, University of Amsterdam, Centre for Educational Research (SCO).

Scribner, S., & Cole, J. (1981). *The psychology of literacy*. Cambridge, MA: Havard University Press.

Sherzer, J. (1987). A diversity of voices: Men's and women's speech in ethnographic perspectives. In S.U. Philips, S. Steele, & C. Tanz (Eds.), *Language, gender and sex in comparative perspective*. New York: Cambridge University Press.

Smith, P.M. (1985). *Language and the sexes in society*. Oxford: Blackwell.

Takala, S. (1983). *Achievement in written composition*. Unpublished manuscript. Urbana, IL: IEA Study of Written Composition.

Takala, S. (1987). Student views on writing in eight countries. In R.E. Degenhart (Ed.), *Assessment of student writing in an international context* (pp. 65-94). Jyväskylä, Finland: Institute for Educational Research.

Theisen, G.L., Anchola, P.P., & Boakari, F.M. (1983). The underachievement of cross-national studies of achievement. *Comparative Education Review, 27*(1), 46-68.

Thorndike, R.L. (1982). *Applied psychometrics*. Boston: Houghton Mifflin.

Thorndike, R.L. (1988). Reliability. In J.P. Keeves (Ed.), *Educational research, methodology, and measurement. An international handbook* (pp. 330-343). Oxford: Pergamon Press.

Törmäkangas, K. (1987). The validity, reliability, and generalizability of ratings of written composition. In R.E. Degenhart (Ed.), *Assessment of student writing in an international context. IFER publication series B: Theory into practice* (Vol. 9) (pp. 107-113). Jyväskylä: Institute for Educational Research.

Törnebohm, H. (1973). *Perspectives on inquiring systems* (Report No. 53). Department of Theory of Science, University of Gothenburg.

Vähäpassi, A. (1982). On the specification of the domain of school writing. *Evaluation in Education, 5*(3), pp. 265-289.

Vähäpassi, A. (1988). The domain of school writing and development of the writing tasks. In T.P. Gorman, A.C. Purves, & R.E. Degenhart, (Eds.), *The international writing tasks and scoring scales. International study of achievement in writing* (Vol. 1) (pp. 15-40). Oxford: Pergamon Press.

Van de Ven, P.H. (1987). Some histories of mother tongue teaching in Western Europe: A comparative framework. *Mother Tongue Education Bulletin*, 2, 40-49.

Van de Ven, P.H. (1988). Some histories of mother tongue teaching in western Europe II: A tentative survey. *Mother Tongue Education Bulletin*, 3, 35-44.

Verma, V., & Pearce, M. (1978). *Users manual for clusters*. London: International Statistical Institute.

Vygotsky, L.S. (1956). *Izbrannye psikhologicheskie isseldovaniia*. Moscow: RSFR Academy of Pedagogical Sciences.

Wagner, D.A. (1987). *The future of literacy in a changing world*. New York: Pergamon Press.

Walker, D.A. (1976). *The IEA six subject survey: An empirical study of education in twenty-one countries*. Stockholm: Almqvist and Wiksell.

Werts, C.E., Breland, H.M., Grandy, J., & Rock, D.R. (1980).   Using longitudinal data to estimate reliability in the presence of correlated measurement errors. *Education and Psychology Measurement, 40,* 19-29.

Wold, H.O. (1982).   Soft modelling techniques.   In K.G. Joreskog & H.O. Wold (Eds.), *Systems under indirect observation: Causality, structure, and prediction,* Vol. 2.   Amsterdam: North Holland Press.

Zeiher, H., Zeiher, H.J., & Gruger, H. (1979).   *Textschreiben als produktives und kommunikatives Handeln. Unterschungen und Konzepte zum Deutschunterricht* (Bd. I).   Stuttgart: Klett.

Appendix A

Sampling Issues

Kari Törmäkangas

The main purpose of this study was to examine the effect on written compositions of such factors as student abilities, teaching practices, school and home. For these purposes data were collected with questionnaires presented to pupils, teachers and school principals, a practice followed in most other projects in IEA. The chosen criterion variable, written composition, was more complicated than the achievement variables in earlier studies and required new solutions in many stages of the study.

For the topics of written composition, nine main tasks were constructed upon which each pupil wrote at least three. These were rated nationally. The organization and analysis of the rating is discussed in Appendix B.

Since the main target of the sampling was the pupil, the sampling figures were calculated on a pupil basis. The original sampling plan consisted of three different age groups. These were 10.5-11.5, 15.5-16.5 and 17.5-18.5 called populations A, B and C respectively. However, due to different school-starting age in the countries, the limits were settled as 10-13, 14-18 and 16-20. Fourteen countries were involved in the study: four countries (Finland, Italy, Sweden, and the USA) collected data for all three age groups and two countries (Hungary and New Zealand) collected data for two age groups. The remaining seven countries collected data only for one age group (mainly Population B; Table 1).

At an early stage of this study, Population B was chosen as main the target population. The samples for Populations A and C are smaller and generally treated as comparison samples for Population B. The sampling was meant to be effected as a two-stage cluster sampling. In most of the countries the schools were selected on the basis of a stratified PPS-sampling (weighting probability proportional to size). However, in some countries the method was not followed exactly and in some cases other sampling methods were used. For example, in Thailand Population C, it was not possible to apply the generally accepted sampling rules. Although the sampling in every country did not follow exactly the same rules, the representativeness of the samples were carefully checked in relation to the whole country, except in Hamburg where the sample was generalized to the state of Hamburg, and in Wales, which was treated as a subsample of England.

Compared to the earlier studies, the most difficult problem was the uniform scoring of the compositions. Double ratings for all pupils were set by the project, but these and the lack of double-rated papers reduced the final achieved sample in some countries. Some of the countries did not rate all of the written compositions, so that the final number of rated students is smaller than in the original sampling plan (The Netherlands and Finland); in some countries each composition was rated only once. The number of complete cases with at least one rated composition per pupil is presented in Table 1.

Table 1

Number of Pupils in Each Age Group in Fourteen Countries.

	Age 10-13	Age 14-18	Age 16-20
CHI		3779	
ENG		1370	
FIN	590	1337	851
HAM		1483	
HUN		2570	1996
IND	2095		
ITA	787	2035	1213
NET		1284	
N-Z	2643	2390	
NIG		3022	
SWE	1175	1616	1340
THA			1312
USA	1396	3266	925
WAL		295	

For some of the countries school questionnaires were returned without any pupil questionnaires. In the following table appear only schools in which at least one pupil is tested, whether a school questionnaire exists or not. Each school is included only once, no matter how many classes were tested in that school. The school frequencies are shown in Table 2.

Table 2

Number of Schools in Three Age Groups

	Age 10-13	Age 14-18	Age 16-20
CHI		100	
ENG		58	
FIN	61	104	57
HAM		56	
HUN		100	77
IND	75		
ITA	42	100	51
NET		107	
N-Z	98	103	
NIG		95	
SWE	48	72	75
THA			65
USA	83	174	99
WAL		12	

The number of teachers follows the number of the schools because normally only one class was selected from each school. The exceptions are Indonesia, where there are two teachers or classes per school (150 altogether),

Finland where six schools have two teachers, and Hamburg with 56 schools and 71 teachers.

Weighting

Weighting is needed to correct the number of observations in each stratum if there are losses in the sample and/or if the proportions of the sample do not match the population proportions. Here the most important stratifying factor was region, although school type was also used in some countries. Although it is well known that there are gender differences, pupil's gender was not used as a stratifying factor in this study. School size was also not used because its influence has been shown to be a minor stratifying factor in earlier studies. However, it was observed as a controlling factor at the first stage of sampling.

Although the sampling design was poor in some of the countries, only England (and Wales) and Thailand were not included in the weighting calculations. In Thailand the actual sample does not match the designed sample, and the correspondence between the sample and the population is poor. In England and Wales, the original set of strata were reduced during the sampling and this was not indicated in the report, so there is no connection between the sample and whole population either. Also the loss from the designed to the achieved sample was quite high in England, where only 58 schools out of the planned oversampling of 120 participated in the study. For the United States, which also oversampled, the achieved samples are: 83 out of planned 110 (Population A), 174 out of 220 (B), and 99 schools out of 110 (C). The weighting was originally planned to be done on state by state basis but since there were only one or two schools per state, such weighting might have been more misleading than aiming for data corrections. The final stratification in the USA used: public and private schools. The proportion of private schools among public schools was 10 % in years 1982-1984 in the USA. This approximation for the public and private schools has been used for all populations. Other kind of losses happened in Finland and in The Netherlands where only part of the actually collected compositions was scored in order to save costs. Thus in Finland the final number of scored pupils was 590 out of the original 1020 in Population A, 1337 (vs. 3022) in Population B, and 851 (vs. 1525) in Population C. In The Netherlands 1284 compositions were scored out of total of 2748 collected. In both cases the scored sample was a rotation in each class.

In this study the designed sample was defined at the school level, but weighting is meaningful only on the pupil level from which the achievement variable(s) are obtained. Population statistics are seldom timed to the sampling moment, as they are usually available about a year later; several years' estimates are often averaged or the last year's figures are used. This information and the samples forms the basis for much of the weighting. Population information for weighting has been estimated in three cases. For the United States, the number of pupils in public and private schools was taken from tables collected for other studies which matched with the percentages given in the sampling plan. In Indonesia, the statistics given in the sampling plan were adjusted when the total number did not match the calculated stratum sums. In Sweden, the statistics for Population B were also used for Population C. Since the proportions of pupils in the strata are more important than the real number of pupils in each stratum, both the proportions of the strata and the absolute number of pupils in the strata have been used depending on the given information.

The weights are defined in the following way. Let N be the size of the whole population and Ni be the size of population stratum i. Let fi be the proportion Ni/N and ni the true achieved value for the stratum, with the total sample sum being n. Now the weight is simply wi = (fin)/ni. Using these weights in calculations, the total number of students will be equal in the weighted and in the initial sample. Table 9 at the end of this appendix gives the achieved sample, the designed sample, and the weights for all the countries and populations. Table 3 shows how far the achieved sample is from the actual population proportion designed. The value of 1.0 means that the sample coincides exactly with the population proportion of the stratum; a figure less than 1.0 indicates too many pupils in the sample from a particular stratum, and a figure more than 1.0, too few pupils in the sample.

For the smaller Populations A and C, weights are not as nicely distributed as for Population B, because the strata were small, and very small losses created heavier weights for some strata and at the same time smaller weights for the rest. However, for Population B, the figures on the totals line approximate a normal distribution.

The weights reveal, however, that the sampled data seldom differ greatly from population proportions, and where this does occur the number of pupils tends to be small, all of which indicates a low weighting effect in the data. Nevertheless, the mean and the weighted mean of each main writing assignment have been calculated and compared with each other (Table 4). Weighting does not make an appreciable difference in the obtained values. When the scale of the rating was from 1 through 5, the highest difference between weighted and unweighted means was .044 for Population A, .043 for Population B and .042 for Population C. Statistical testing is not needed to see that these means are essentially the same, and that stratum-based weighting is not necessary in this study. Since England, Thailand, and Wales had poor weighting information, they are missing from the table.

Table 3

The Distribution of Stratum Weights
by Country in Each Population

	-0.70	0.71-0.90	0.91-1.10	1.11-1.30	1.31+
POP A					
FIN	2	1	2	4	
IND		1	1		1
ITA		3		2	
N-Z	2	1	2		
SWE	7	2	2	2	3
USA			1	1	
Total	11	8	8	9	4
%	28	20	20	22	10
POP B					
CHI		1	5		
FIN		1	4	2	
HAM		3	2	2	1
HUN	1	2	6	3	
ITA		1	3		1
NET		1	3	1	
N-Z	1	1	3	1	
NIG		1	1	3	
SWE	5	3	3	3	3
THA	1			2	1
USA		1	1		
Total	8	16	31	17	6
%	10	20	40	22	8

Table 3 (Cont'd.)					
	-0.70	0.71-0.90	0.91-1.10	1.11-1.30	1.31+
POP C					
FIN		1	4	1	
HUN	1	2	3	3	1
ITA		2	2		1
SWE	3	3	1	1	5
THA	1			2	1
USA			1		1
Total	5	8	11	7	9
%	12	20	28	18	22

Table 4

The Differences between Weighted and Unweighted
Means and Standard Deviations

POP A	Letter or form		Retelling a story		Description process		Narrative story		Argument	
	Mean	StD	Mean	StD	Mean	StD	Mean	StD	Mean	StD
FIN	.001	.002	.011	.000	.020	.007	.009	.016	.017	.008
IND	.002	.003	.007	.007	.020	.009	.005	.004	.010	.021
ITA	.014	.005	.026	.002	.019	.002	.023	.001	.044	.005
N-Z	.006	.004	.007	.003	.014	.005	.013	.003	.014	.001
SWE	.006	.012	.000	.000	.000	.000	.013	.003	.005	.005
USA	.000	.001	.001	.001	.000	.000	.001	.001	.002	.001

Table 4 (Cont'd.)

POP B	Letter or form		Narrative story		Argument		Reflective essay		Letter of advice	
	Mean	StD	Mean	StD	Mean	StD	Mean	StD	Mean	StD
CHI	.003	.001	.009	.001	.005	.003	.005	.000	.008	.001
FIN	.000	.001	.001	.000	.005	.006	.004	.002	.005	.001
HAM	.010	.002	.017	.009	.015	.006	.017	.001	.017	.000
HUN	.012	.003	.005	.005	.003	.005	.001	.000	.006	.001
ITA	.007	.000	.025	.000	.027	.004	.016	.005	.022	.003
NET	.003	.001	.000	.001	.003	.001	.000	.001	.000	.000
N-Z	.022	.003	.030	.002	.036	.001	.027	.008	.043	.004
NIG	.000	.007	.006	.002	.026	.002	.012	.006	.003	.007
SWE	.004	.008	.005	.002	.007	.009	.000	.005	.012	.000
USA	.004	.008	.005	.002	.007	.009	.000	.005	.012	.000

POP C	Letter or form		Summary		Argument		Reflective essay		Letter of advice	
	Mean	StD	Mean	StD	Mean	StD	Mean	StD	Mean	StD
FIN	.004	.004			.001	.002	.005	.001	.007	.000
HUN	.031	.005			.015	.004	.025	.009	.029	.006
ITA	.012	.004	.010	.001	.021	.016	.017	.018	.019	.005
SWE	.016	.004			.032	.010	.010	.005	.031	.004
USA	.027	.005			.027	.009	.014	.006	.042	.001

In most countries girls achieved better than boys, and if there are disproportionately more girls in the sample, the overall mean achievement for such a country might look better than it actually is. Gender thus seems to be an important weighting factor at least in some of the countries and should be examined. The information needed here is the gender distribution within each stratum, but it was not collected from the participating countries so that the proportion can only be examined for the whole population.

Weighting by gender is not excluded, however, from the analysis, for there are at least two possibilities to estimate the population mean. Most of the countries have given the gender distribution in the whole population. This can be as fixed for each stratum and the differences within stratum can be treated as errors. The other possibility is to use a fifty-fifty distribution of boys and girls. Because the proportion of gender can vary year by year, so that sometimes there are more boys than girls and vice versa, the equal proportions can be taken as unbiased estimates to which the sample figures are related.

In Table 5 the gender differences have been examined using a two-tailed t-test to check whether the mean is significantly different between boys and girls. Because the number of boys and girls in the sample follow the population proportion closely, only clear differences would indicate that weighting is needed. Therefore, the .001 significance level has been chosen to point out such differences.

Table 5

Significance Levels of the Difference between Boys
and Girls in Writtten Composition.
Two-tailed *t*-test Probability Values for 5 Tasks.

POP A	Letter or form	Retelling a story	Description process	Narrative story	Argument
FIN	.000	.002	.000	.000	.008
IND	.001	.030	.134	.000	.498
ITA	.000	.852	.557	.029	.242
N-Z	.000	.000	.000	.000	.000
SWE	.000			.000	.000
USA	.002	.000		.053	.008

Table 5 (Cont'd.)

POP B	Letter or form	Narrative story	Argument	Reflective essay	Letter of advice
CHI	.000	.000	.011	.000	.000
ENG	.000	.000	.013	.010	.000
WAL	.000	.004	.025	.010	.000
FIN	.000	.000	.000	.000	.000
HAM	.000	.072	.121	.107	.000
HUN	.000	.000	.000	.000	.000
ITA	.000	.000	.000	.000	.000
NET	.000	.000	.005	.000	.000
N-Z	.000	.029	.000	.000	.000
NIG	.001	.582	.105	.046	.423
SWE	.000	.000	.000	.000	.000
USA	.000	.000	.000	.000	.000

POP C	Letter or form	Summary	Argument	Reflective essay	Letter of advice
FIN	.000		.000	.000	.000
HUN	.000		.180	.000	.000
ITA	.065	.080	.000	.000	.018
SWE	.000		.000	.000	.000
THA	.811	.004	.000	.080	.016
USA	.025		.024	.049	.050

In Population A the difference between boys and girls is clear in New Zealand and Sweden for all tasks. In Finland there are three such tasks (out of five) and in Italy, Indonesia and USA only one task. In Population B there are five countries where there are differences in all tasks. Four tasks were found in Chile, The Netherlands and New Zealand, three tasks in England, two in Hamburg and Wales, while Nigeria had no differences between gender. In Population C, Finland and Sweden have significant differences in the means in all tasks. In Hungary there is one equal mean in task 6 and three equal means in Italy. In Thailand there is only one clear difference. In this population, the USA seems to have equal means.

Table 6 has been calculated to show these differences if weighting by gender is done where differences clearly occur. Again the differences between unweighted and weighted means are close to zero. We should note that on a scale of 1-5 averaged across two raters, the first decimal is more or less uncertain and the second decimal close to insignificant. The second is the highest level where weighting might produce some influence. Weighting on the stratum or gender basis, therefore, does not cause a statistically significant influence on the results and is not used.

Table 6

The Differences of Means Weighted and Unweighted
by Gender in Selected Countries

A	Letter or form		Retell a story		Description process		Narrative story		Argument	
	Mean	StD	Mean	StD	Mean	StD	Mean	StD	Mean	StD
FIN	.003	.002	.011	.001	.004	.002	.012	.005	.007	.003
N-Z	.004	.001	.002	.003	.004	.004	.003	.001	.003	.005
SWE	.003	.000	.000	.000	.000	.000	.002	.000	.002	.000
B										
FIN	.007	.001	.003	.001	.001	.004	.009	.008	.006	.000
HUN	.001	.006	.004	.003	.007	.009	.001	.000	.002	.006
ITA	.010	.003	.010	.002	.007	.004	.004	.005	.004	.003
SWE	.004	.000	.004	.000	.002	.000	.001	.000	.004	.000
USA	.012	.002	.003	.002	.010	.006	.017	.004	.017	.005
C										
FIN	.000	.000	.000	.000	.000	.000	.004	.001	.000	.000
SWE	.001	.002	.001	.001	.000	.000	.000	.000	.007	.006

The determining of design effect was based on the work done by Kish (1965). Previous work in this area in IEA has been done by Peaker (1975). In this particular study, deft instead of deff was used. The square root of design effect (deff) gives the design factor (deft), which is used to correct other estimates (mean, confidence interval etc.). These coefficients have been calculated using the Clusters-program by Verma and Pearce (1977) for all of the three populations and presented in table form (Table 7). The formulas used are presented in the above manual (Verma and Pearce, 1977).

Because of the unequal school sizes roh-coefficient is selected instead of rho to describe intraclass correlation and homogeneity within countries. The rho is traditionally used in IEA studies. However, the difference between roh and rho is quite small (Rossi, Wright and Anderson 1983). The calculations have been made using the same program as above. The basic requirements for the calculation of roh was that the number of pupils in a school must be more than 6. This was not achieved in all of the countries for rotated compositions and so Table 10 includes blanks for these cells.

Table 7

Design Factors (Deft) for Three Populations and Fourteen Countries
(Two Unrotated Tasks in Each Population)

	Letter/Description		Narrative task	
POP A	Deft	Roh	Deft	Roh
FIN	1.109	.029	1.362	.029
IND	1.697	.138	2.666	.138
ITA	2.158	.261	2.340	.290
N-Z	1.340	.033	1.824	.096
SWE	1.594	.068	1.693	.082
USA	1.659	.129	1.825	.158

Table 7 (Cont'd.)				
	Letter/Description		Letter of advice	
POP B	Deft	Roh	Deft	Roh
CHI	2.410	.150	3.286	.313
ENG	2.630	.269	3.374	.530
WAL	2.781	.290	3.501	.526
FIN	1.269	.054	1.627	.147
HAM	1.667	.077	1.966	.129
HUN	1.749	.149	1.996	.227
ITA	1.569	.097	2.025	.189
NET	1.872	.235	2.155	.363
N-Z	1.961	.136	1.738	.228
NIG	2.691	.235	2.915	.347
SWE	1.415	.048	1.937	.135
USA	1.742	.120	2.152	.265
POP C	Deft	Roh	Deft	Roh
FIN	1.317	.073	1.422	.101
HUN	1.555	.087	1.736	.106
ITA	2.469	.271	1.906	.291
SWE	2.109	.439	1.936	.393
THA	2.383	.247	1.651	.205
USA	1.515	.154	1.627	.202

The sampling error for "Letter of Advice" task for Population B is apparently higher than for other tasks and so are the rohs. There are three defts above 3.0 and two rohs more than 0.5. This indicates larger differences between schools for this task as compared with the others (although the n and standard deviation are also needed to judge the situation).

Using the figures we may calculate the optimal sample size assuming a 5 % sampling error in standard deviation and 95% confidence level. The calculated number of students for and equivalent simple random sample is 400. Only Population B has been taken as a basis for sampling error calculations and two tasks completed by the majority of pupils have been selected as criterion variables. Effective sample size is estimated using formula nc = ns(1 + (n-1)*roh), where nc is the effective cluster sample, ns is the corresponding simple random sample and n is the mean cluster size.

Table 8

The Effective Sampling Size and Sampling Error as a
Percent from the Standard Deviation: Population B

	Letter/Description			Letter of advice		
	Achieved	Effect.	Sampling	Achieved	Effect.	Sampling
	sample	sample	error %	sample	sample	error %
CHI	3779.	2320.	3.9	3779.	4319.	5.3
ENG	1370.	2767.	7.1	1370.	4555.	9.1
WAL	295.	3103.	16.2	295.	4903.	20.4
FIN	1337.	644.	3.5	1337.	1059.	4.4
HAM	1483.	1108.	4.3	1483.	1546.	5.1
HUN	2570.	1222.	3.5	2570.	1589.	3.9
ITA	2035.	986.	3.5	2035.	1640.	4.5
NET	1284.	1406.	5.2	1284.	1852.	6.0
N-Z	2390.	1537.	4.0	2390.	1212.	3.6
NIG	3022.	2891.	4.9	3022.	3398.	5.3
SWE	1616.	797.	3.5	1616.	1496.	4.8
USA	3266.	1216.	3.0	3266.	1852.	3.8

The selected tasks are different: the Letter/ Description task created very low deff and roh coefficients, and the "Letter of Advice" created the highest deffs and rohs almost for every country. The optimal sample size is obviously between the two values given above. The sampling error is less than 5% in every country except in England, where the collected sample was almost half of the designed sample and in Wales which was only a subgroup in England. The values for Nigeria are at the upper limit and all other countries are clearly below it. Excluding out of topic and other missing scores the sampling error for each main task and for each population is presented in Table 10. As expected, the sampling error is high for Populations A and C where there were smaller samples than for Population B. Also rotated tasks for Population B have sampling errors of more than 5% of the standard deviation in most cases.

The data bank and documentation

The IEA Written Composition Study data banks are located in The Hague and in Jyväskylä, Finland and Albany, USA. All data (pupil, teacher and school background and the ratings in the compositions concerning the individual pupil) have been compiled into one merged file. In connection with the cleaning, checking and calculations, the national options and divergences from international format have been documented for each country. This documentation has been made separately for each background questionnaire and for each variable. A separate rating file is also available.

Table 9

The Stratum Weights, Desired and Achieved Sample for Each
Country and Population

Chile

POP B							
Stratum	1	2	3	4	5	6	Total
Desired	354	737	1892	145	190	460	3779
Achieved	327	790	1880	149	211	422	3779
Weight	1.083	.932	1.006	.974	.902	1.089	1.000

England
　　Stratum information missing.

Finland

POP A										
Strat.	11	12	21	22	31	32	41	42	51	52	Total
Des.	74	74	70	22	101	27	121	58	77	40	590
Ach.	62	0	61	33	85	26	109	80	75	59	590
Wt.	1.198	0.000	1.153	.661	1.186	1.019	1.110	.720	1.027	.684	1.000

POP B							
Strat.	11	13	23	31	33	41	53	Total
Des.	73	65	101	193	187	501	216	1337
Ach.	62	63	96	191	207	534	184	1337
Wt.	1.179	1.039	1.050	1.012	.902	.938	1.175	1.000

Table 9 (Cont'd.)

Finland (Cont'd.)

POP C							
Strat.	11	13	31	33	41	53	Total
Des.	55	87	142	97	368	102	851
Ach.	58	73	150	101	355	114	851
Wt.	.953	1.185	.944	.964	1.036	.894	1.000

Hamburg

POP B								
Strat.	1	2	3	4	5	6	7	8	Total
Des.	558	74	52	45	105	459	172	19	1484
Ach.	634	82	62	41	87	398	165	14	1483
Wt.	.879	.899	.838	1.098	1.205	1.153	1.042	1.375	1.000

Hungary

POP B						
Strat.	1	2	3	4	5	6	7
Des.	432	292	227	209	144	53	287
Ach.	383	292	212	177	136	175	237
Wt.	1.128	1.000	1.068	1.178	1.061	.872	1.022

Table 9 (Cont'd.)

POP B (Cont'd.)					
Strat.	8	9	10	11	12	Total
Des.	287	237	219	143	61	2570
Ach.	237	232	204	210	148	2570
Wt.	1.208	1.020	1.074	.679	.409	1.000

POP C											
Strat.	1	2	3	4	5	6	7	8	9	10	Total
Des.	345	233	247	201	228	185	157	152	155	94	1996
Ach.	245	202	235	177	204	196	198	180	168	191	1996
Wt.	1.407	1.153	1.051	1.137	1.115	.941	.791	.845	.923	.490	1.000

Indonesia

POP A				
Stratum	1	2	3	Total
Desired	1215	463	418	2096
Achieved	1316	533	247	2096
Weight	.923	.868	1.691	1.000

Table 9 (Cont'd.)

Italy

POP A					
Strat.	1	2	3	4	5	Total
Des.	194	133	136	177	145	785
Ach.	221	101	119	192	152	785
Wt.	.879	1.316	1.142	.921	.951	1.000

POP B					
Strat.	1	2	3	4	5	Total
Des.	501	415	364	402	341	2023
Ach.	519	414	459	393	238	2023
Wt.	964	1.003	.792	1.024	1.432	1.000

POP C					
Strat.	1	2	3	4	5	Total
Des.	293	203	266	243	208	1213
Ach.	324	224	290	162	213	1213
Wt.	.904	.904	.916	1.502	.978	1.000

Table 9 (Cont'd.)

Netherlands

POP B						
Strat.	1	2	3	4	5	Total
Des.	151	249	496	186	203	1284
Ach.	168	240	492	168	216	1284
Wt.	.899	1.035	1.007	1.105	.938	1.000

New Zealand

POP A						
Strat.	1	2	3	4	5	Total
Des.	1646	648	161	94	95	2643
Ach.	1492	597	193	152	209	2643
Wt.	1.103	1.085	.834	.616	.452	1.000

POP B							
Strat.	1	2	3	4	5	6	Total
Des.	1483	120	230	222	235	100	2390
Ach.	1334	110	215	215	286	230	2390
Wt.	1.111	1.095	1.071	1.032	.820	.433	1.000

Table 9 (Cont'd.)

Nigeria

	POP C					
Strat.	1	2	3	4	5	Total
Des.	1356	630	397	232	407	3022
Ach.	1225	857	403	198	339	3022
Wt.	1.106	.734	.985	1.174	1.200	1.000

Sweden

	POP A									
Strat.	1	2	3	4	5	6	7	8	11	13
Des.	39	12	18	148	278	20	28	206	206	19
Ach.	56	28	37	111	296	28	46	175	0	27
Wt.	.695	.413	.494	1.331	.939	.717	.600	1.177	0.000	.708

	POP A (Cont'd.)							
Strat.	14	15	20	21	22	23	24	29	Total
Des.	1	1	3	158	103	7	48	87	1175
Ach.	22	0	23	122	103	25	23	53	1175
Wt.	.053	0.000	.147	1.294	.998	.280	2.094	1.637	1.000

	POP B									
Strat.	1	2	3	4	5	6	7	8	11	13
Des.	54	16	27	202	377	26	38	291	291	27
Ach.	95	22	28	169	341	17	23	306	0	34
Wt.	.567	.726	.950	1.197	1.106	1.509	1.651	.951	0.000	.808

Table 9 (Cont'd.)

				POP B (Cont'd.)					
Strat.	14	15	20	21	22	23	24	29	Total
Des.	2	8	4	216	136	9	66	116	1616
Ach.	22	25	29	173	135	25	81	91	1616
Wt.	7.94	.337	.144	1.249	1.009	.356	.812	1.272	1.000

					POP C				
Strat.	1	2	3	4	5	6	7	8	11	13
Des.	46	14	23	172	321	22	32	248	248	248
Ach.	24	24	49	97	434	9	43	179	0	0
Wt.	1.913	.567	.462	1.776	.740	2.428	.752	1.385	0.000	0.000

				POP C (Cont'd.)					
Strat.	14	15	20	21	22	23	24	29	Total
Des.	248	7	7	184	116	116	56	99	1340
Ach.	0	17	0	241	121	0	26	76	1340
Wt.	0.000	.422	0.000	.763	.958	0.000	2.155	1.297	1.000

Thailand   Weighting not unique.

USA

	POP A			POP B			POP C		
Strat.	1	4	Total	2	5	Total	3	6	Total
Des.	1269	128	1397	2967	299	3266	840	85	925
Ach.	1289	108	1397	2932	334	3266	905	20	925
Wt.	.984	1.183	1.000	1.011	.894	1.000	.928	4.232	1.000

Wales   Stratum information missing.

Table 10

The Standard Deviation, Design Factor, Degree of Homogeneity,
Achieved and Effective Samples, and Sampling Error as Percentage of
Standard Deviation for Each Population and Task in Every Country
(* = below 5%)

	Task	StD	Deft	Roh	Ach.	Effect.	Err %	< 5%
POP A								
FIN	1	1.15	1.109	0.029	549	493	0.047	*
	3	0.78	1.242	0.000	172	9999	0.095	
	4	0.93	1.162	0.000	187	9999	0.085	
	5	0.92	1.362	0.105	556	740	0.058	
	6	0.88	0.996	0.000	156	9999	0.080	
IND	1	0.92	1.697	0.138	1098	1151	0.051	
	3	0.85	1.661	0.334	470	1108	0.077	
	4	1.00	1.408	0.000	326	9999	0.078	
	5	0.85	2.666	0.270	1773	2841	0.063	
	6	0.75	1.549	0.000	424	9999	0.075	
	8	0.69	3.134	0.423	1641	3936	0.077	
ITA	1	1.07	2.158	0.261	630	1862	0.086	
	3	1.00	1.300	0.000	189	9999	0.095	
	4	1.05	1.882	0.379	324	1416	0.105	
	5	0.97	2.340	0.290	689	2186	0.089	
	6	1.06	1.348	0.000	157	9999	0.108	
N-Z	1	1.21	1.340	0.033	2490	722	0.027	*
	3	0.95	1.149	0.044	801	527	0.041	*
	4	0.98	1.354	0.111	835	733	0.047	*
	5	1.03	1.824	0.096	2469	1329	0.037	*
	6	1.07	1.292	0.101	747	667	0.047	*

Table 10 (Cont'd.)

	Task	StD	Deft	Roh	Ach.	Effect.	Err%	<5%
SWE	1	0.96	1.594	0.068	1144	1020	0.047	*
	5	0.82	1.693	0.082	1146	1151	0.050	*
	6	0.70	1.803	0.100	1125	1296	0.054	
USA	1	0.84	1.659	0.129	1208	1102	0.048	*
	3	0.97	1.345	0.123	630	725	0.054	
	5	0.82	1.825	0.158	1309	1335	0.050	*
	6	0.77	1.382	0.161	553	767	0.059	

POP B

	Task	StD	Deft	Roh	Ach.	Effect.	Err %	< 5%
CHI	1	0.83	2.410	0.150	3303	2320	0.042	*
	5	0.94	1.942	0.277	1099	1508	0.059	
	6	0.98	1.980	0.291	1102	1564	0.060	
	7	0.92	1.883	0.251	1113	1414	0.056	
	9	0.88	3.286	0.313	3235	4319	0.058	
ENG	1	0.91	2.630	0.269	1335	2767	0.072	
	4	0.99	2.174	0.411	584	1896	0.090	
	5	0.89	1.925	0.419	432	1473	0.093	
	6	1.01	1.979	0.452	432	1557	0.095	
	7	0.98	2.015	0.488	422	1630	0.098	
	9	0.98	3.374	0.530	1194	4555	0.098	
FIN	1	1.02	1.269	0.054	1278	644	0.035	*
	2	0.95	1.000	0.000	381	9999	0.051	
	4	1.05	1.373	0.137	776	756	0.049	*
	5	1.00	1.066	0.000	431	9999	0.051	
	6	1.00	1.180	0.000	408	9999	0.058	
	7	1.00	1.266	0.000	426	9999	0.061	
	9	1.04	1.627	0.147	1270	1059	0.046	*

	Task	StD	Deft	Roh	Ach.	Effect.	Err %	< 5%
				Table 10 (Cont'd.)				
HAM	1	0.77	1.667	0.077	1345	1108	0.045	*
	5	0.78	1.405	0.138	452	792	0.066	
	6	0.85	1.211	0.069	436	588	0.058	
	7	0.82	1.344	0.119	436	724	0.064	
	9	0.83	1.966	0.129	1483	1546	0.051	
HUN	1	0.96	1.749	0.149	1479	1222	0.045	*
	3	1.09	1.411	0.000	493	9999	0.064	
	4	0.91	1.335	0.000	596	9999	0.055	
	5	0.92	1.339	0.157	607	720	0.054	
	6	0.74	1.325	0.000	575	9999	0.055	
	7	0.86	1.305	0.129	644	679	0.051	
	9	0.87	1.996	0.227	1414	1589	0.053	
ITA	1	0.97	1.569	0.097	1614	986	0.039	*
	2	0.92	1.219	0.000	386	9999	0.062	
	4	0.92	1.454	0.149	846	847	0.050	*
	5	0.91	1.454	0.144	872	844	0.049	*
	6	1.05	1.273	0.000	427	9999	0.062	
	7	0.92	1.264	0.000	473	9999	0.058	
	8	0.99	1.489	0.000	166	9999	0.116	
	9	0.89	2.025	0.189	1743	1640	0.049	*
NET	1	0.82	1.872	0.235	1248	1406	0.053	
	5	0.79	1.286	0.000	399	9999	0.064	
	6	0.72	1.520	0.000	412	9999	0.075	
	7	0.68	1.369	0.000	390	9999	0.069	
	9	0.76	2.155	0.363	1180	1852	0.063	

	Task	StD	Deft	Roh	Ach.	Effect.	Err %	< 5%
				Table 10 (Cont'd.)				
N-Z	1	1.04	1.961	0.136	2256	1537	0.041	*
	4	1.10	1.875	0.256	1116	1404	0.056	
	5	1.05	1.518	0.214	730	922	0.056	
	6	1.06	1.580	0.247	727	1003	0.059	
	7	1.04	1.512	0.221	701	913	0.057	
	9	1.11	1.738	0.228	2390	1212	0.036	*
NIG	1	0.74	2.691	0.235	2557	2891	0.053	
	2	0.91	3.154	0.349	2480	3988	0.063	
	5	0.70	1.222	0.082	651	597	0.048	*
	6	1.16	1.637	0.000	534	9999	0.071	
	7	1.04	2.051	0.000	489	9999	0.093	
	9	0.95	2.915	0.347	2101	3398	0.064	
SWE	1	0.96	1.415	0.048	1564	797	0.036	*
	5	1.07	1.300	0.106	541	676	0.056	
	6	0.89	1.423	0.159	535	807	0.062	
	7	0.88	1.172	0.000	397	9999	0.059	
	9	0.90	1.937	0.135	1536	1496	0.049	*
USA	1	0.84	1.742	0.120	3134	1216	0.031	*
	5	0.81	1.483	0.222	1114	880	0.044	*
	6	0.87	1.499	0.248	1049	896	0.046	*
	7	0.88	1.477	0.000	954	9999	0.048	*
	9	0.92	2.152	0.265	3266	1852	0.038	*

Table 10 (Cont'd.)

	Task	StD	Deft	Roh	Ach.	Effect.	Err %	< 5%
POP C								
FIN	1	0.82	1.330	0.000	323	9999	0.074	
	6	0.79	1.317	0.073	632	695	0.052	
	7	0.85	1.422	0.101	633	808	0.057	
	8	0.80	1.045	0.000	168	9999	0.081	
	9	0.83	1.137	0.000	324	9999	0.063	
HUN	1	0.82	1.281	0.081	687	656	0.049	*
	6	0.73	1.555	0.087	1332	967	0.043	*
	7	0.70	1.736	0.106	1536	1201	0.044	*
	9	0.68	1.379	0.162	504	756	0.061	
ITA	1	0.99	1.122	0.000	237	9999	0.073	
	2	1.00	1.185	0.000	250	9999	0.075	
	6	0.92	2.469	0.271	1011	2438	0.078	
	7	0.98	1.906	0.291	512	1448	0.084	
	8	0.98	1.732	0.246	465	1197	0.080	
	9	0.94	1.657	0.193	513	1103	0.073	
THA	1	0.66	2.172	0.398	672	1881	0.084	
	2	0.70	1.487	0.138	637	886	0.059	
	6	0.72	2.383	0.247	1298	2277	0.066	
	7	0.71	1.651	0.205	613	1089	0.067	
	9	0.74	1.799	0.248	650	1293	0.071	
SWE	1	0.94	1.796	0.289	643	1290	0.071	
	6	0.97	2.109	0.439	655	1787	0.082	
	7	1.00	1.936	0.393	592	1500	0.080	
	9	0.94	2.023	0.394	655	1645	0.079	

Table 10 (Cont'd.)								
	Task	StD	Deft	Roh	Ach.	Effect.	Err %	< 5%
USA	1	0.82	1.361	0.168	534	743	0.059	
	6	0.88	1.515	0.154	826	917	0.053	
	7	0.90	1.627	0.202	804	1054	0.057	
	9	0.89	1.267	0.000	246	9999	0.081	

Appendix B

The Achieved Quality of Essay Ratings

Rainer H. Lehmann

Ratings Files

This appendix makes use of special rating files which treat individual ratings of essays as cases, to preserve full information of what went on in the scoring. It is a record of the coded judgments of specially trained raters, who did their work on randomly distributed essays without any knowledge as to student characteristics. Much effort was invested to make these judgments truly independent of each other. Therefore, the set of scores awarded by one rater to a single essay is the primary unit of information. Whatever is inferred from this as a student score needs to be justified, so we can know how to talk about students' "achievement" in written composition.

The data stored on the international rating files possess a rather complex structure, outlined in four main areas below.

Students

Each record containing any rater's codes for a single essay carries a unique student identification code, including country, population, stratum, school, and class membership. This information was hidden from the raters; tasks, for instance, which were given to more than one population, were to be rated in a single procedure, with the essays from the differing age groups thoroughly mixed so as to avoid mitigating effects of prior rater expectations. In order to look at the raters, we selected only compositions that had two or three independent ratings (with some exceptions as noted). Since we were only interested in those papers with scale scores, those that the raters refused to score in cases of nonresponse, illegibility, or evasion of the task assigned, an essay received one of these codes from at least one of the raters, that was also excluded.

In a few very rare cases, errors in the identification codes implied exclusion of the case. Thus the numbers of students referred to in this chapter are generally slightly smaller than those given elsewhere and may not be representative of students, but they are representative of raters.

Tasks

The design of the study included provisions for rotating certain tasks randomly among the students tested, so that all combinations of tasks occur with approximately equal frequencies without every student having to complete every task. Some of the pairs of tasks, therefore, are nonexistent. Moreover, some of the tasks left the students with a choice between various options, so that even the nonempty cells in the array may contain extremely few cases. Therefore, the following analyses do not distinguish between the options within a task, and where a complete block design is required, rotated forms are treated as being parallel, so as to present meaningfully aggregated and sufficiently robust estimates. Again, in some extremely rare cases students or essays were excluded, because the task identification implied some error in the implementation of the design or, more likely, some coding error. Thus, the number of tasks/essays per student can vary from one to four, including a nationally optional task, if any was given.

Ratings

Although each record bears a code identifying the rater, his or her personal identity is of little concern here (unfortunately, no background data were gathered). It is easy to see that particularly in those countries where large numbers of scorers were used, the consideration of all possible combinations of raters would have produced by far too much detail. Also, conscious efforts to randomize the allocation of essays to raters were explicitly motivated by the aim to minimize any individual rater's influence on the estimation of student writing achievement. The methods used to attain this goal varied from country to country. Figure 6.1 gives two examples of how the compositions were distributed among the raters.

It will be noted that both approaches guarantee approximately equal frequencies for existing pairs of raters, but only the "Star Design" ensures that all possible combinations occur. In most countries the same jury was used across all tasks within a country, so as to avoid the confounding of jury and task effects. In any event, only the distinction between first and second (and, occasionally, third) rating matters here.

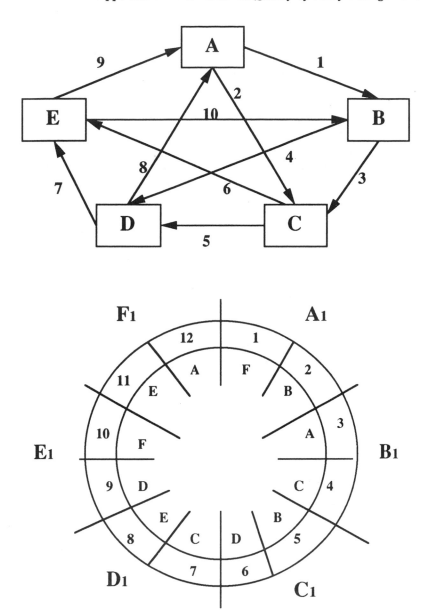

Figure 1: Distribution of Compositions among Raters

Rating Aspects

The International Scoring Guide prescribed that each rating incorporate at least four internationally defined marks: (a) An "Overall Impression Score," to be awarded immediately after the first reading of the text; (b) a mark on "Quality and Scope of Content"; (c) a rating of "Structure and Organization"; and (d) a score on "Style and Appropriateness of Tone." As an international option for some tasks, two subscores could be added to each of these scores, except the "Overall Impression Score". So the number of analyzable codes per rating varies between four and ten, depending on the task and the country's decision to use the more elaborate scoring method. Any incomplete set of codes was deleted from the analysis. It may also be mentioned that in one instance, use will be made of "Grammar Scores" (based on error counts, but projected on the same five-point scale as used for the international measures), as well as scores for "Handwriting." Since these are not generally included in the international rating files, suffice it to mention that such measures exist on only some of the national data tapes.

It is this four-dimensional structure -- several aspects per rating, at least two ratings per essay, one to four texts per student -- which is analyzed. It should be noted, though, that the exact details may vary from country to country. Table 1 gives a summary of the basis for the analysis: number of essays (with at least two interpretable ratings) by country and task and, as a first overview as to the achieved reliability of ratings, the product-moment correlations for the existing pairs of "overall impression" ratings.

From these summary data, we note that the achieved inter-rater agreement varies more between countries than it does between tasks. In particular, it does not seem to depend substantially on the "length" of the essays (the time allowed for completion of the task); the short tasks are rated just as or even slightly more reliably than the longer ones. The students' presumed lack of familiarity with some of the tasks does not appear to have affected the quality of the ratings. The "letter of advice" was certainly quite an unfamiliar assignment for students in most countries -- after all, it was included in the study primarily with content-analytic perspectives in mind -- and it has the highest median correlation in both Populations B and C! Curiously, in some countries the average quality of ratings is considerably lower for the Population C data sets than for the respective Population B files; the same holds true (although to a lesser extent) for the Population A ratings in these countries. Since strong counter examples exist, there is no compelling reason to suspect a systematic effect of populations. These first observations suggest the need for a more in-depth analysis of the ratings, country-by-country and population-by-population.

Table 1

Achieved Interrater Agreement for Averages across Four
Rating Aspects (Product-Moment Correlation with
Two Independent Ratings) By Country and Task

No. of cases per task is included in parentheses

POP A	Func.	Para.	Descr.	Narr.	Arg.
FIN	.60 (372)	.41 (127)	.72 (162)	.50 (416)	.49 (114)
IND	.88 (904)	.88 (506)	-	.86 (1.849)	.71 (406)
ITA	.63 (602)	.54 (188)	.57 (299)	.54 (691)	.56 (147)
N-Z[ab]	.92 (274)	.91 (81)	.97 (74)	.96 (270)	.96 (83)
SWE	.69 (835)	-	-	.65 (1.119)	.62 (967)
USA[c]	.62 (46)	.45 (49)	-	.62 (111)	.67 (50)
Median[d]	.63	.50	.72	.62	.67

[a] two independent ratings for part of the data set only
[b] partly consensus scores
[c] median correlation from three pairs of ratings
[d] excluding New Zealand

Table 1 (Cont'd.)

POP B	Func.	Descr.	Narr.	Arg.	Refl.	Exp.
CHI [ag]	.82 (703)	-	.86 (226)	.88 (234)	.78 (249)	.84 (703)
ENG [b]	.57 (1097)	.66 [c] (473)	.60 (375)	.72 (390)	.62 (381)	.67 (1097)
FIN [b]	.66 (671)	.68 [c] (340)	.50 (210)	.54 (223)	.62 (235)	.80 (671)
HAM [bd]	.82 (1169)	-	.88 (424)	.83 (393)	.91 (408)	.93 (1169)
HUN [ef]	.89 (1460)	.89 (591)	.93 (602)	.87 (565)	.90 (619)	.90 (1404)
ITA [b]	.54 (645)	.42 [c] (203)	.48 (318)	.61 (153)	.53 (175)	.48 (645)
NET [be]	.71 (972)	-	.48 (322)	.66 (333)	.64 (317)	.68 (972)
N-Z [gh]	.96 (222)	.98 (112)	.97 (87)	.96 (84)	.92 (81)	.96 (125)
NIG [i]	NA	-	NA	NA	NA	NA
SWE [b]	.73 (1283)	-	.71 (473)	.65 (481)	.68 (330)	.70 [e] (1283)
USA [g]	.69 (1151)	-	.65 (268)	.91 (570)	.87 (310)	.97 (843)
WAL [bj]	.48 (235)	.64 [c] (109)	.52 (77)	.44 (83)	.35 (75)	.60 (235)
Median	.70	.66	.62	.69	.66	.75

[a] at least 2 tasks completed   [b] at least 3 tasks completed
[c] at least 4 tasks completed   [d] nationally opt. task: $r = .89$
[e] med. corr., 3 pairs of ratings   [f] internationally opt. task: $r = .91$
[g] 2 indep. rat. (part of data set only) [h] partly consensus scores
[i] too few cases   [j] internationally opt. task: $r = .53$

Table 1 (Cont'd.)

POP C	Func.	Sum.	Arg.	Refl.	Open	Exp.
FIN	.43 (316)	-	.35 (586)	.51 (543)	.48 (146)	.61 (307)
HUN[a]	.87 (699)	-	.85 (1340)	.83 (1537)	-	.82 (502)
ITA	.49 (108)	.47 (177)	.46 (689)	.43 (341)	.46 (336)	.29 (307)
SWE	.66 (705)	-	.70[a] (638)	.75 (615)	-	.67 (712)
THA	.51 (666)	.55 (636)	.51 (1297)	.84 (605)	-	.90 (643)
USA[b]	.54 (75)	-	.62 (72)	.52 (70)	-	-
Median	.52	.51	.56	.63	.47	.67

[a] median corrleation from three pairs of ratings
[b] two independent ratings for part of the data set only

Analyzing the Quality of Essay Ratings - Some Theoretical Considerations

It has been mentioned that all of the rating variables to be analyzed here were coded on a five-point scale, with no value labels attached. In every instance, code 1 represents the extreme category for low performance, while code 5 stands for the top achievement level. Strictly speaking (i.e., from the perspective of measurement theory), these variables are only defined at the ordinal level, since equidistance between adjacent scale points is not given. The use of parametric statistical techniques seems precluded, therefore.

In practice, however, much research on the quality of writing assessment has been published in terms of parametric statistics. At the other extreme, some authors have reported simple percentages of agreement between raters, in addition to or instead of correlations, probably to enable a wide public to draw easy comparisons (see, for example, Applebee, Langer, & Mullis, 1986, pp. 94f.). The question is, what to do?

To make matters even more complicated, it can be argued that the use of product-moment-correlations (such as the ones reported in Table 1) does not account for possible mean differences between raters: differences in leniency or stringency, as they are often perceived in -- or insinuated against -- teachers. As a way out, one could also control the regression coefficients where the additive constant can be interpreted in conjunction with the slope as a measure of differential leniency (cf. Törmäkangas, 1987). While this approach would solve the latter problem, the fundamental objections of strict measurement theorists against the use of any parametric techniques are still not addressed.

If one is prepared, at least for a moment, to set aside these objections of principle, as the majority of researchers in the field appears to be, another aspect may be worth pursuing. Provided that parametric statistics render essentially the same conclusions as are produced by nonparametric methods, the parametric approach could have the advantage of allowing additional insights. More specifically, techniques based on the analysis of variance (ANOVA), probably first introduced to the area of writing assessment by Gosling (1966), render a powerful set of tools which prove to be generally superior to correlational methods. On this basis, it is possible to derive from the classical definition of measurement theory,

$$\text{Reliability} = \frac{\text{true variance}}{\text{observed variance}}$$

precise specifications for a potentially unlimited number of situations. In particular, the problem of inter-rater agreement, which correlational statistics can handle only for pairs of raters, is then treated as a very simple special case. Since this situation has already been covered to some extent by the findings presented in Table 1, the case with two (or three) independent ratings may be suitable both for an introduction into the methods used and for comparisons between the various statistical approaches for estimating inter-rater reliability. Those readers interested in the derivation of the respective formulae and in computational detail may wish to consult the excellent introduction provided in Thorndike (1982, 1988).

A necessary precondition for the application of ANOVA is, at least in principle, a full data matrix, in the present case with the two factors "Essay" and "Rating" (first vs. second [vs. third]). Having $k = 2,3,...$ ratings for each of the N essays, there are $k \times N$ cells, each containing a single score, so that there is no within-cell variance. In the present example, the "Overall Impression Scores" are used, and there are countries with 2 and others with 3 ratings per essay. The total variance of all these $k \times N$ scores can now be partitioned into three constituents. Formally, the following variance components (and their respective mean squares [*MS*]) are defined:

1. the essay component, standing for the variation in overall quality;
2. the rating component, representing mean (leniency) differences between the two or three rounds of scoring; and
3. the residual component, that is, the interaction term essay x rating, indicating the influence of inter-rater disagreement.

Any differences of mean leniency between first and subsequent ratings, which may have occurred in spite of the above illustrated efforts to avoid them, are, of course, to be considered as error variance, so that both of the following hold true:

Error variation = rating variation + residual variation;

True variation = total (observed) variation - rating variation - residual variation.

Dividing the true variation thus obtained by the observed total variation renders the reliability of sum or average scores obtained from the multiple ratings. Since some of the participating countries, however, did not implement multiple scoring on their entire sets of essays, but preferred -- or were forced -- to restrict it to a control routine on certain subsets, it is also of interest to know how much faith can be invested into the single ratings. Their reliability can be estimated under the assumption that the control scoring was performed on true random samples. The following equations (with k = number of ratings) hold:

$$\text{Reliability of multiple ratings} = \frac{MS_{\text{Essays}} \, MS_{\text{Error}}}{MS_{\text{Essays}}}$$

$$\text{Reliability of single ratings} = \frac{MS_{\text{Essays}} \, MS_{\text{Error}}}{MS_{\text{Essays}} + (k-1)MS_{\text{Error}}}$$

The latter measure is also known as "intra-class correlation", and it has been proposed occasionally as an appropriate indicator for the reliability of essay marking (Zeiher, Zeiher, & Gruger, 1979).

In order to assess both the quality of the data sets contributed to the IEA study and the influence of the estimation mode, the respective intraclass correlation coefficients are listed for the participating countries and the three populations (Table 2), excluding those data sets where the number of cases is insufficient (Nigeria) or where complete independence of ratings is not given (New Zealand). The computations are based on all compositions with multiple ratings ("overall impression" scores only); that is, task was assumed to be irrelevant here, as justified on the basis of Table 1.

An examination of these results shows that percentages of pairwise agreement - be it exact or "loose" ($\pm$ 1 scale point) - cannot be taken to be good indicators or substitutes for reliability estimates in a well-defined sense. No further use will be made of them here.

Secondly, it is apparent that the objections against the application of parametric statistics are based on very little substance. In most of the cases, the difference between Spearman's rank order correlation coefficient and the intra-class correlation is below .01, and it never exceeds .03!

Finally, the close congruence of product-moment correlations and intra-class correlations (both estimates for the reliability of single ratings) is truly remarkable.   Such correspondence is to be expected if the rating component is small and if the linear relationship between first and second rating, implied by the correlational approach, is well approximated, both of which conditions were attained in most countries by an appropriate scoring design. Under such conditions, then, the correlational method (which is much easier to implement computationally) renders very good direct estimates of the reliability of single ratings, which provides a justification *a posteriori* for starting out in this chapter with product-moment correlations in Table 1. In addition, product-moment correlations can be used to estimate the reliability of sum or average scores from two or more ratings by inserting them into the Spearman-Brown formula for increasing the test length, as control calculations convincingly show. For the triple ratings in the Netherlands and Sweden, Population B, for instance, this formula would give .7768 and .8249, as compared with the tabulated values of .7693 and .8239, respectively.

The major advantage of the ANOVA approach, however, lies in the fact that it can be generalized to situations with more than just two factors involved. As will be seen shortly, a systematic investigation of the quality of writing assessment requires more than just an analysis of rater agreement on a single rating aspect. The following will, therefore, be based largely on the technique of partitioning the observed variance into its components which -- even if they be considered "error variance" -- have a great deal to say about the character of the ratings produced by the IEA Study of Achievement in Written Composition.

Table 2

Achieved Inter-Rater Agreement For Overall-Impression
Scores by Country and Statistic Used
(All Compositions with Multiple Ratings, Irrespective of Task)

POP A	N of compositions	% strict agreement	% loose agreement	Spearman's rho
FIN	1191	43.9	88.2	.5395
IND	3665	64.3	99.2	.7620
ITA	1930	38.5	86.2	.5400
SWE[a] (SWE[b])	2102 968	50.9 52.7[c]	95.1 96.3[c]	.6477 .5584[c]
USA	256	60.2	96.1	.6494
	product-moment correlation	reliability of single rating	reliability of double rating	reliability of triple rating
FIN	.5346	.5328	.6952	
IND	.7617	.7614	.8645	
ITA	.5395	.5372	.6989	
SWE[a] (SWE[b])	.6563 .5651[c]	.6563 .5642[c]	.7925 .7214[c]	.7944
USA	.6598	.6593	.7947	

[a] all compositions with double ratings (Argument only, if third task is missing)
[b] compositions with triple ratings only (Argument)
[c] average from three possible pairs of ratings

Table 2 (Cont'd.)

POP B	N of compositions	% strict agreement	% loose agreement	Spearman's rho
CHI	3087	61.9	96.7	.6930
ENG	4317	45.2	90.8	.6032
FIN	3600	47.2	91.3	.6672
HAM	5286	75.5	99.1	.8021
HUN[a]	5689	68.7[d]	98.8[d]	.8256[d]
ITA	5331	39.9	87.6	.4922
NET[a]	3482	46.6[d]	91.6[d]	.5371[d]
SWE[b] (SWE⁹)	4101 487	53.0 48.5[d]	94.6 92.9[d]	.7201 .6127[d]
USA	1248	48.2	94.4	.5040
WAL	1044	31.5	91.3	.4211
	product-moment corr	reliability of single rating	reliability of double rat.	reliability of triple rat.
CHI	.6962	.6932	.8188	
ENG	.6158	.6157	.7622	
FIN	.6689	.6688	.8015	
HAM	.8080	.8077	8936	
HUN[a]	.8278[d]	.8273[d]	.9049[d]	.9344
ITA	.4916	.4916	.6591	
NET[a]	.5371[d]	.5278[d]	.6905[d]	.7693
SWE[b] (SWE⁹)	.7160 .6109[d]	.7158 .6102[d]	.8344 .7577[d]	.8239
USA	.5070	.5060	.6720	
WAL	.4402	.4395	.6106	

Table 2 (Cont'd.)

POP C	N of compositions	% strict agreement	% loose agreement	Spearman's rho
FIN	1898	40.6	86.7	.3855
HUN[a]	4080	70.4[d]	98.6[d]	.7537[d]
ITA	1958	36.4	81.7	.4088
SWE[b] (SWE[c])	2073 638	47.3 47.1[d]	93.6 93.0[d]	.6612 .6444[d]
THA	3847	58.8	95.9	.5870
USA	218	43.1	93.1	.4859
	product-moment correlation	reliability of single rating	reliability of double rating	reliability of triple rating
FIN	.4150	.4150	.5866	
HUN[a]	.7601[d]	.7599[d]	.8617[d]	.9030
ITA	.4169	.4177	.5893	
SWE[b] (SWE[c])	.6692 .6664[d]	.6678 .6663[d]	.8008 .7995[d]	.8561
THA	.5981	.5954	.7464	
USA	.5208	.5145	.6794	

[a] all compositions rated by three raters
[b] all compositions with double ratings (Argument only, if third rating is missing)
[c] compositions with triple ratings only (Argument)
[d] average from three possible pairs of raters

The Reliability of the Analytical Ratings

The recommendation to use multiple marking in the assessment of student writing is often justified with the argument that the individual ratings operate just like items on a test: the more individual marks, the higher the reliability, because sums or averages tend to polish out at least some of the erratic components of the single mark. Discounting for a moment the problem of validity, the same argument can be used to defend the analytical scoring scheme applied in the study. If the raters can express analytically strengths and weaknesses of an essay, the reliability of sums or averages calculated from the analytic scores will increase. It may, however, also be that the analytical scores for content, organization, and style contain true diagnostic information, which is likely to be the case when several raters deviate independently and in the same direction on a particular rating aspect. In this situation, it would be clearly inappropriate to capitalize on the polishing effect of aggregate statistics, and the total information should be used instead.

Which interpretation of the relative merits of analytical scoring fits the present data better, can be investigated empirically. In order to do this, the preliminary two-factorial ANOVA model has to be generalized to a three-dimensional model with essays as cases and Rating (first vs. second) and Rating Aspect (overall impression, content, organization, style) as facets. Again, the array of data contains a single code in each cell (zero within-cell variance), but now six variance components are defined:

1. variation between the Rating Aspects, as resulting from averaging across the two rounds of scoring and the total N of essays (main effect A);

2. variation between the Ratings, derived from the means of four scores and N essays (one for the first, one for the second round of scoring; main effect R);

3. interaction between Essay and Rating Aspect (E x A), which can be interpreted, if high, as a sign of true diagnostic scoring;

4. interaction between Essay and Rating (E x R), which is a measure of differential assessment between the two rounds of scoring, but across all four rating aspects;

5. interaction between Rating Aspect and Rating (A x R), indicating aspect-specific differences in leniency between the two rounds of scoring; and

6. residual variation (E x A x R).

Table 3 (bottom of each subtable) presents each of these components (sigma^2) in percent of the total variance. These terms can be used in various ways to produce reliability estimates, depending on the assumptions one is prepared to make with respect to the role of the rating aspects and the raters (cf. the numerous variants presented in Thorndike, 1988, pp. 335-340).

Table 3

Achieved Reliabilities for Overall Impression Scores
(Global Marks) and Analytical Scores by Country
(All Compositions with Multiple Ratings, Irrespective
of Task; Constituent Variance Components in Percent)

POP A	N of compos.	total var.	overall impress.	single aspect	4 random aspects	4 fixed aspects
FIN	1191	1.10	.70	.65	.73	.73
IND	3665	.85	.86	.74	.88	.88
ITA	1930	1.43	.70	.64	.72	.72
SWE[a]	2102	.98	.79	.71	.80	.80
(SWE[b])	968	.70	.72	.70	.80	.80
USA	256	.84	.79	.75	.83	.83
Median			.76	.71	.80	.80

POP A	Essay	Aspect	Rating	Essay x Aspect	Essay x Rating	Aspect x Rating	Ess. x Asp. x Rating
FIN	49	1	-	3	31	16	
IND	68	1	-	9	8	15	
ITA	48	1	-	3	30	17	
SWE[a]	55	1	-	4	21	19	
(SWE[b])	47	-	-	6	24	24	
USA	62	-	-	5	21	13	
Median	52	1	-	4	23	17	

[a] all compositions with double ratings (Argument only, if third rating is missing)
[b] compositions with triple ratings only (Argument)

Table 3 (Cont'd.)

POP B	N of compos.	total var.	overall impress.	single aspect	4 random aspects	4 fixed aspects
CHI	3087	.85	.82	.68	.81	.81
ENG	4317	1.23	.76	.68	.77	.77
FIN	3600	1.33	.80	.70	.80	.80
HAM	5286	.76	.89	.78	.90	.90
HUN[a]	5689	1.19	.93	.83	.93	.93
ITA	5331	1.15	.66	.59	.68	.68
NET[a]	3472	1.00	.77	.62	.79	.79
SWE[b]	4101	1.18	.83	.76	.84	.84
(SWE[c])	487	1.02	.82	.78	.85	.85
USA	1248	.78	.67	.59	.70	.70
WAL	1044	1.28	.61	.58	.66	.67
Median			.80	.68	.81	.81

POP B	Essay	Aspect	Rating	Essay x Aspect	Essay x Rating	Aspect x Rating	Ess. x Asp. x Rating
CHI	56	1	-	11	15	-	16
ENG	54	1	-	2	26	-	16
FIN	59	1	-	5	21	-	15
HAM	70	-	-	11	7	-	13
HUN[a]	71	1	-	10	6	-	12
ITA	43	-	-	3	32	-	22
NET[a]	42	1	1	10	17	-	29
SWE[b]	63	-	-	3	19	-	16
(SWE[c])	56	-	-	3	25	-	17
USA	45	-	-	5	29	-	21
WAL	42	2	2	3	34	-	18
Median	56	1	-	5	21	-	16

Table 3 (Cont'd.)

POP C	N of compos.	total var.	overall impress.	single aspect	4 random aspects	4 fixed aspects
FIN	1898	.97	.57	.51	.62	.62
HUN[a]	4080	.82	.90	.72	.88	.88
ITA	1958	1.26	.59	.49	.59	.59
SWE[b]	2073	1.17	.80	.70	.80	.80
(SWE[c])	638	1.15	.86	.82	.88	.88
THA	3847	.66	.75	.61	.72	.73
USA	218	.75	.68	.60	.71	.71
Median			.75	.61	.72	.73

POP C	Essay	Aspect	Rating	Essay x Aspect	Essay x Rating	Aspect x Rating	Ess. x Asp. x Rating
FIN	38	-	-	3	39	-	21
HUN[a]	60	-	-	16	10	-	16
ITA	35	1	-	4	39	-	22
SWE[b]	57	-	-	3	21	-	18
(SWE[c])	62	-	-	2	22	-	15
THA	50	3	-	4	26	-	18
USA	45	1	1	5	24	-	23
Median	50	-	-	4	24	-	18

[a] compositions with triple ratings only
[b] all compositions with double ratings (Argument only, if third rating is missing)
[c] compositions with triple ratings only (Argument)

An inspection of the table shows that nowhere, except in Chile, Hamburg, Hungary and The Netherlands (Population B), and Hungary (Population C) has the Essay-by-Aspect interaction term reached or exceeded 10 percent of the total variance, while it is as low as 2 percent in some other countries and populations, with an overall median of 5 percent or below. So, if it is the aim to produce comparable reliability estimates for all countries and population, it is probably not advisable to include the interaction between Essay and Rating Aspect as part of the true variation: For most data sets, indications are that the analytical scoring has contributed little beyond providing an option to express special strengths and weaknesses, but with limited specific agreement among the raters.

This corresponds well with another observation. Rating Aspect has rarely produced a main effect associated with more than 1 percent of the total variation; indeed, it was to be expected that the raters would tend intuitively to orient themselves at identical scale midpoints for all aspects (as was at least implicitly suggested by the International Benchmark Set). Therefore, it is practically of no importance whether Rating Aspect is treated as a fixed or random factor. Both estimates (top of subtables) render generally higher values than the respective reliabilities of two independent "overall impression" scores alone, but since the average reliabilities for a single rating aspect (interpolated in the random model) are lower than the latter, the "polishing effect" again appears to be the dominant advantage of the analytical scoring method used in the study.

A tentative conclusion emerges from an investigation of those variance components associated with Rating. There is hardly any main effect for this facet, because the scoring designs have rather effectively eliminated this error source, but the Essay-by-Rating interaction (*general* rater disagreement) and the residual term (*differential* rater disagreement) indicate the substantial influence of rater disagreement on the achieved reliabilities. It is remarkable that general disagreement is in most countries and populations the larger of these two components. Where this is not so -- Indonesia (Population A), Chile, Hamburg, Hungary and The Netherlands (Population B), Hungary (Population C) -- there is also a relatively large Essay-by-Aspect interaction (standing, as will be recalled, for rater *agreement* in diagnostic differentiation), and most of these data sets are associated with rather high reliabilities, even without considering the Essay-Aspect-interaction as a source of true variation. So, it seems likely that at least here, the analytical categories have served to reduce the general disagreement. The distinction between a more diagnostic, truly analytical rating behavior, which consciously tries to avoid within-essay halo effects, and a more holistic one, profiting from the "polishing effect," might be referred to as one of *rating styles*. This concept will have to be borne in mind when looking at the problems of validity and generalizability of essay ratings.

For two of the data sets, it was possible to use a subsample (the narrative, argumentative, and reflective tasks) to investigate the question of whether the above mentioned subcategories of the rating aspects have resulted in a further increase of reliabilities (Hamburg and the Netherlands, Population B). While for Hamburg, the Spearman-Brown extrapolation was precisely matched (reliabilities of .94 for ten categories as against .87 for four aspects; two rounds of scoring), this was not the case for the Dutch jury. There, the introduction of additional aspects led to considerable differences in standards for the categories, as inferred from the value of 16% for the aspect-by-rating interaction term. Consequently, the averages from ten categories, two rounds, attained only a reliability of .58 instead of the predicted .71.

It would have been easy to justify an estimation mode which combines the essay-by-rating component with the residual term, that is, general and differential rater disagreement are then considered as a single source of error variation. This method would have produced slightly higher reliability estimates for the average score; the preference was to work within the more conservative -- and more specific -- approach. Likewise, the inclusion of the essay-by-aspect interaction component in the true variation would have resulted in higher achieved reliability estimates, and again the more conservative option was chosen. So, the values given in Table 3 may be considered lower boundaries for the reliability of the ratings and their respective averages. Although future work with these data will have to take into account the considerable between-country differences, it may be informative to compare across-country medians with figures given by Breland (1983, p.10) for inter-rater reliabilities to be expected on the basis of the state-of-the-art as summarized by him. Typically, the country contributions to the IEA study compare favorably with these standards.

The Vaildity of the Analytical Ratings - Some Indirect Evidence

It has to be stated at the very beginning of this section: The IEA files do not contain any variable against which to validate the ratings externally. So, it is not possible to study questions of the predictive or concurrent validities of the ratings, save by analyzing the relationships between ratings referring to different tasks. As will be seen, this approach produces at least some indirect evidence as to what has been measured. Table 5 presents the intertask correlations.

Table 4

Achieved Reliabilities for Aggregated Scores in
Comparison with Expected Values Reported by
Coffman and Breland, by Number of Ratings Involved

N of ratings source	1	2	3
Coffman	.38	.56	.65
Breland	.64	.70	.78
IEA	.61	.76	.84

Table 5

Intertask Correlations for Overall Impression Scores
(Averages from Two Ratings), by Country

POP A	Para.	Descr.	Narr.	Arg.
Finland Functional Paraphrase Description Argument	.24	.32	.28 .32 .39 .39	.24
Indonesia Functional Paraphrase Argument	.23		.27 .36 .43	.22
Italy Functional Paraphrase Description Argument	.31	.40	.36 .40 .49 .48	.39
New Zealand[a] Functional Paraphrase Description Argument	.31	.33	.36 .39 .45 .41	.30
Sweden[b] Functional Argument			.52 .54	.47
USA[a] Functional Paraphrase Argument	.22		.24 .36 .34	.23

[a] single ratings included
[b] third rating included, if available (Argument)

Table 5 (Cont'd.)

POP B	Sum.	Para.	Desc	Narr.	Arg.	Refl.	Open	Exp.
Chile								
Functional				.10	.42	.25		.30
Expository				.40	.37	.44		
England								
Functional			.44	.47	.50	.46		.52
Description				.40	.58	.54		.55
Expository				.53	.61	.57		
Finland								
Functional	.22		.41	.41	.43	.42		.46
Summary				.34	.24	.28		.35
Description				.41	.35	.56		.57
Expository				.50	.48	.64		
Hamburg								
Functional				.18	.30	.29		.30
Expository				.24	.25	.30		
Hungary[a]								
Functional		.53	.41	.50	.43	.46		.58
Paraphrase				.42	.55	.51		.61
Description				.36	.31	.43		.45
Expository				.62	.58	.62		
Italy								
Functional	.29		.25	.34	.24	.28	.44	.32
Summary					.34			.41
Description				.46				.40
Reflective							.51	
Expository				.49	.43	.49	.31	
Netherlands[a]								
Functional				.35	.40	.45		.38
Expository				.49	.55	.55		
New Zealand[b]								
Functional			.36	.28	.28	.31		.36
Description				.48	.44	.47		
Expository				.36	.39	.43		

Table 5 (Cont'd.)								
POP B	Sum.	Para.	Desc	Narr.	Arg.	Refl.	Open	Exp.
Sweden[c]								
Functional				.58	.59	.46		.52
Expository				.59	.63	.59		
USA[b]								
Functional				.23	.22	.32		.26
Expository				.35	.40	.41		
Wales								
Functional	.52		.61	.64	.70	.57		.58
Summary				.56	.69	.57		.63
Description				.62	.60	.71		.77
Expository				.67	.64	.65		

[a] averages from three ratings
[b] single ratings included
[c] third rating included, if available (Argument)

Table 5 (Cont'd.)

POP C	Arg.	Refl.	Open	Exp.
Finland				
Functional	.24	.25		
Argument		.25		.30
Reflective				.39
Hungary				
Functional	.22	.29		
Argument		.34		.34
Reflective				.45
Italy				
Functional	.19	.42	-.04	
Summary	.32	.53	.38	
Persuasive		.48	.44	.38
Reflective				.40
Proc. Desc.				.34
Sweden[b]				
Functional	.43	.50		
Argument				.59
Reflective				.53
Thailand				
Functional	.27	.33		.22
Summary	.14	.15		.24
Argument		.37		.33
USA[a]				
Functional	.20	.16		
Argument		.58		.31
Reflective				.40

[a] single ratings included
[b] third rating included, if available (Argument)

There are considerable national differences between these correlations. Interestingly, it is not the case that higher reliabilities (as listed in Tables 2 and 3 above) are necessarily accompanied by higher inter-task correlations as one would normally expect. Even more intriguing, perhaps, there appears to be a rather close connection between the rating styles of national juries (as first defined in the context of discussing the results of Table 3) and the intertask correlations: the more a national jury has emphasized the different rating aspects (as indicated by the Essay-by-Aspect interaction term), the lower tend to be the intertask correlations. This tendency is not so implausible as may seem at first sight; after all, the intertask correlations were computed on the basis of the global "overall impression" scores, and, therefore, a more holistic approach to the rating of student essays is likely to correspond better to this particular mode of investigating the meaning of the ratings across tasks. Nevertheless, there may well be more involved. It is possible, at least theoretically, that the difference between a clearly differentiated analytic approach and a more holistic rating style implies a fundamental difference in the meaning of the judgments: while the former will have to stress text characteristics, the latter may - or, perhaps, is even likely to - capitalize more on stable student traits. This question will have to be taken up again below (cf. the evidence presented in chapter 8).

It is also clear, however, that the nature of the tasks involved has also had some influence on the inter-task correlations. While it does not appear that these differences can be easily related to the theoretical grid of "domains of school writing" (Vähäpassi, 1982) originally developed to provide a framework for the study, some observations do stand out.

At the Population A level, the highest inter-task correlation within a given country is always associated with the narrative task, whereas the pragmatic tasks display the lowest coefficients. It will be noted that this finding does not correspond to any observed differences in interrater agreement (cf. Table 1), so that an explanation in terms of statistical effects of attenuation can be ruled out. That provides some reason to reconsider the issue of text length: While it was stated above that the ratings for the short assignments do not appear to be less reliable than corresponding ones for the longer tasks, there is some evidence now to suggest that longer assignments might produce more valid judgments. In fact, disregarding for the moment the very special case of the expository letter of advice, which will be discussed shortly, the analyses of the data on the other two populations appear to give full support for this hypothesis. Longer assignments do seem to be better predictors for writing performance on other tasks than shorter ones.

The expository letter - the "letter of advice to a friend" spelling out what needs to be done to obtain good marks for one's writing - is special, indeed. It was administered with relatively little time allowed for completion

(20 minutes), but it is the nature of this task which makes it so interesting. To articulate in writing one's own perceptions of the relevant criteria of good writing requires a reflective mode, and it will be fairly safe to expect raters to award high marks on this task only if the response provides significant evidence for reflection. (Content analytic techniques applied to the Hamburg data have shown that this is indeed the case.) Thus, it is quite remarkable to find that for both Populations B and C, this particular task is generally associated with the highest intertask correlations and that the highest coefficient within the array for a country is usually the one connecting the task with the reflective task! It seems that these findings confirm the notion of a school-specific writing culture: The fact that the scores in general are highest for those students who know best how to express the teachers' - the raters' - expectations as to good writing can certainly be interpreted as an indication not only for the existence, but also for the effectiveness of such system of mutual expectations.

As far as the magnitude of the coefficients is concerned, the intertask correlations are more or less in line with (or even slightly higher than) what could be expected. In his state-of-the-art report of 1983, Breland has compiled the results from eight studies on the predictive and concurrent validities of essay scores (pp. 13f.). His tables would provide medians of .23 for concurrent correlations with verbal intelligence tests, etc., and of .30 for predictive correlations (e.g., with course marks, excluding the secondary analysis of Werts, Breland, Grandy, & Rock, 1980), which leads to rather modest expectations to begin with, even if it is also clear from this material that correlations will tend to be higher to the extent that the validation criterion resembles the indicators of writing achievement used.

Very sporadically, the concurrent validity of analytical rating aspects has been investigated differentially (cf. Breland, 1983, p. 17, Table 11). In such studies, higher values were found regularly for language-related characteristics (style and grammar, for instance) than for measures of content quality and structure. This finding is confirmed in IEA rating files. If rating aspects are interpreted as "traits" and writing assignments as "methods" to measure them, it is possible to compute "convergent validity coefficients" (Campbell & Fiske, 1959; Marsh, 1988). As can be seen from Table 6, these are generally higher for Style than they are for Content and Organization.

That leads to the question of the construct validity of the analytical scoring scheme as a whole. The labels for the rating aspects in the International Scoring Guide, common across all tasks, and parallel phrasings in the respective circumscriptions seem to suggest that these aspects are invariant against text genres and tasks. This is an assumption, however, which warrants testing. It was not possible to do this for all data sets, but principal component analyses could be performed on the rating files from Hamburg and Sweden (Population B) in order to clarify the factorial structure of 18 variables, six each from three tasks (Functional vs. Narrative, Argumentative, Reflective [combined] vs. Expository letter). The rating aspects included were: Overall Impression, Content, Organization, Style, Grammar, and Handwriting/ Neatness.

Table 6

Convergent Validity Coefficients for Averages from Two or More Ratings, by Country and Rating Aspect

POP A	$\underline{N}$ of task comb.	Overall Impress	Content	Organ.	Style and Tone	$\underline{X}$
FIN	7	.3126	.2251	.3604	.3760	.3185
IND	5	.3014	.2734	.2642	.2870	.2815
ITA	7	.4039	.3053	.3530	.4202	.3706
N-Z[a]	7	.3636	.3119	.3556	.3679	.3497
SWE[b]	3	.5118	.3900	.4257	.4904	.4545
USA[a]	5	.2763	.2162	.2666	.2785	.2594
Median		.3325	.2893	.3543	.3720	

[a] including single ratings
[b] including third rating, where available (Argument)

Table 6 (Cont'd.)

POP B	N of task comb.	Overall Impress	Content	Organ.	Style and Tone	X
CHI	7	.3238	.2233	.2812	.2740	.2756
ENG	12	.5158	.4171	.4631	.4988	.4737
FIN	17	.4096	.3667	.4032	.4283	.4020
HAM	7	.2666	.2132	.2308	.3144	.2563
HUN[a]	17	.4924	.3723	.4320	.4714	.4420
ITA	16	.3745	.3161	.3510	.3534	.3488
NET[a]	7	.4544	.2426	.3071	.3739	.3445
N-Z[b]	11	.3768	.3187	.3720	.3916	.3648
SWE[c]	7	.5655	.4659	.4713	.5154	.5045
USA[b]	7	.3133	.2602	.2729	.2738	.2800
WAL	17	.6306	.4659	.5117	.6469	.5638
Median		.4096	.3187	.3720	.3916	

POP C	N of task comb.	Overall Impress	Content	Organ.	Style and Tone	X
FIN	5	.2869	.2559	.2708	.2768	.2726
HUN[a]	5	.3283	.2300	.2696	.2807	.2772
ITA	11	.3489	.2737	.3313	.3019	.3140
SWE[c]	4	.5146	.4597	.4544	.4926	.4803
THA	8	.2562	.2271	.2274	.2350	.2364
USA[b]	5	.3259	.2935	.3052	.3078	.3090
Median		.3271	.2646	.2880	.2913	

[a] triple ratings
[b] including single ratings
[c] including third rating, where available (Argument)

The respective results were quite unambiguous: Apart from Handwriting and -- for Hamburg only -- Grammar, the factors are clearly task factors! Moreover, the different weights/eigenvalues of the first principal component demonstrated again the existence of different rating styles. Apparently, the Swedish jury has been guided more strongly by characteristics of language (also visible from the fact that there is no independent grammar factor here, but high loadings of Grammar on the task factors instead), while the Hamburg jury differentiated more between Content/Organization and Style and made "quality and scope of content" decisive for their "overall impression" scores. It was also implied by the results that stylistic characteristics and the ability to write grammatically correctly are relatively near to each other, even if this relation was almost entirely masked by halo effects in Sweden. Taking it all together, however, these findings confirm basically the distinction of Quellmalz, Capell & Chou (1982) between a task-specific "coherence" factor (content and organization) and an independent "mechanics" factor. Conversely, the validity of the IEA ratings is certainly enhanced by the fact that it was possible, on that basis, to replicate important findings from earlier research.

The Generalizability of the Ratings

The IEA study comprised quite a number of different tasks, and it is rare in the field of writing assessment to find a corpus with more than a single text from each student, such as here. The tasks given do not stand for themselves. They were developed to cover as wide a range of school writing as seemed possible under the anticipated time limits and under the constraints of an international project with very diverse participating school systems. They were also meant to cover as wide a range of student abilities as possible. So the question is almost unavoidable: To what extent can the essay ratings be generalized across tasks into a single estimate of student writing achievement?

Technically, this question can be treated as a special topic of the problem of reliability; it can be investigated adequately with the aid of variance components analysis, if there are at least two sets of ratings per student. It was deemed appropriate here, however, to discuss first the question of the validity of the analytical ratings, because it follows directly from these analyses (as was already suggested by the findings from Section 3) that average scores computed from the rating aspects for Overall Impression, Content, Organization, and Style are adequate measures of the quality of an essay as perceived by the raters.

So the technique of characterizing the specifics of each rating file by its constituent variance components can now be resumed, but with a change in the design, of course. The "cases" (unit of analysis) are now students, and the facets are Task (strictly speaking "assignment," because rotated tasks had to be combined in order to have a complete block design) and Rating. In accordance with the overall design of the study, both Task and Rating (first vs. second round of scoring) are treated as random factors. It is to be noted that only the averages across the four main rating aspects are entered into the computations.

Now, the following variance components are defined:

1.   Variation of student achievement, computed from the averages across two, three, or four tasks, and two independent ratings (main effect S);

2.   Variation associated with differences between the mean ratings for the different tasks/assignments (main effect T);

3.   Variation between first and second rating (main effect R);

4.   Student-by-essay interaction, interpretable as an indicator for fluctuations in the performance level across tasks to the extent that they were perceived by both judges (S x T);

5.   Student-by-rating interaction which indicates systematic changes in scoring standards for certain (groups of) students between scoring rounds (S x R);

6.   Task-by-rating interaction, a measure of differential changes of standards at the task level between scoring rounds (T x R); and

7.   Residual variation, which encompasses all 'erratic' rater disagreement (S x T x R).

Table 7 presents the respective data; the generalizability coefficient (top right column) was computed in accordance with the stated specifications, and the variance components (bottom) are again the $sigma^2$ terms converted to percentages of the total variance, which is also given.

As was stated above, the problem of the generalizability of essay ratings can be understood as a special topic in the study of reliabilities; it represents a certainly necessary, however rarely pursued question: What is the degree of precision with which we can make inferences as to a single, general measure of writing achievement, if we assume that the tasks/assignments are a random sample from the universe of all possible tasks considered relevant? An inspection of the figures given in Table 7 must have rather sobering effects. If "general writing achievement" (or "general writing ability", for that matter) is a meaningful concept -- and many programmatic texts (e.g., preambles of mother tongue curricula) seem to start out from that assumption -- and if the measurement of general writing achievement was an important aim of the study, then this has been achieved only moderately well.

Table 7

Achieved Generalizabilities for Averages across Four
Rating Aspects on the Basis of Multiple Writing Assignments
("Essays") and Multiple Ratings by Country
(Constituent Variance Components in Percent)

POP A	*N* of assign.	*N* of ratings	*N* of students	Total Variance	General-izability
FIN	3	2	255	1.10	.50
IND	3	2	307	.72	.61
ITA	3	2	327	1.12	.61
SWE[a]	3	2	982	.90	.66
Median					.61

POP A	Student	Essay	Student x Essay	Student x Rating	Student x Essay x Rating
FIN	21	3	42	-	36
IND	32	1	56	-	12
ITA	26	3	24	2	44
SWE[a]	32	18	21	-	29
Median	32	3	33	-	32

[a] for Argument first and second rating only

Table 7 (Cont'd.)

POP B	N of assign.	N of ratings	N of students	Total Variance	General- izability
CHI	2	2	733	.69	.38
ENG	3	2	1097	1.01	.76
FIN	3	2	671	1.11	.70
HAM	3	2	1169	.65	.55
HUN	3	3	942	1.12	.68
ITA	3	2	645	.94	.62
NET	3	3	972	.70	.65
SWE[a]	3	2	1283	1.01	.72
Median					.68
ENG	4	2	473	1.04	.77
FIN	4	2	340	1.10	.75
HAM[b]	4	2	1088	.62	.62
HUN	4	3	373	1.00	.72
ITA	4	2	203	.89	.70
Median					.72

Table 7 (Cont'd.)

POP B	Student	Essay	Student x Essay	Student x Rating	Student x Essay x Rating
CHI (2)	23	-	62	4	10
ENG (3)	42	-	22	-	37
FIN (3)	38	4	27	1	31
HAM (3)	26	5	57	-	12
HUN[c] (3)	34	10	28	1	13
ITA (3)	28	-	23	1	48
NET (3)	29	4	30	1	33
SWE[a] (3)	42	5	27	-	27
Median	34	4	27	1	31
ENG (4)	38	-	23	1	38
FIN (4)	37	3	27	1	32
HAM (4)	29	3	56	-	11
HUN	36	11	41	-	12
ITA (4)	29	-	18	1	52
Median	36	3	27	1	32

[a] all compositions with double rating (Argument only, if third rating is missing)
[b] including nationally optional task
[c] also 4% for rater component and 11% for essay x rater component

Table 7 (Cont'd.)

POP C	*N* of assign.	*N* of ratings	*N* of students	Total Variance	General-izability
FIN	3	2	454	.78	.55
HUN	3	3	904	.61	.48
ITA	3	2	212	1.00	.64
SWE[a]	2	2	1196	1.03	.64
THA	3	2	1224	.52	.50
Median					.55

POP C	Student	Essay	Student x Essay	Student x Rating	Student x Essay x Rating
FIN	22	-	23	1	56
HUN	22	22	43	-	12
ITA	27	1	16	1	55
SWE[a]	41	-	28	1	30
THA	19	2	42	-	39
Median	22	1	28	1	39

[a] for Argument first and second rating only

When looking for causes, it is helpful to analyze the variance components contributing true and error variance. It is obvious that inter-rater disagreement (the residual term) is only one -- and in some countries, a rather minor -- source of error variance. Clearly, the fluctuations of student performance between tasks (S x T interaction) have a major influence -- and in some countries they constitute the largest variance component of all. Since the generalizability coefficient takes into account all these components, it is easily seen that a low level of rater disagreement and a low level of within-student achievement variation are required to obtain better results. More texts would also have helped, of course, and it may be worth remembering that the nature of the assignments does seem to be related to their power of allowing valid predictions of achievement in different assignments (cf. the discussion of Table 5).

The rating files as such do not allow us to identify external reasons for the observed student fluctuation of achievement over tasks. It is possible that context factors are involved where larger student-task interactions are involved, for example, class- or school-specific opportunities to learn. So this must be left for further investigations. It is, however, possible and even likely that the rating styles which have emerged from the previous analyses are also to be considered here. When comparing the essay-by-aspect interaction terms from Table 3 with the student-by-task interaction terms from Table 7, there is an almost perfect correlation of rank orders, and of course the between-country differences in inter-task correlations have illustrated basically the same phenomenon. This, then, suggests the following tentative explanation: The clearer the distinction between content and language (i.e., variable task requirements and general expectations as to "good language") the lower the emphasis on student characteristics which are relatively stable across the different tasks.

If this interpretation is correct, it has far-reaching implications for the study of writing achievement. It follows directly that all correlations with a measure of writing achievement as a criterion will depend on the specific rating style of the jury and, further, that the explained variances in multiple regression analyses and causal models will be immediately affected. The last chapters of this volume provide ample material to test this hypothesis, but the reader should be forewarned that the present analysis has produced sufficient evidence against any superficial comparison not only of mean achievement levels, but also of effect sizes between countries.

Conclusions

The reported analyses of the international rating files from the IEA study allow us to draw the following conclusions:

1. The internationally standardized scoring procedures produced ratings from independent and "blind" (i.e., uninformed as to any student characteristic) operating scorers. These for most countries and populations are reliable in accordance with the state of the art. Most rating files fit the model of analytical scoring as a way to provide repeated, equivalent measures which increase the overall reliability when averages of the existing rating aspects are used.

2. Some indirect evidence could be produced as to the validity of the analytical scoring scheme. Whereas writing achievement must be primarily defined with respect to specific tasks completed, there are traces of a distinction between content-related and language-related text characteristics.

3. For most countries and populations, it does not seem justified to aggregate ratings across tasks into a single measure of "general writing achievement." Unexplained variations of writing achievement within-students, between-tasks lead in most cases to rather low generalizability estimates. It seems advisable, therefore, to perform multivariate analyses at the level of individual tasks.

4. The national juries differ clearly in what has here been suggested to be called "rating style": Some juries have distinguished more clearly than others between the analytical rating aspects. This has had demonstrable effects on the inter-task correlations. It is hypothesized that a more pronounced analytic rating style with its emphasis on content qualities of the text as opposed to language ability of the student will be associated with lower external correlations and will therefore preclude superficial comparisons of effect sizes across countries.

In one sentence, then: While exploratory investigations into background factors influencing writing achievement are certainly possible and warranted, if interpreted with care, complex multivariate analyses such as causal models with latent constructs will not be directly comparable and are best understood as exemplary "case studies."

Contributors

Mary E. DeMasi
The University at Albany, State University of New York

R. Elaine Degenhart
The University of Hamburg

Michael S. Green
The University at Albany, State University of New York

Wilfried Hartmann
The University of Hamburg

Rainer H. Lehmann
The University of Hamburg

Alan C. Purves
The University at Albany, State University of New York

Hannu Saari
Institute for Educational Research, University of Jyväskylä

Ruth Schick
The University at Albany, State University of New York

Sauli Takala
Institute for Educational Research, University of Jyväskylä

Kari Törmäkangas
Institute for Educational Research, University of Jyväskylä

275

Index